Security without Obscurity

A Guide to Confidentiality, Authentication, and Integrity

Security without Obscurity

Obscurity

A Guide to
Confidentiality, Authentication,
and Integrity

J. J. Stapleton

CRC Press
Taylor & Francis Group
Boca Raton London New York

CRC Press is an imprint of the
Taylor & Francis Group, an **informa** business

AN AUERBACH BOOK

CRC Press
Taylor & Francis Group
6000 Broken Sound Parkway NW, Suite 300
Boca Raton, FL 33487-2742

© 2014 by Taylor & Francis Group, LLC
CRC Press is an imprint of Taylor & Francis Group, an Informa business

No claim to original U.S. Government works

Printed on acid-free paper
Version Date: 20140311

International Standard Book Number-13: 978-1-4665-9214-8 (Hardback)

Library of Congress Cataloging-in-Publication Data

Stapleton, Jeffrey James.
    Security without obscurity : a guide to confidentiality, authentication, and integrity / Jeffrey James Stapleton.
        pages cm
    Summary: "The traditional view of information security includes three cornerstones: confidentiality, integrity, and availability, also known as the CIA of information security. As the field has become more complex, both novices and professionals with years of experience need a good reference book outlining the basics. Rather than focusing on compliance or policies and procedures, this book takes a top-down approach. Providing insight from the author's experience developing dozens of standards, the book starts with the fundamentals to bridge the understanding gaps--approaching information security from the bedrock principles of CIA. "-- Provided by publisher.
    Includes bibliographical references and index.
    ISBN 978-1-4665-9214-8 (hardback)
    1. Data protection--Standards. 2. Information technology--Security measures. 3. Computer security. 4. Computer networks--Security measures. I. Title.

QA76.9.A25S734 2014
005.8--dc23   2014006006

Visit the Taylor & Francis Web site at
http://www.taylorandfrancis.com

and the CRC Press Web site at
http://www.crcpress.com

This book is dedicated in historical order to those who mentored me, inspired me, or just plain tolerated my incessant questions. To my former bosses at MasterCard—Fred Liner, Allen Tweedy, Roger Altevogt, Chuck Davis, and Jim Kennedy—who gave me the freedom to learn from my mistakes, encouraged me in all of my endeavors, and opened the door into the fascinating world of cryptography and standards. Also to Bill Poletti, who keeps trying to explain politics and the business side of payments—I think I almost got it. To my former associates at RSA: George Soerheide, who was once described as putting the "gentle" in gentleman (we still miss you); Bob Mannal, who educated me in the mysterious realm of marketing, mergers, and acquisition; and special thanks to Burt Kaliski for welcoming me into RSA Labs. To my former associates at KMPG: Al Van Ranst, who supported me in the participation of X9 and ISO standards; Bob Mannal, who still seems surprised I hired him as my boss; and Mark Lundin, who taught me about accounting and auditing. And over the years, to all of the various X9 and ISO workgroup members, many of whom I call friends. I got to travel to many cities and countries, and have made acquaintances around the world. My particular appreciation goes to Carl Campbell and Dennis "Abe" Abraham for taking me under their wings in my early days of standards and patiently educating me about symmetric and asymmetric cryptography. My special thanks go to my book reviewers Ralph Poore, Bill Poletti, and Clay Epstein for their comments and suggestions. Extra appreciation goes to Ralph Poore for his insights and recommendations, and my publisher Rich O'Haney for his expertise and advice. And of course to my wife, Linda, who has supported me over all these years, made friends with everyone I have ever met, gets invited to all of the standards meetings, and brings me along to the dinners and parties. They always did like her best.

Contents

About the Author

Jeff J. Stapleton has over thirty years experience developing and assessing payment systems and security techniques, including cryptography and biometrics. His career includes the major card brands (MasterCard, Visa, American Express, and Discover) for payment systems and security assessments; big-four accounting firm experience performing security assessments of applications, systems, and products; working with large and medium-sized financial institutions providing risk assessments and security compliance audits; and developing policies, practices, and procedures for security systems.

Jeff has participated in developing ISO and X9 security standards for over twenty years within the financial services industry. For the first five years, he participated on several X9 workgroups and has been an industry liaison and U.S. expert several times for various ISO workgroups. In addition, he has been chair of the X9F4 Cryptographic Protocols and Application Security Workgroup for fifteen years. His experience includes participation on several X9 and ISO workgroups and development of over three dozen ISO and X9 standards. Some of the standards have multiple parts, which add to the overall count.

- X9.8 PIN Management and Security [38]
- X9.24 Key Management [42]

- X9.31 Digital Signatures Using Reversible Public Key Cryptography (rDSA) [43]
- X9.42 Public Key Cryptography for the Financial Services Industry Agreement of Symmetric Keys Using Discrete Logarithm Cryptography [44]
- X9.45 Enhanced Management Controls Using Digital Signatures and Attribute Certificates
- X9.49 Secure Remote Access to Financial Services [46]
- X9.52 Triple Data Encryption Algorithm Modes of Operation
- X9.55 Public Key Cryptography for the Financial Services Industry: Extensions to Public Key Certificates and Certificate Revocation Lists
- X9.57 Public Key Cryptography for the Financial Services Industry: Certificate Management
- X9.62 Public Key Cryptography for the Financial Services Industry: The Elliptic Curve Digital Signature Algorithm (ECDSA) [47]
- X9.63 Public Key Cryptography for the Financial Services Industry: Key Agreement and Key Transport Using Elliptic Curve Cryptography [48]
- X9.68 Digital Certificates for Mobile/Wireless and High Transaction Volume Financial Systems
- X9.69 Framework for Key Management Extensions [49]
- X9.73 Cryptographic Message Syntax—ANS.1 and XML [50]
- X9.79 Public Key Infrastructure (PKI) [51]
- X9.84 Biometric Information Management and Security [54]
- X9.95 Trusted Time Stamp Management and Security [55]
- X9.98 Lattice-Based Polynomial Public Key Establishment Algorithm for the Financial Services Industry [57]
- X9.111 Penetration Testing [58]
- X9.112 Wireless Management and Security [59]
- X9.117 Secure Remote Access—Mutual Authentication [60]
- X9.122 Secure Consumer Authentication for Internet Payments [61]
- X9.125 Cloud Services Compliance Data [62]
- TR-37 Migration from DES [64]
- TG-3 Retail Financial Services Compliance Guideline [65]

- TG-4 Recommended Notation for DEA Key Management In Retail Financial Networks [63]
- TG-7 Initial DEA Key Distribution for Pin Entry and Transaction Originating Devices
- TG-9 Abstract Syntax Notation & Encoding Rules for Financial Industry Standards

Some of these X9 standards were transitioned to ISO standards and have since been retired. A few of the X9 standards have been withdrawn due to changes in technology [9]. Others have been updated by X9F workgroups with newer participation lists that might not include Mr. Stapleton's name. The list of international standards is also provided.

- ISO 9564 PIN Management and Security [99]
- ISO 11568 Banking—Key Management (retail) [102]
- ISO 12812 Mobile Banking and Payments [103]
- ISO 13491 Banking—Secure Cryptographic Devices (retail) [104]
- ISO 13492 Financial Services—Key Management Related Data Element—Application and Usage of ISO 8583 Data Elements 53 and 96 [105]
- ISO 19092 Financial Services—Biometrics—Security Framework [109]

Jeff has published articles in various information security journals, several IEEE papers, PKI Forum notes, and is a contributing author to several books on biometrics and cryptography. He is also a patent holder for cryptographic solutions.

- *Biometrics*. John D. Woodward Jr., Nicholas M. Orlans, and Peter T. Higgins. Contributing authors: Dr. Martin Libicki, Kapil Raina, Richard E. Smith, Jeff Stapleton, and Dr. Valorie Valencia. McGraw-Hill/Osborne, 1999. ISBN 0-07-222227-1.
- *A Biometric Standard for Information Management and Security*. Stephen M. Matyas Jr. and Jeff Stapleton. Computers & Security, Elsevier Science, 2000.
- *PKI*. Thomas Austin. Contributing authors: Santosh Chokhani, Roseann Day, Todd Glassey, Sven Hammar, Diana Kelley, Sathvik Krishnamurthy, Steve McIntosh,

Samir Nanavati, Ruven Schwartz, Jeff Stapleton. A Wiley Tech Brief, 2001. ISBN 0-471-35380-9. [30]

- "PKI Note: Biometrics." Jeff Stapleton. PKI Forum, 2001.
- "PKI Note: CA Trust." Jeff Stapleton. PKI Forum, 2001.
- "PKI Note: Smart Cards." Eric Longo and Jeff Stapleton. PKI Forum, 2002.
- "Digital Signature Paradox." Jeff Stapleton, Paul Doyle, and Steven Teppler Esq. IEEE Workshop on Information Assurance and Security. U.S. Military Academy, West Point, NY, 2005.
- "Cryptographic Transitions." Jeff Stapleton and Ralph Poore. IEEE 1-4244-0359-6/06, 2006. [72]
- "Digital Signatures Are Not Enough." Jeff Stapleton and Steven Teppler. *The ISSA Journal*, January 2006.
- "Cryptography as a Service." Jeff Stapleton. *The ISSA Journal*, January 2009.
- "The PCI DSS: Friend or Foe?" Jeff Stapleton. *The ISSA Journal*, April 2009.
- "PAN Encryption: The Next Evolutionary Step?" Jeff Stapleton. *The ISSA Journal*, June 2009. [12]
- "Tokenization and Other Methods of Security Cardholder." Ralph Poore and Jeff Stapleton. *(ISC)2 Information Security Journal*, 2010.
- Chapter 17: "Trusted Time Stamps." Jeff Stapleton. In *Information Security Management Handbook*, 6th edition, Volume 4, edited by Harold F. Tipton. Auerbach Publications, 2010. ISBN 978-1-4398-1903-6.
- Chapter 23: "Cryptographic Message Syntax (CMS)." Jeff Stapleton. In *Information Security Management Handbook*, 6th edition, Volume 5, edited by Harold F. Tipton, Auerbach Publications, 2011. ISBN 978-1-46650850-7.
- "The Art of Exception." Jeff Stapleton and Ben Cobb. *The ISSA Journal*, July 2011.
- U.S. Patent 7,941,668. "Method and System for Securely Managing Application Transactions Using Cryptographic Techniques." Jeff J. Stapleton, Bradley L. Morrison, and Arnold G. Werschky. U.S. Patent Office, May 2011.
- "Brief History of PKI." Jeff Stapleton. *The ISSA Journal*, September 2012.

- Chapter 20: "Elliptic Curve Cryptosystems." Jeff Stapleton. In *Information Security Management Handbook*, 6th edition, Volume 6, edited by Harold F. Tipton. Auerbach Publications, 2012. ISBN 978-1-4398-9313-5.
- Chapter 16: "Cloud Cryptography." Jeff Stapleton. In *Information Security Management Handbook*, edited by Richard O'Hanley. Auerbach Publications, 2013.

Jeff has also authored various white papers for customers on debit card payments, key management, data loss prevention (DLP) solutions, and format-preserving encryption (FPE). He is a CISSP® and a former Certified TG-3 Assessor (CTGA®) and a PCI Qualified Security Assessor (QSA®). The CTGA and QSA are only viable for security consultants in active practice. He has also been a frequent public speaker at information security conferences, seminars, and webinars.

1

INTRODUCTION

1.1 About This Book

1.1.1 Audience for This Book

This book was written for several reasons. First, over my career, I have had to research numerous, seemingly disjointed topics, only to discover two consistent trends: Things are quite often designed or built in a knowledge vacuum, and the same mistakes get made over and over. I attribute this to several issues, one of which is the simple truth that everyone cannot know everything, and this is especially true when it comes to information security. In 2002, Donald Rumsfeld was quoted [70] describing the known and the unknown conditions in his report to the North Atlantic Treaty Organization (NATO):

> Now what is the message there? The message is that there are no "knowns." There are things we know that we know. There are known unknowns. That is to say there are things that we now know we don't know. But there are also unknown unknowns. There are things we don't know we don't know. So when we do the best we can and we pull all this information together, and we then say well that's basically what we see as the situation, that is really only the known knowns and the known unknowns. And each year, we discover a few more of those unknown unknowns.

Scenarios for information technology might include a Web designer who knows nothing about general security, a business analyst designing a new application who may know nothing about the current state of protocol vulnerabilities, or a software engineer using cryptography who may know nothing about key management. The consequence of not knowing about information security is that applications and systems are consistently vulnerable to rudimentary attacks. And even if systems or applications are designed with security in mind, the next modification or enhancement performed by another group—without benefit or knowledge of the prior group—will invariably open or unlock the analogous security window or door that was previously secured.

Another reason why knowledge is lacking and mistakes are repeated is simple economics. Lack of resources, funding cuts, accelerated schedules, and interruption by higher priority projects all affect the end quality. Failure to implement, failure to test or fix, and failure to deploy are all symptoms of trying to do more with less, but this really results in doing less with less. Developers might not understand how to meet security requirements, so the solution is ignored. Testers often address functionality but not security controls. Development environments are often sufficiently different from their counterpart production environments that security solutions are overlooked in testing or do not work in production.

Second, another reason for writing this book is to share my compiled knowledge and observations about information security that I've gathered over the years. I've been incredibly fortunate to have several excellent mentors and acquaintances in my career, many whom I call friends, who taught me something new almost every day of my life. They were especially helpful in showing me how to apply cryptography solutions to achieve the desired security goal and at the same time how to manage cryptographic keys appropriately. I recognize that these same folks continue to educate me, even as I write this book.

This book also promotes the importance of security standards; however, even these tend to be segmented into different industries, technologies, and applications. So the third reason for writing this book is to provide a roadmap of various security standards and their applicability to confidentiality, integrity, and authentication. This book also discusses the use of cryptography in each security area and stresses the importance of managing cryptographic keys in a secure fashion.

The fourth reason for writing this book is to help stem the tide of what I call the "lowest common denominator" security. In mathematics, the lowest common denominator (LCD) is used to adjust adding a group of fractions with differing denominators: $^1/_2 + ^1/_3 = ^3/_6 + ^2/_6 = ^5/_6$, so "6" is the LCD, whereas some larger values would work just as well. However, LCD has also become an idiom referring to the minimal solution or the set of least common attributes. Unfortunately "LCD security" seems to be an industry trend to apply the lowest possible cost and often the least effective security controls. Granted, spending

$1 million to protect a $1,000 asset is not reasonable. At the same time, spending $1 million to protect a $1-billion asset is very reasonable. Ignoring security policy and practices, circumventing procedures, or cutting back on security controls are all actions for disaster.

Sometimes an analogy can help clarify a concept, and information security is no exception. Consider the construction of a house. Any building needs a solid foundation on which to erect a frame, and then install walls, doors, windows, and a roof. In the context of information technology, the foundation includes information security standards. The walls, doors, windows, and roof all need fasteners to secure them to the frame. However, much like security, one fastener does not fit all needs. For example, studs are put together with heavier nails than wood trim; wood trim is not tacked using shingle nails; pipes are installed using brackets; and electrical lines are installed using staples. If the right fastener is not used for the right job, then to use another analogy within an analogy, what is built is merely a house of cards. Likewise, the right security control needs to be used for the right job; otherwise, systems, applications, and individuals are at risk.

This book can be used by information security professionals, application developers, information technologists, business analysts, manufacturers, or even end users. Information security professionals have an overall knowledge base with expertise typically in only a few areas, so this book can be used as a reference and refresher material. For example, the (ISC)2 Certified Information Systems Security Professional (CISSP®) program [3] is organized into ten domains, with emphasis on two of the ten areas. The certification does not expect a professional to be an expert in every area.

Application developers need to design and implement security controls; information technologists need to operate and monitor security controls; and business analysts need to understand the security controls to manage risk. Thus, they all need a basic understanding of what the security controls can provide (the good), what security controls cannot provide (the bad), and the complexities of using security controls (the ugly); so for them, this book can be used as both a primer and a reference material.

Manufacturers need to design and produce solutions and services that meet industry standards with reasonable security controls. Both manufacturers and their customers implementing products or using services can use this book as a reference and as refresher material. End users who rely on applications, whether developed in-house or provided by vendors, can also benefit from this book as both a primer and reference material.

Information security is not a destination; rather it is a journey, both in learning and in doing. It is not something to be taken lightly; you either have good security or you have bad security. The "good enough" approach does not work; this has been proven time and time again. The security breaches, stolen identities, lost data, and fraud that appears in the news is only the tip of the real iceberg. Such problems will not heal themselves; it takes dedication to stay a step ahead of the bad guys. The good guys have everything to worry about, but each bad guy can focus on one thing and keep probing until another vulnerability is discovered or exploited. Good security also includes good cryptography.

1.1.2 Guide to This Book

This book organizes security controls into three major areas: confidentiality, integrity, and authentication. These areas have been chosen as the primary categories to discuss information security, although they are not necessarily aligned with other well-recognized credential programs. For example, the (ISC)2® Certified Information Systems Security Professional (CISSP®) program [3] organizes security into ten domains.

1. Access control
2. Telecommunications and network security
3. Information security governance and risk management
4. Software development security
5. Cryptography
6. Security architecture and design
7. Security operations
8. Business continuity and disaster recovery planning
9. Legal, regulations, investigations, and compliance
10. Physical (environmental) security

Confidentiality, integrity, and authentication play significant roles in each of these domains, so many of the same controls are applicable to more than one domain. Other categories have been used to address information security. For example, there is the well-known security triad of confidentiality, integrity, and availability (CIA) for an information technology (IT)-focused approach.

- *Confidentiality* is typically described as the security controls required to prevent the disclosure of information to unauthorized individuals or systems. However, the controls applicable for data transmission versus data storage differ considerably. Further, different data classifications have different levels of controls. For example, protecting cryptographic keys is different than protecting passwords, and protecting passwords is different than protecting account numbers.
- *Integrity* is typically described as the security controls required to ensure that data cannot be modified or substituted undetectably. Access controls can restrict read-and-write operations to authorized entities but cannot guarantee intentional or inadvertent changes. Further, different controls are applicable for data transmission versus data storage.
- *Availability* is typically described as the security controls required to ensure that information remains accessible at all times. However, the issues for system and resource reliability include capacity planning, operations management, business continuity, and disaster recovery, which are all topics that are beyond the scope of just information security controls. There is always a balance between closed security and open systems. Therefore, while availability is an important information technology (IT) metric, *authentication*—inclusive of authorization and accountability—is a more appropriate subject for information security controls.

While data confidentiality and integrity are fundamental information security controls, other controls such as authentication, authorization, and accountability (AAA) are equally important. This book reorganizes security controls organized into the following topics:

- *Confidentiality* (Chapter 2): These security controls protect data from unauthorized access when in transit, process, or storage. Transit occurs when data are transmitted between two points. Process occurs when data are resident in the memory of a device. Storage occurs when data are stored on stationary or removable media. Note that the states of transit, process, and storage align with the PCI Data Security Standard (DSS) [190] for cardholder data.

- *Integrity* (Chapter 4): These security controls protect data from undetected modification or substitution when in transit or storage. Data in process is a necessary unstable state where data are being intentionally changed; however, this is where software assurance plays an important role.
- *Authentication* (Chapter 3): These security controls verify entity access to system resources, including data and applications. There is a distinction between regular data and authentication data, also called *authentication credentials*. Authentication controls include authorization and accountability.

This book also addresses several other important topics to help round out the overall discussion of information security controls.

- *Nonrepudiation* (Chapter 5): A combination of integrity and authentication controls provable to a third party; however, there are technical and legal aspects that do not necessarily align.
- *Privacy* (Chapter 6): A combination of confidentiality and authentication controls for regulatory and legal issues whose scope is across multiple industries, including health care and financial services.

Cryptography is used in almost every information security control such as data encryption, message authentication, or digital signatures. This book dedicates an entire chapter to one of the most important controls for any information security program, and, unfortunately, one of the most overlooked areas.

- *Key management* (Chapter 7): These security controls properly administer cryptographic keys throughout their life cycle and consist of key generation, key distribution, key usage, key backup and recovery, key revocation, key termination, and possibly key archive.

This book tends to focus on the financial services industry; however, since other industries face similar vulnerabilities and environments [62], most of the security issues and controls discussed are equally applicable.

1.2 Standards

1.2.1 Standards Organizations

It is essential that security practitioners have an appreciation of the organizations that develop security-related standards in order to better understand the proliferation, association, and disassociation between standards. Figure 1.1 shows the relationships between various standards bodies. The organizations are sorted into two broad categories: formal and informal groups, and the formal groups are further arranged into international and domestic groups in the United States. Formal organizations are recognized by other groups and have country-level membership linking national standards groups to international groups. Informal organizations tend to be autonomous and self-recognizing.

There are three international peer organizations that develop international standards for the world, i.e., for approximately 200 countries and 1,000 cooperating organizations, including consortiums, associations, other private-sector entities and academic institutions.

- The International Telecommunication Union (ITU, www.itu. int), founded in 1865, is the United Nations (UN) specialized agency for information and communication technologies (ICT).

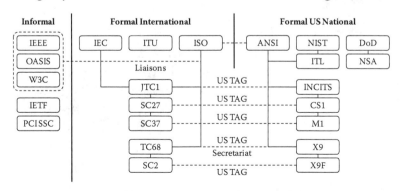

Figure 1.1 Standards organizations.

- The International Electrotechnical Commission (IEC, www. iec.ch), founded in 1906, develops international standards for electrical, electronic, and related technologies, collectively called *electrotechnology*.
- ISO (www.iso.org), founded in 1947, develops international standards for a wide variety of topics organized into over 275 technical committees, including Technical Committee 68 for financial services. ISO is not an acronym; its name is derived from the Greek word *isos*, meaning "equal." ISO has published almost 20,000 standards. The ISO site lists 161 member countries, 112 of which are full participating members with their own national standards body.

The IEC and ISO have collectively established joint technical committees, including JTC1 for Information and Communication Technology (ICT). JTC1 has more than twenty subcommittees and workgroups, including SC27 for information technology security techniques and SC37 for biometrics. The ISO Technical Committee 68 for financial services has roughly sixteen subcommittees and workgroups, including SC2 for information security.

Membership in ISO currently includes over 100 member bodies, where each country has its own national standards body. For the United States, this is the American National Standards Institute (ANSI, www.ansi.org), which is the official U.S. representative to ISO, IEC, ITU, and many other organizations. ANSI itself does not develop standards; rather, it accredits other organizations to develop standards in a specific area, with over 200 accredited standards-developer organizations. Among these U.S. groups are

- InterNational Committee for Information Technology Standards (INCITS, www.incits.org) for information and communications technologies (ICT). INCITS is the U.S. technical advisory group (TAG) to JTC1. Further, the INCITS subcommittee Cyber Security (CS1) is the TAG to JTC1/SC27 information security, and the INCITS subcommittee Biometrics (M1) is the TAG to JTC1/SC37. Other INCITS subcommittees are the TAGs to other JTC1 subcommittees.
- Accredited Standards Committee X9 (ASC X9, www.x9.org) for the financial services industry. X9 is both the U.S. TAG

and TC68 secretariat. Further, the X9F information security subcommittee is the TAG to TC68/SC2. Other X9 subcommittees are TAGs to other TC68 subcommittees.

- National Institute of Standards and Technology (NIST, www.nist.gov). Information Technology Lab (ITL) is a division of NIST that is accredited by ANSI. NIST also develops Federal Information Processing (FIPS) Publications, Special Publications (SP), and Internal Reports (IR), but these are not ANSI-accredited standards. The Department of Defense (DoD) along with the National Security Agency (NSA) develops its own security standards. However, both NSA and NIST participate on INCITS, X9, JTC1, and ISO security workgroups.

There are many standards groups that are recognized worldwide by information technology professionals and information security experts but are not formally accredited standards developers. However, some of these informal groups are recognized by ISO and other formal groups as cooperating organizations that essentially have liaison status. Many of these groups have developed ICT standards that employ or rely on security techniques such as cryptography or security standards that define security protocols.

- The Institute of Electrical and Electronics Engineers (IEEE, www.ieee.org) is a professional association with more than 400,000 members in more than 160 countries. IEEE publishes technical literature in electrical engineering, computer science and electronics, and international standards for telecommunications, information technology, and power generation products and services. IEEE has liaison status with ISO.
- The Organization for the Advancement of Structured Information Standards (OASIS, www.oasis-open.org) is a not-for-profit consortium that drives the development, convergence, and adoption of open standards. OASIS has over 80 committees addressing various ICT and security technologies. OASIS has liaison status with ISO.
- The World Wide Web Consortium (W3C, www.w3c.org) is an international community of over 300 member organizations developing Web and Extensible Markup Language (XML) standards. W3C has liaison status with ISO.

- The Internet Engineering Task Force (IETF, www.ietf.org) is an open and free international community of network designers, operators, vendors, and researchers to produce relevant technical and engineering documents for the Internet architecture. Its mission statement is further defined in RFC 3935 [91], which identifies security as a core principle: "Considering security is one of the core principles of sound network engineering for the Internet. Apart from that, it's not relevant to this memo." The IETF does not have liaison status with ISO.
- The Payment Card Industry Security Standards Council (PCI SSC, www.pcisecuritystandards.org) is a global forum launched in 2006 to develop and manage PCI security standards and its associated programs. American Express, Discover Financial Services, JCB International, MasterCard Worldwide, and Visa Inc. are the five founding global payment brands. PCI operates with its own executive committee and manages its own technical workgroups and task forces, along with special interest groups (SIG) and board of advisors composed of members from over 600 participating organizations.

This list of formal and informal standards groups is not all-inclusive. While there are many other international and national organizations that develop, publish, and maintain security-related standards, there are simply too many to list. Each has its own history and achievements that deserve recognition in its own regard but whose discussion is beyond the scope of this book. This book tends to focus on the financial services industry; however, most of the security issues discussed in this book are applicable to many other industries, including health care, government, and many others.

1.2.2 ISO TC68 Financial Services

The overview of any standards group is always a snapshot in time, and this is equally true for ISO Technical Committee 68 (TC68). Established in 1948, the secretariat for TC68 is ANSI, which has been delegated to X9. Of the 161 ISO members, TC68 has thirty-one participating countries and forty-five observing countries. The thirty-one participating countries (and their national standards body) include Algeria (IANOR), Armenia (SARM), Australia (SA), Austria (ASI), Barbados (BNSI), Brazil (ABNT), Bulgaria (BDS), Canada (SCC), China (SAC), Denmark (DS), Finland (SFS), France (AFNOR), Germany (DIN), India (BIS), Italy (UNI), Japan (JISC), Kenya (KEBS), Korea–Republic of (KATS), Luxembourg (ILNAS), Netherlands (NEN), Norway (SN), Portugal (IPQ), Russian Federation (GOST R), Singapore (SPRING SG), South Africa (SABS), Sweden (SIS), Switzerland (SNV), Tunisia (INNORPI), Turkey (TSE), United Kingdom (BSI), and of course the United States (ANSI) as the TC68 secretariat. The structure of TC68 has several short-term and long-term task groups (TG), advisory groups (AG), subcommittees, and workgroups (WG).

- TC68/TG1 Payment: Payment Standards Evaluation Group (SEG)
- TC68/AG1 Advisory group on registration authorities (AGRA)
- TC68/TG6 Technical Support for ISO 20022 Universal Financial Industry Message Scheme
- TC68/TG5 Cards and Related Retail Financial Services
- TC68/TG2 Securities: Securities Standards Evaluation Group (SEG)
- TC68/TG4 Foreign Exchange (FX) Standards Evaluation Group (SEG)
- TC68/TG3 Trade Services: Trade Finance Standards Evaluation Group (SEG)
- TC68/CAG Chairman's advisory group
- TC68/WG4 Management of ISO 20022 Universal Financial Industry Message Scheme
- TC68/WG5 ISO 20022 Semantic Models
- TC68/WG6 Legal Entity Identifier (LEI)
- TC68/WG7 ISO 20022 *Registration Management Group* (RMG)

Administrative activities are typically performed in task groups and advisory groups. Standards development and documentation management is relegated to workgroups. Workgroups can be formed within the primary technical committee or subcommittee. Subcommittees are established to focus on specific areas. TC68 currently has the following long-standing subcommittees.

- TC68/SC2 Security develops standards for protecting financial transactions and financial services. Adopters of SC2 security standards include Australia, China, Germany, Japan, United Kingdom, and United States. SC2 has published seventeen ISO standards.
- TC68/SC4 Securities and Related Financial Instruments develops standards for tradable assets, including cash, entity ownership, and contractual rights for receiving and delivering cash or other financial instruments. SC4 has published eleven ISO standards.
- TC68/SC7 Core Banking develops standards for banking inclusive of retail, commercial and wholesale, and depository and financial transaction–based services and consumer credit products and services. SC7 has published thirteen ISO standards.

TC68 subcommittees and workgroups have published four dozen ISO financial industry standards, and of those standards SC2 has published seventeen standards. The following SC2 security standards are listed in numerical order along with the abstracts from the ISO website (www.iso.org).

- ISO 9564 Financial services—Personal Identification Number (PIN) management and security [99]
  Part 1: Basic principles and requirements for PINs in card-based systems
  Part 2: Approved algorithms for PIN encipherment
  Part 4: Guidelines for PIN handling in open networks
  Abstract: ISO 9564 – Part 1 specifies the basic principles and techniques which provide the minimum security measures required for effective international personal identification number (PIN) management. These measures are applicable to those institutions responsible for implementing techniques for the management and protection of PINs during their creation, issuance, usage, and deactivation. This standard is applicable to

the management of cardholder PINs for use as a means of cardholder verification in retail banking systems in, notably, automated teller machine (ATM) systems, point-of-sale (POS) terminals, automated fuel dispensers, vending machines, banking kiosks, and PIN selection/change systems. It is applicable to issuer and interchange environments.

Abstract: ISO 9564 – Part 2 specifies algorithms for the encipherment of personal identification numbers (PINs). Based on the approval processes established in ISO 9564-1, these are the data encryption algorithm (DEA) and the RSA (Rivest-Shamir-Adleman) encryption algorithm.

Abstract: ISO/TR 9564 – Part 4 provides guidelines for personal identification number PIN handling in open networks, presenting finance industry best-practice security measures for PIN management and the handling of financial-card-originated transactions in environments where issuers and acquirers have no direct control over management, or where no relationship exists between the PIN entry device and the acquirer prior to the transaction.

- ISO 11568 Banking—Key management (retail) [102]

  Part 1: Principles

  Part 2: Symmetric ciphers, their key management and life cycle

  Part 4: Asymmetric cryptosystems—Key management and life cycle

    Abstract: ISO 11568 – Part 1 specifies the principles for the management of keys used in cryptosystems implemented within the retail-banking environment. The retail-banking environment includes the interface between a card-accepting device and an acquirer, an acquirer and a card issuer, and an ICC and a card-accepting device. This standard is applicable both to the keys of symmetric cipher systems, where both originator and recipient use the same secret key(s), and to the private and public keys of asymmetric cryptosystems, unless otherwise stated. The procedure for the approval of cryptographic algorithms used for key management is specified.

Abstract: ISO 11568 – Part 2 specifies techniques for the protection of symmetric cryptographic keys in a retail financial services environment using symmetric cryptosystems and the life-cycle management of the associated symmetric keys. The techniques described in this part of ISO 11568 enable compliance with the principles described in ISO 11568-1. For the purposes of this document, the retail financial services environment is restricted to the interface between: (1) a card-accepting device and an acquirer; (2) an acquirer and a card issuer; and (3) an ICC and a card-accepting device.

Abstract: ISO 11568 – Part 4 specifies techniques for the protection of symmetric and asymmetric cryptographic keys in a retail financial services environment using asymmetric cryptosystems and the life-cycle management of the associated asymmetric keys. The techniques described in this part of ISO 11568 enable compliance with the principles described in ISO 11568-1. For the purposes of this document, the retail financial services environment is restricted to the interface between: (1) a card-accepting device and an acquirer; (2) an acquirer and a card issuer; and (3) an ICC and a card-accepting device.

- ISO 13491 Banking—Secure cryptographic devices (retail) [104]

  Part 1: Concepts, requirements, and evaluation methods

  Part 2: Security compliance checklists for devices used in financial transactions

  Abstract: ISO 13491 – Part 1 specifies the requirements for secure cryptographic devices (SCDs) based on the cryptographic processes defined in ISO 9564, ISO 16609, and ISO 11568. This standard has two primary purposes: (1) to state the requirements concerning both the operational characteristics of SCDs and the management of such devices throughout all stages of their life cycle, and (2) to standardize the methodology for verifying compliance with those requirements.

Abstract: ISO 13491 – Part 2 specifies checklists to be used to evaluate secure cryptographic devices (SCDs) incorporating cryptographic processes, as specified in parts 1 and 2 of ISO 9564, ISO 16609, and parts 1 to 6 of ISO 11568, in the financial services environment. IC payment cards are subject to the requirements identified in this part of ISO 13491 up until the time of issue, after which they are to be regarded as a "personal" device and outside of the scope of this document.

- ISO 13492 Financial services—Key management related data element—Application and usage of ISO 8583 data elements 53 and 96 [105]

   Abstract: ISO 13492 describes a key-management-related data element that can be transmitted either in transaction messages to convey information about cryptographic keys used to secure the current transaction, or in cryptographic service messages to convey information about cryptographic keys to be used to secure future transactions. This standard addresses the requirements for the use of the key-management-related data element within ISO 8583, using the following two ISO 8583 data elements: security-related control information (data element 53) or key management data (data element 96).

- ISO/TR 13569 Financial services—Information security guidelines [106]

   Abstract: ISO Technical Report 13569 provides guidelines on the development of an information security program for institutions in the financial services industry. It includes discussion of the policies, organization and the structural, legal and regulatory components of such a program. Considerations for the selection and implementation of security controls, and the elements required to manage information security risk within a modern financial services institution, are discussed. Recommendations are given that are based on consideration of the institutions' business environment, practices, and procedures. Included in this guidance is a discussion of legal and regulatory compliance issues, which should be considered in the design and implementation of the program.

- ISO/TR 14742 Financial services—Recommendations on cryptographic algorithms and their use

    Abstract: ISO Technical Report 14742 provides a list of recommended cryptographic algorithms for use within applicable financial services standards prepared by ISO/TC68. It also provides strategic guidance on key lengths and associated parameters and usage dates. The focus is on algorithms rather than protocols, and protocols are in general not included in ISO/TR 14742. This standard deals primarily with recommendations regarding algorithms and key lengths.

- ISO 15782 Certificate management for financial services [107]

    Part 1: Public key certificates

    Part 2: Certificate extensions

    Abstract: ISO 15782 – Part 1 defines a certificate management system for financial industry use for legal and natural persons that includes credentials and certificate contents; Certification Authority systems, including certificates for digital signatures and for encryption key management, certificate generation, distribution, validation, and renewal; authentication structure and certification paths; and revocation and recovery procedures. This standard also recommends some useful operational procedures (e.g., distribution mechanisms, acceptance criteria for submitted credentials). This ISO standard originated as the ANSI standard X9.57 submitted by the United States.

    Abstract: ISO 15782 – Part 2 specifies extensions to the definitions of public-key certificates and certificate revocation lists in ISO 15782-1. This standard includes specifications of the extension fields, descriptions of the underlying requirements, and descriptions of their intended use. This ISO standard originated as the ANSI standard X9.55 submitted by the United States.

- ISO 16609 Financial services—Requirements for message authentication using symmetric techniques [108]

   Abstract: ISO 16609 specifies procedures, independent of the transmission process, for protecting the integrity of transmitted banking messages and for verifying that a message has originated from an authorized source. It also specifies a method by which block ciphers can be approved for use in the authentication of banking messages. In addition, because of the necessity for both members in a communicating pair to use the same means for data representation, it defines some methods for data representation. A list of block ciphers approved for the calculation of a message authentication code (MAC), as well as the method to be used to approve additional block ciphers, is also provided. The authentication methods it defines are applicable to messages formatted and transmitted both as coded character sets and as binary data.

- ISO/TR 19038 Banking and related financial services—Triple DEA—Modes of operation—Implementation guidelines

   Abstract: ISO Technical Report 19038 provides the user with technical support and details for the safe and efficient implementation of the Triple Data Encryption Algorithm (TDEA) modes of operation for the enhanced cryptographic protection of digital data. The modes of operation described therein are specified for both enciphering and deciphering operations. The modes described in this technical report are implementations of the block cipher modes of operation specified in ISO/IEC 10116 using the triple DEA algorithm (TDEA) specified in ISO/IEC 18033-3.

- ISO 19092 Financial services—Biometrics—Security framework [109]

   Abstract: ISO 19092 describes the security framework for using biometrics for authentication of individuals in financial services. It introduces the types of biometric technologies and addresses issues concerning their application. ISO 19092:2008 also describes the architectures for implementation, specifies the minimum security requirements for effective management, and provides control objectives and recommendations suitable for use by a professional practitioner. This ISO standard originated as the ANSI standard X9.84 submitted by the United States.

- ISO 21188 Public key infrastructure for financial services— Practices and policy framework [110]

  Abstract: ISO 21188 sets out a framework of requirements to manage a PKI (public key infrastructure) through certificate policies and certification practice statements and to enable the use of public key certificates in the financial services industry. It also defines control objectives and supporting procedures to manage risks. This standard facilitates the implementation of operational, baseline PKI control practices that satisfy the requirements for the financial services industry in a contractual environment; however, application of this document to other environments is not specifically precluded. This ISO standard originated as the ANSI standard X9.79 submitted by the United States.

The security standards published by SC2 workgroups do not address all confidentiality methods, all authentication methods, or all integrity methods. Historically, the SC2 security standards addressed PIN authentication, MAC integrity, and related key management methods for PIN and MAC keys. Standards for biometric security and public key infrastructure (PKI) were added to expand the scope of security practices for the financial services industry. The TC68/SC2 security standards address four areas.

- PIN and biometrics for person authentication
- Message authentication codes (MAC) for data integrity and authenticity
- Key management for PIN and MAC methods
- PKI policy and practices for certification authorities (CA)

PIN and biometrics are discussed further in Chapter 3 (Authentication); MAC is discussed in Chapter 4 (Integrity); and keys and PKI are discussed extensively in Chapter 7 (Key Management).

1.2.3 ASC X9 Financial Services

The overview of any standards group is always a snapshot in time, and this is equally true for the Accredited Standards Committee (ASC) X9. The ANSI accredited X9 committee develops, maintains, and promotes standards for the financial services industry, including security standards. The scope of X9 includes both U.S. domestic ANSI standards and international ISO standards. ASC X9 is an independent nonprofit corporation comprised of its board, operational and technical subcommittees, and working groups. The X9 board is the consensus body, voting on acceptance of X9 standards for submittal to ANSI to become American National Standards. The X9 committee organizes its technical subcommittees and workgroups into subject matter expert areas, and has the following long-standing subcommittees:

- X9AB Payments subcommittee develops standards for payments systems that facilitate interoperability among traditional and emerging payment technologies, processing both domestically and globally. Payments include traditional paper checks, electronic checks, and retail methods including traditional bank cards, electronic benefits, and other alternate techniques. This subcommittee has the double letter "AB" designation from its historical merger of the legacy retail banking "A" and the check "B" subcommittees.
- X9C Corporate Banking subcommittee is an umbrella term for treasury, finance, and cash management functions within a corporation and for banking services offered to corporations. Corporate banking is separate from capital-raising, mergers advice, or risk mitigation; corporate banking consists of daily cash movements among numerous accounts, handling foreign-currency transactions, financing short-term trade balances, and processing customer payments.
- X9D Securities subcommittee develops standards for electronic institutional trade communications for the securities

industry, securities data dictionary, procedures, information requirements, and paper documents related to securities processing.
- X9F Data and Information Security subcommittee develops security standards to reduce financial data security risk and vulnerability.

As mentioned previously, ASC X9 is both the ISO secretariat and the United States (US) technical advisory group (TAG) to TC68. Accordingly, X9 subcommittees and workgroups also have the international role as TAG to individual TC68 subcommittees and workgroups, as shown in Figure 1.2.

The X9 subcommittees and workgroups structure generally reflects the TC68 subcommittees and workgroups; however, the mapping is not one-to-one. The TAG roles below the committee levels are informal but nonetheless are important to manage the TC68 relationships.

- X9AB Payments subcommittee is the TAG to SC7 Core Banking, which includes bank cards, mobile banking and payments, business identification codes, and international currency codes.

While the X9C Corporate Banking subcommittee is relatively new within X9 and does not have a corresponding TC68 subcommittee, its scope easily fits into SC7 Core Banking.

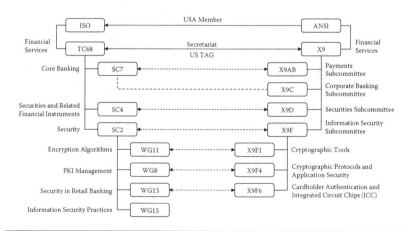

Figure 1.2   X9 and TC68 subcommittees and workgroups.

- X9D Securities subcommittee is the TAG to SC4 Securities and Related Financial Instruments, which includes number schemes, classification of financial instruments, their short names and abbreviations, and market identification codes (MIC). The primary focus of X9D is supporting maintenance of ISO 20022 Financial Services – UNIversal Financial Industry message scheme.
- X9F Security subcommittee is the TAG to SC2 Security, which includes public key infrastructure (PKI), encryption algorithms, retail banking security, and information security practices.

Within the X9F and SC2 security subcommittees and workgroups, there are further alignments where TAG roles come into play by subject matter experts of each group.

- X9F1 Cryptographic Tools is the TAG to TC68/SC2/WG11 Encryption algorithms used in banking applications.
- X9F4 Cryptographic Protocols and Application Security workgroup is the TAG to TC68/SC2/WG8 Public key infrastructure management for financial services.
- X9F6 Cardholder Authentication and Integrated Circuit Chips (ICC) is the TAG to TC68/SC2/WG13 Security in retail banking.

At present, there is no corresponding X9F workgroup relating to TC68/SC2/WG15 Information Security Practices, although if a work item required U.S. attention, it would likely be assigned to an existing X9F workgroup or possibly an ad hoc workgroup.

Previously, security within X9 was addressed separately by each subcommittee. The TC68 model of having a centralized SC2 security subcommittee seemed to be working, so X9F was allocated. Historically, X9F had six workgroups, allocated and numbered sequentially.

- X9F1 was originally established to develop digital signature and hash algorithms in parallel with NIST, and establish requirements for certificate management. This workgroup continues to work on various symmetric, asymmetric, and hash algorithms, prime number and random number generation methods, and a wide variety of key management schemes. Both NIST and NSA are members of X9F1 along with several financial institutions and cryptography vendors.

- X9F2 was established to develop general information security guidelines for the financial services industry. The effort culminated in the publication of X9 Technical Guideline #5 (TG-5) Information Security Guideline for Financial in March 1992, which was subsequently internationalized by TC68/SC2/WG15 and published as ISO/TR 13569 Financial Services—Information Security Guidelines. X9F2 was disbanded and TG-5 was replaced by TR 13569.

- The original X9E9 workgroup for wholesale banking security was transitioned as X9F3, and since the industry differences between retail and wholesale banking were no longer significant, the X9E subcommittee was formally disbanded, and its workload was folded into the X9A Retail Banking subcommittee, which as mentioned previously eventually merged with the X9B Checks subcommittee to become the X9AB Payments committee. The X9F3 mission was to develop cryptographic protocols based on the X9F1 work, and eventually X9F3 was merged into X9F4.

- X9F4 was originally established prior to the World Wide Web to develop an online banking application standard for telephone and dial-up access, but its scope was expanded to include Internet access. Since then, X9F4 has developed numerous other application security standards, including biometrics, trusted time stamps, penetration testing, and others. The merger of the X9F3 work expanded the scope of X9F4 to include cryptographic protocols, and the merger of the X9F5 work further expanded the X9F4 work to include PKI standards.

- X9F5 was established to develop PKI standards. The effort resulted in the publication of X9.79 Public Key Infrastructure—Policy and Practices Framework. Other parts were added later, so this was renamed as X9.79 PKI – Part 1: Policy and Practices Framework. This ANSI standard was subsequently internationalized by TC68/SC2/WG8 and published as ISO 21188 PKI—Policy and Practices Framework. The same ANSI standard was also adopted by the American

Institute of Certified Public Accountants (AICPA) and the Canadian Institute of Chartered Accountants (CICA) and published as the Webtrust for CA accounting standard. With its original X9.79 work completed, the X9F5 workgroup was disbanded. As the other X9.79 parts became new work items, the PKI related standards were reassigned to X9F4.

- The original X9A3 Retail Banking Security workgroup was transitioned as X9F6 to continue its work on cardholder authentication and ICC. Its primary focus is on payment systems and PIN management, including encryption, key management for PIN-related cryptographic keys, and cryptographic hardware related to PIN processing.

The complete list of X9 standards can be found in the Catalog of American National Standards, Technical Reports and Guidelines, available at www.x9.org. The following X9F security standards are listed in numerical order along with the abstracts from the X9 catalog [66]:

- X9/TG-9 Abstract Syntax Notation and Encoding Rules for Financial Industry Standards

  Abstract: This tutorial guideline helps the user to understand Abstract Syntax Notation One (ASN.1), the international standard language for defining and encoding data elements in the open systems environment. ASN.1 provides for a more precise specification of message fields and other data, improving interoperability and reducing costs. TG-9 familiarizes the reader with the ASN.1 concepts in ISO/IEC 8824, Specification of ASN.1, and ISO/IEC 8825, Specification for Basic Encoding Rules for ASN.1, without requiring the reader to read the international documents.

- X9/TR-31 Interoperable Secure Key Exchange Key Block Specification for Symmetric Algorithms

  Abstract: Describes a method consistent with the requirements of ANS X9.24 Retail Financial Services Symmetric Key Management Part 1 for the secure exchange of keys and other sensitive data between two devices that share a symmetric key exchange key. This method may also be used for the storage of keys under asymmetric key. This document is not a security standard and is not intended to establish security requirements. It is intended instead to provide an interoperable method of implementing security requirements and policies.

- X9/TR-37 Migration from DES [64]

  Abstract: This X9 technical report discusses the transition and security issues of migrating from single-length DES to triple DES and newer technologies that include the following topics: (1) transition from X9.9 Message Authentication Codes (MAC) to newer technology providing integrity protection for wholesale financial messages (or other financial messages); (2) transition from X9.23 Message Encryption to newer technology providing encryption protection for wholesale financial messages (or other financial messages); (3) transition from X9.17 Key Management to newer technology providing key management in support of the wholesale financial industry; (4) measures to ameliorate the risks inherent in X9.9, X9.23, and X9.17 during the transition period; and (5) general use of Message Authentication Codes (MAC), data encryption, specific use of PIN encryption, and general use of key management. Note that this document is an X9 technical report; it is not an American national standard and, as such, does not define requirements or technical implementations.

- X9/TR-39 (formerly TG-3) Retail Financial Services Compliance Guideline Part 1: PIN Security and Key Management [65]

  Abstract: This guideline applies to all organizations using the Triple Data Encryption Algorithm (TDEA) for the encryption of PINs used for retail financial services such as POS and ATM transactions, messages among retailers and financial institutions, and interchange messages among acquirers, switches, and card issuers. The guideline should be completed by all organizations acquiring or processing transactions containing PINs, from the terminal driving system to the authorizing entity. The guideline control objectives address security controls from the PIN entry device to the interface delivering the transaction to the authorizing entity. When this guideline is completed by a device manufacturer, the control objectives are intended to evaluate the manufacturing environment and the device's ability to be implemented in a manner compliant with X9.8 and X9.24.

- X9.8-1 Personal Identification Number (PIN) Management and Security Part 1: PIN Protection Principles and Techniques for Online PIN Verification in ATM and POS Systems [38]

  Abstract: Part 1 of this two-part standard specifies the basic principles and techniques that provide the minimum security measures required for effective international PIN management. These measures are applicable to those institutions responsible for implementing techniques for the management and protection of PINS. PIN protection techniques are applicable to financial transaction card-originated transactions in an online environment and include a standard means of interchanging PIN data. These techniques are applicable to those institutions responsible for implementing techniques for the management and protection of the PIN at automated teller machines (ATM) and acquirer-sponsored point-of-sale (POS) terminals.

- X9.24-1 Retail Financial Services Symmetric Key Management, Part 1: Using Symmetric Techniques [42]

  Abstract: This part of ANS X9.24 covers both the manual and automated management of keying material used for financial services such as point-of-sale (POS) transactions (debit and credit), automated teller machine (ATM) transactions, messages among terminals and financial institutions, and interchange messages among acquirers, switches, and card issuers. This part of this standard deals exclusively with management of symmetric keys using symmetric techniques. This part of this standard specifies the minimum requirements for the management of keying material. Addressed are all components of the key management life cycle, including generation, distribution, utilization, storage, archiving, replacement, and destruction of the keying material. An institution's key management process,

whether implemented in a computer or a terminal, is not
to be implemented or controlled in a manner that has less
security, protection, or control than described herein.

- X9.24-2 Retail Financial Services Symmetric Key
Management, Part 2: Using Asymmetric Techniques for the
Distribution of Symmetric Keys [42]

  Abstract: This part of ANS X9.24 covers the management of
  keying material used for financial services such as point-of-
  sale (POS) transactions, automatic teller machine (ATM)
  transactions, messages among terminals and financial
  institutions, and interchange messages among acquirers,
  switches, and card issuers. The scope of this part of X9.24
  may apply to Internet-based transactions, but only when
  such applications include the use of a TRSM (as defined
  in Section 7.2 of ANS X9.24, Part 1) to protect the private
  and symmetric keys. This part of ANS X9.24 deals with
  management of symmetric keys using asymmetric techniques and storage of asymmetric private keys using symmetric keys. Additional parts may be created in the future
  to address other methods of key management.

  This part of ANS X9.24 specifies the minimum requirements
  for the management of asymmetric keying material and
  TDEA keys used for ensuring the confidentiality and
  integrity of the private keys of asymmetric key pairs when
  stored as cryptograms on a database. Addressed are all
  components of the key management life cycle, including
  generation, distribution, utilization, storage, archiving,
  replacement, and destruction. Requirements for actions to
  be taken in the event of key compromise are also addressed.
  This part of ANS X9.24 presents overviews of the keys
  involved in the key transport and key agreement protocols,
  referencing other ANSI standards where applicable.

- X9.42 Public Key Cryptography for the Financial Services
Industry: Agreement of Symmetric Keys Using Discrete
Logarithm Cryptography [44]

  Abstract: This standard specifies schemes for the agreement
  of symmetric keys using Diffie-Hellman and MQV algorithms. It covers methods of domain parameter generation,

domain parameter validation, key pair generation, public key validation, shared secret value calculation, key derivation, and test message authentication code computation for discrete logarithm problem-based key agreement schemes. These methods may be used by different parties to establish a piece of common shared secret information such as cryptographic keys. The shared secret information may be used with symmetrically keyed algorithms to provide confidentiality, authentication, and data integrity services for financial information, or used as a key-encrypting key with other ASC X9 key management protocols.

- X9.44 Public Key Cryptography for the Financial Services Industry: Key Establishment Using Integer Factorization Cryptography [45]

  Abstract: This standard specifies key establishment schemes using public key cryptography based on the integer factorization problem. Both key agreement and key transport schemes are specified. The schemes may be used by two parties to transport or agree on shared keying material. The keying material may be used to provide other cryptographic services that are outside the scope of this standard, e.g., data confidentiality, data integrity, and symmetric-key-based key establishment. The key pair generators may be used in other standards based on the integer factorization problem.

- X9.62 Public Key Cryptography for the Financial Services Industry: The Elliptic Curve Digital Signature Algorithm (ECDSA) [47]

  Abstract: This standard defines methods for digital signature (signature) generation and verification for the protection of messages and data using the Elliptic Curve Digital Signature Algorithm (ECDSA). The ECDSA shall be used in conjunction with an approved hash function, as specified in X9 Registry Item 00003, Secure Hash Standard (SHS). The hash functions approved at the time of publication of this document are SHA-1, SHA-224, SHA-256, SHA-384, and SHA-512. This ECDSA standard provides methods and criteria for the generation of public and private keys that are required by the ECDSA and the procedural controls required for the secure use of the algorithm with these keys. This ECDSA standard also provides methods and criteria for the generation of elliptic curve domain parameters that are required by the ECDSA and the procedural controls required for the secure use of the algorithm with these domain parameters.

- X9.63 Public Key Cryptography for the Financial Services Industry: Key Agreement and Key Transport Using Elliptic Curve Cryptography [48]

  Abstract: This standard specializes ISO/IEC 11740-3 "Information Technology—Security Techniques—Key Management—Part 3: Mechanisms using asymmetric techniques" for use by the financial services industry. This standard defines key establishment schemes that employ asymmetric cryptographic techniques. The arithmetic operations involved in the operation of the schemes take place in the algebraic structure of an elliptic curve over a finite field. Both key agreement and key transport schemes are specified. The schemes may be used by two parties to compute shared keying data that may then be used by symmetric schemes to provide cryptographic services, e.g., data confidentiality and data integrity.

- X9.69 Framework for Key Management Extensions [49]

  Abstract: This standard defines methods for the generation and control of keys used in symmetric cryptographic algorithms. The standard defines a constructive method for the creation of symmetric keys by combining two or more secret key components. The standard also defines a method for attaching a key usage vector to each generated key that prevents abuses and attacks against the key. The two defined methods can be used separately or in combination.

- X9.73 Cryptographic Message Syntax—ASN.1 and XML [50]

  Abstract: This standard specifies a cryptographic syntax scheme that can be used to protect financial transactions, files, and other messages from unauthorized disclosure and modification. The cryptographic syntax scheme is based on an abstract Cryptographic Message Syntax (CMS) schema whose concrete values can be represented using either a compact, efficient, binary encoding, or as a flexible, human-readable, XML markup format.

- X9.79 Public Key Infrastructure (PKI), Part 4: Asymmetric Key Management [51]

  Abstract: This standard addresses the management and security of asymmetric keys for protecting financial information and other associated data independent of the asymmetric algorithm, schemes, or public key cryptography proto-col. An asymmetric key pair consists of a mathematically related private key and public key that are jointly created using an asymmetric key generation algorithm. Only the public key (often encapsulated within an X.509 certifi-cate issued by a certification authority) is distributed to the relying party. Note that all public key certificates (e.g., X.509 certificates) are one type of public key credentials, and for the purposes of this standard, the term *certificate* includes all types of public key credentials.

- X9.80 Prime Number Generation Primality Testing and Primality Certificates [52]

  Abstract: In the current state of the art in public key cryptog-raphy, all methods require, in one way or another, the use of prime numbers as parameters to the various algorithms. This document presents a set of accepted techniques for generating primes. It is intended that ASC X9 standards that require the use of primes will refer to this document, rather than trying to define these techniques on a case-by-case basis. Standards, as they exist today, may differ in the methods they use for parameter generation from those specified in this document. It is anticipated that as each existing ASC X9 standard comes up for its five-year review, it will be modified to reference this document instead of specifying its own techniques for generating primes. This standard defines methods for generating large prime num-bers as needed by public key cryptographic algorithms. It also provides testing methods for testing candidate primes presented by a third party. This standard allows primes to be generated either deterministically or probabilistically, where: (a) a number shall be accepted as prime when a probabilistic algorithm that declares it to be prime is in error with probability less than 2^{-100} or (b) a deterministic prime shall be generated using a method that guarantees that it is prime. In addition to algorithms for generating primes, this standard also presents primality certificates for some of the algorithms where it is feasible to do so. The syntax for such certificates is beyond the scope of this document. Primality certificates are never required by this standard. Primality certificates are not needed when a prime is generated and kept in a secure environment that is managed by the party that generated the prime.

- X9.82 Random Number Generation [53]

  Abstract: Part 1 of this standard, Overview and Basic Principles, defines techniques for the generation of random numbers that shall be used whenever ASC X9 standards require the use of a random number or bit string for cryptographic purposes.

  Abstract: Part 3 of this standard, Deterministic Random Bit Generators, defines mechanisms for the generation of random bits using deterministic methods.

- X9.84 Biometric Information Management and Security for the Financial Services Industry [54]

  Abstract: This standard describes the security framework for using biometrics for authentication of individuals in financial services. It introduces the types of biometric technologies and addresses issues concerning their application. This standard also describes the architectures for implementation, specifies the minimum security requirements for effective management, and provides control objectives and recommendations suitable for use by a professional practitioner.

- X9.92 Public Key Cryptography for the Financial Services Industry Digital Signature Algorithms Giving Partial Message Recovery—Part 1: Elliptic Curve Pintsov-Vanstone Signatures (ECPVS)

  Abstract: This standard defines methods for digital signature generation and verification for the protection of messages and data giving partial message recovery. This document is Part 1 of this standard, and it defines the Elliptic Curve Pintsov-Vanstone Signature (ECPVS) digital signature algorithm. Part 2 of this standard defines the Finite Field Pintsov-Vanstone Signature (FFPVS) digital signature algorithm. ECPVS is a signature scheme with low message expansion (overhead) and variable-length recoverable and visible message parts. ECPVS is ideally suited for short messages, yet is flexible enough to handle messages of any length. The ECPVS shall be used in conjunction with an approved hash function and an approved symmetric encryption scheme. In addition, this ECPVS standard provides the criteria for checking the message redundancy. Supporting examples are also provided.

- X9.95 Trusted Time-Stamp Management and Security [55]

  Abstract: This standard specifies the minimum security requirements for the effective use of time stamps in a financial services environment. Within the scope of this standard, the following topics are addressed: requirements for the secure management of the time-stamp token across its life cycle, comprised of the generation, transmission and storage, validation, and renewal processes. The requirements in this standard identify the means to securely and verifiably distribute time from a national time source down to the application level; the requirements for the secure management of a Time Stamp Authority (TSA); the requirements of a TSA to ensure that an independent third party can audit and validate the controls over the use of a time-stamp process; the techniques for the coding, encapsulation, transmission, storage, integrity, and privacy protection of time-stamp data; and the usage of time-stamp technology.

- X9.97-1 Financial Services—Secure Cryptographic Devices (Retail) Part 1: Concepts, Requirements, and Evaluation Methods [56]

  Abstract: This part of ANS X9.97 specifies the requirements for Secure Cryptographic Devices that incorporate the cryptographic processes defined in ISO 9564, ISO 16609, and ISO 11568. This part of ANS X9.97 has two primary purposes: (1) to state the requirements concerning both the operational characteristics of SCDs and the management of such devices throughout all stages of their life cycle and (2) to standardize the methodology for verifying compliance with those requirements. Appropriate device characteristics are necessary to ensure that the device has the proper operational capabilities and provides adequate protection for the data it contains. Appropriate device management is necessary to ensure that the device is legitimate, that it has not been modified in an unauthorized manner, e.g., by "bugging," and that any sensitive data placed within the device (e.g., cryptographic keys) has not been subject to disclosure or change.

- X9.97-2 (Identical to ISO 13491-2: 2005) Banking—Secure cryptographic devices (retail) Part 2: Security compliance checklists for devices used in financial transactions [56]

  Abstract: This part of the standard specifies checklists to be used to evaluate secure cryptographic devices (SCDs) incorporating cryptographic processes, as specified in parts 1 and 2 of ISO 9564, ISO 16609, and parts 1 to 6 of ISO 11568, in the financial services environment. IC payment cards are subject to the requirements identified in this part of ISO 13491 up until the time of issue, after which they are to be regarded as a "personal" device and outside of the scope of this document.

- X9.98 Lattice-Based Polynomial Public Key Encryption Algorithm Part 1: Key Establishment; Part 2: Data Encryption [57]

  Abstract: This standard specifies the cryptographic functions for establishing symmetric keys using a lattice-based polynomial public key encryption algorithm and the associated parameters for key generation. The mechanism supported is *key transport*, where one party selects keying material and conveys it to the other party with cryptographic protection. The keying material may consist of one or more individual keys used to provide other cryptographic services outside the scope of this standard, e.g., data confidentiality, data integrity, or symmetric-key-based key establishment. It also specifies key pair generators and corresponding key pair validation methods supporting the key transport schemes.

- X9.102 Symmetric Key Cryptography for the Financial Services Industry—Wrapping of Keys and Associated Data

  Abstract: This standard specifies four key wrap mechanisms based on ASC X9–approved symmetric key block ciphers whose block size is either 64 bits or 128 bits. The key wrap mechanisms can provide assurance of the confidentiality and the integrity of data, especially cryptographic keys or other specialized data.

- X9.111 Penetration Testing within the Financial Service Industry [58]

  Abstract: This standard specifies recommended processes for conducting penetration testing with financial service organizations. This standard describes a framework for specifying, describing, and conducting penetration testing, and then relating the results of the penetration testing. This standard allows an entity interested in obtaining penetration testing services to identify the objects to be tested, specify a level of testing to occur, and to set a minimal set of testing expectations.

- X9.112-1 Wireless Management and Security Part 1: General Requirements [59]

  Abstract: This standard describes risks related to wireless systems and legacy networks opened by the wireless environment, defines requirements for managing wireless systems in a secure fashion, defines requirements for policy management, provides control objectives for evaluating wireless systems, provides information regarding cryptography relating to wireless technology, provides background information on other wireless standards, lists other wireless-related standards recognized by X9, and provides information regarding the Office of the Comptroller of Currency (OCC) advisory letter Risk Management of Wireless Networks.

- X9.117 Secure Remote Access—Mutual Authentication [60]
  Abstract: This standard defines a taxonomy, requirements, operating principles, controls objectives, techniques, and technical approaches to enable financial institutions (FI) to support secure remote access.

The security standards published by X9F cover a wide variety of confidentiality, authentication, and integrity methods, including key management. Existing standards are mandatorily reviewed every five years, which can result in its (a) withdrawal as no longer relevant, (b) enhancement to address newer issues, or (c) reaffirmation with no changes. For example, in 1999 three X9 standards (X9.9 MAC, X9.17 Key Management, and X9.23 Message Encryption) were withdrawn due to their dependency on DES and the industry migration to a stronger algorithm, namely Triple DES (3DES). New work items are submitted and balloted by the X9 committee and, if approved, are assigned to a new or existing workgroup.

One of the more common complaints is that standardization takes too long. There are several reasons why developing a new standard can take years.

- First and foremost, standards are developed by unpaid volunteers, who must balance their full-time day jobs and families. Most participants use their evenings or weekends to write or review standards. Rarely are full-time or even part-time technical editors available to write hundreds or thousands of sentences, draw diagrams, craft charts, review material drafted by others, and provide constructive comments to improve the documents.
- Secondly and just as important, subject matter experts (SME) are necessary to ensure the material is correct, complete, and consistent. Finding, recruiting, and retaining volunteer SME can often be problematic. Not all SME agree on the issues or the solutions. Negotiations and diplomacy are an important aspect of every standards-development effort, and many participants have their own overt and covert agendas. Debates, heated discussion, and sometimes antagonism are part and parcel of any workgroup, whether it is between representatives from different countries, companies, or just individuals who fundamentally disagree on an issue.

- Thirdly, standards development is a consensus process. Formal and sometimes informal workgroup ballots are necessary. For example, in ISO development, the initial document is a working draft (WD), which, to become a committee draft (CD), requires a ballot. For the document to be promoted from a CD to a draft international standard (DIS) requires another ballot. And for a final draft international standard (FDIS) to become an international standard, a final ballot is required. The X9 development process is similar. Workgroup ballots are not required but are often used to determine if the draft is ready for a subcommittee ballot. Once the ballot comments have been resolved, the draft is then ready for an X9 committee ballot. And once those ballot comments have been resolved, the draft must undergo an ANSI review before it is promoted to a newly approved ANSI standard. So in addition to the original development time and the comment resolution times, the ballot process itself can take many months.

It is important to recognize that consensus does not mean unanimous agreement. Although most standards are by majority approval with no negative votes, this is not always the case. Some negative votes with their "no" comments cannot be resolved. When this occurs, the voter is notified that the workgroup has been unable to address the comments but that sufficient votes have approved the standard and that it will be published despite the negative vote. Most voters cast a negative vote with comments in the hopes of improving the draft standard, while occasionally others sometimes are taking a position or making a public statement.

1.2.4 Standards Depreciation

There is an interesting industry phenomenon that occurs around standards, as they tend to be depreciated from their publication to implementation. Figure 1.3 shows a typical four-phased implementation cycle beginning with the publication of a standard in the "design" phase. Once the standard is published, manufacturers develop or enhance a hardware or software product that is compliant with the standard. Once the product becomes available, implementers purchase

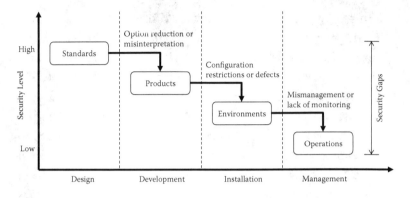

Figure 1.3 Standards implementation cycle.

or lease the product and install it for use within their environment. Once the installation is completed, the product is used and managed within the environment. However, as the security requirements and recommendations migrate across the standards implementation cycle, they are often overlooked, misinterpreted, or affected by product defects or mismanagement of the product in its operational environment.

The following stages of the standards implementation cycle are described in general terms with no particular methodology, developmental tool, system, or programming language in mind. These descriptions are based on empirical evidence observed over years of experience performing product evaluations, security assessments, and information security audits.

- *Design* is when solutions to meet the business, functional, and nonfunctional requirements are determined and integrated on paper. Business requirements are those necessary features that the product must offer to be usable and successful within a given market. The functional requirements are the technical aspects of the product that enable the business features, and the nonfunctional requirements are basically everything else to make the product reliable, including security, availability, regulatory, legal, and contractual issues.

  Industry standards are one of the many inputs into the design phase that influence hardware, firmware, or software components. Hardware considerations include power, emissions, weight, and size restrictions. Firmware considerations include power, memory, and storage limitations. Software considerations include protocols, languages, and toolkits for communications, interoperability, and functionality. During design, assumptions and dependencies can affect the later development, installation, and management phases. This is especially true for security issues, typically lumped into non-functional requirements, relating to confidentiality, integrity, and authentication. Industry security standards are often considered "best practices," implying that something less is acceptable. In reality, industry security standards are written using "shall" for mandatory requirements, and "should" for recommendations. Thus, designing to only the "shall" requirements is really the minimally acceptable practices, whereas designs that address both the "shall" and "should" requirements and recommendations are actually following best practices.

- *Development* is when the hardware is created, the code is written, and everything is tested to ensure that things work as designed and, further, that things don't work as designed. The former is easier, whereas the latter is much more difficult to accomplish. For example, checking that a given input produces an expected output is deterministic and far easier than to ascertain that any random input does not trigger a known or unknown vulnerability. Establishing an assurance level that hardware or software products do not contain any vulnerability that might allow an adversary to attack an application or network component is not an easy task. However, hardware or software assurance is a complicated endeavor addressed by other fields of study and is subsequently outside the scope of this book.

  During the development stage, problems sometimes occur that affect the design. Limitations of resources, funding, or technology can impact deadlines such that features or functionality are removed from the current project, thereby affecting the product. Worse, testing might be curtailed such that problems go undiscovered or lesser known bugs are relegated to later releases. This can likewise affect security-related controls, such that the best practices are weakened to "good enough" practices, and the product is shipped to market on time. Another security-related issue is the misinterpretation of a security standard. Sometimes security requirements are stated without a complete explanation of their justification to prevent educating bad actors, such that the developer implements a security control incorrectly, thereby creating vulnerabilities. Other times, the security standard might include an error, something as simple as a typo, which affects the product. For example, in a real-world scenario, an overlooked missing "if statement" in the software caused a major security flaw that required an immediate modification to the product.

- *Installation* is when the product is configured and deployed, including both testing and production environments. All products come with system and application parameters that must be configured; however, products right "out of the box" also have default parameter values established by the vendor. Vendor defaults might be based on the most common usage of the product as determined by the sales and marketing teams, or even the last set of quality assurance (QA) parameters used right before the product was packaged and shipped to market. The most infamous vendor default is, of course, passwords that if left unchanged allow a knowledgeable adversary to log on and misuse the installed product.

In addition to vendor defaults, products must work within their respective environments, which might not have been thoroughly tested as discussed in the development phase. Particular mainframe, midrange, or desktop hardware or operating systems might not support all features of the application. An organization's configuration policy and practices might not support specific Ethernet ports or protocols. Network components such as switches, routers, and firewalls might be incompatible with some of the application features such that some functions might not operate correctly or not at all. Another consideration is differences that might exist between the test and the production environments. Things that work properly in a test environment might not operate exactly the same in a production environment due to slight differences between the two.

- *Management* is when the product is running in its operational environment, authentication and authorization access controls are in place, monitoring controls are activated, and audit logs are captured and reviewed. However, access-control lists must be kept current. Control lists must be reviewed periodically and also updated as needed, such as when employees change roles or depart the organization. Monitoring of system controls, invalid logon attempts, vulnerability scans, and patch management need to be in place with appropriate alerts. Audit logs need to be collected and analyzed in real time to maintain proper controls, and the logs need to be retained for forensics purposes as part of an incident response plan.

  When products are not managed properly, things can go astray without anyone watching. Old accounts can be left active and thus be susceptible to misuse. Current accounts can be attacked when users are on vacation or sabbatical. Unapplied patches or aged antivirus files can allow vulnerabilities to be exploited. Changes can inadvertently expose the system to attack, and the lack of regular vulnerability scans allows such weaknesses to go undetected. Audit logs can contain sufficient information to detect attacks; however, such events often go unnoticed, as the logs are only reviewed when an incident becomes recognized.

Thus there are often security gaps between what the standards require and recommend versus what products can actually offer and achieve. For lack of a better term, we refer to this observable fact as *standards attrition*. Part of the problem lies in the fact that there are typically no standards certification programs for vendors to have their products formally evaluated. For example, NIST runs both the cryptographic algorithm validation program (CAVP) and its cryptographic module validation program (CMVP) by relying on accredited laboratories. NIST accredits the laboratories to perform the algorithm and module evaluations in accordance with the NIST standards and derived test specifications. However, other standards bodies such as ISO TC68 and ASC X9 do not have such validation programs; therefore, buyers are dependent on vendors assessing their own products.

This is not to say that ANSI does not have an accreditation process to establish validation programs, but to date no such programs exist.

Another aspect of the attrition problem is the general lack of education and awareness. To be fair, there are so many standards, organizations, and industry segments that it is simply not possible to follow and be cognizant of everything. Conversely, a payment-application developer needs to know about financial services security standards and develop compliant products. Likewise, a security service implementer needs to know about information security standards and operate the service securely. Consequently, organizations need to invest appropriate time and money in security standards development and education of its software developers, engineers, architects, managers, and auditors.

1.3 Risk Assessment

There are many risk models addressing all sorts of issues such as threats, probabilities, consequences, impacts, effects, weaknesses, defenses, exposures, liabilities, or vulnerabilities. Some models attempt to qualify risk as costs in monetary amounts, while others rely on an abstract quantity. However, it is often difficult to assign costs for various types of risks. Thus, for the purposes of this book, we will use a relative score based on various criteria. As a basis for performing a risk assessment, we describe risk based on the ANSI standard X9.49 Secure Remote Access [46] risk analysis framework. Risks were categorized into four groups for losses or expenses based on direct or indirect costs in funds, resources, or revenues.

- Direct monetary loss is due to theft or fraud due to exploitation of one or more vulnerabilities.
- Indirect productivity loss is due to costs of incident response and remediation.
- Reputational loss is due to public exposure decreasing customer or business revenues.
- Legal loss is due to liabilities and responses addressing compliance to legal, regulatory, or contractual obligations or other civil actions.

The challenge is to quantify risks relative to each other such that similar risks have comparable ratings across disparate applications

Table 1.1   Risk Equations

IR	Intrinsic risk = Threat × Vulnerability × Probability × Impact
AT	Adjusted threat = Threat − Controls
AV	Adjusted vulnerability = Vulnerability − Controls
AP	Adjusted probability = Probability − Controls
AI	Adjusted impact = Impact − Controls
AR	Adjusted risk = AT × AV × AP × AI

operating in equivalent environments. As shown in Table 1.1, risk scores for each category can be calculated based on equations using the subjective parameters of threats, vulnerabilities, probabilities, and impacts. Note that some risk models do not separate vulnerabilities or probabilities from threats, nor do they merge vulnerabilities into the probability estimate. The mathematical nature of the relationship between each of the risk factors has been debated for many years, and likely will continue to be debated for many more to come. Addition, multiplication, set theory, matrices, or other mathematical functions have been postulated, but for the purposes of this book, intrinsic risk (IR) is simply the product of the threat, vulnerability, probability, and impact estimates. The adjusted risk (AR) is a similar product of the adjusted threats (AT), adjusted vulnerabilities (AV), adjusted probabilities (AP), or adjusted impacts (AI).

Each of the threats, vulnerabilities, probabilities, or impacts might be adjusted by one or more combinations of preventive, detective, or recovery controls. Security controls can be expressed as preventive, detective, or recovery types. Preventive controls are pre-attack countermeasures that can avert or oppose attacks. Detective controls are current or postattack methods that can sense, alert, or analyze attacks. Recovery controls are postattack mechanisms that include compensations to present repayments, cover damages, or provide alternative processing. Controls can reduce the intrinsic risks by affecting threats, vulnerabilities, probabilities, or resulting impacts.

- Preventive controls can reduce threats, vulnerabilities or probabilities
- Detective controls can reduce probabilities or impacts
- Recovery controls can reduce impacts

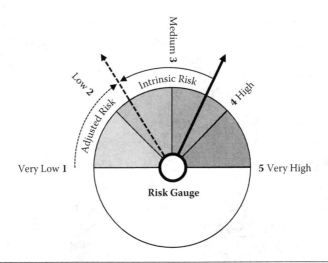

Figure 1.4   Risk gauge.

Figure 1.4 is a graphic interpretation between the intrinsic risk and the adjusted risk. The risk gauge shows the five increasing risk values: 1 = very low risk, 2 = low risk, 3 = medium risk, 4 = high risk, and 5 = very high risk. In this example, an intrinsic risk of 3.5 is shown as a solid arrow, and the adjusted risk of 2.25 is shown as a dotted arrow. The risk gauge shows the remaining adjusted risk as compared to the original intrinsic risk. Gauges such as these provide a quick visual, easily interpreted and understood, and can be created for individual risks, aggregate risks, or grouped by application or regional areas.

The following sections discuss the intrinsic and adjusted risk parameters: threats, vulnerabilities, probabilities, and impacts. Controls used to create the adjusted risk parameters are also addressed, along with an example risk assessment, using a set of illustrative parameter scores.

1.3.1 Threat Analysis

Threats are potential attacks on systems, applications, protocols, or network components that ultimately result in data disclosure, modification, or injection. Inadequate system controls allow hackers to take over servers or infiltrate databases. Unprotected applications might be manipulated or commandeered. Weak protocols can be manipulated to steal information or usurp a session from the legitimate user. Mismanaged network components such as firewalls or routers

Table 1.2 Threat Scores

THREAT SCORE	THREAT LEVEL	TYPE OF ATTACK
5	Very high	Examples include the compromise of a long-term cryptographic key or administrative authentication data that enables unauthorized access or modification to large volumes of identification or confidential data
4	High	Examples include compromise of short-term cryptographic keys or user-authentication data that enables unauthorized access or modification to significant volumes of identification or confidential data
3	Medium	Examples include unauthorized access or modification to identification or confidential data
2	Low	Examples include unauthorized access or modification to proprietary data
1	Very low	Examples include unauthorized access or modification to public data

might be penetrated to allow malware infiltration or data exfiltration. Exposed information might include cryptographic keys for encryption, authentication data such as passwords, identity information such as account numbers, or other types of data. [58]

Compromised cryptographic keys can be used to undo various security controls. For example, encryption keys can be misused to decrypt data; integrity keys can be misused to undetectably modify data; and signature keys can be misused to falsify identity or messages and to alter legal documents. Further, exposed passwords can be misused to unlawfully access systems, applications, or network components. In general, stolen identification data can be misused to enable identity theft or identity fraud. Note that identity theft is when an adversary steals your credentials versus actually using the stolen credentials to perpetrate fraud. Table 1.2 provides an example threat risk score, using a simple range of 1 for very low to 5 for very high, consistent with the risk gauge shown in Figure 1.4.

Ultimately, a realized threat results in one or more instances of (a) direct monetary loss, (b) indirect productivity loss, (c) reputational loss, or (d) legal liability. However, the business logic needs to be understood to determine related threats. Some examples include, but are certainly not limited to: an exposed password that might enable the illegal transfer of funds from its legitimate account to a fraudulent account; a data breach requiring an extensive investigation that consumes valuable resources; the public disclosure of a security incident that affects stock prices; and a compromise that could result in a class action lawsuit that incurs legal costs, fines, and possibly settlement amounts. Ultimately all of these result in financial loss.

- *Confidentiality*: Given an application, its business logic, and operating environment, what are the threats related to unauthorized data disclosure?
- *Integrity*: Given the same application logic and processing environment, what are the threats related to unauthorized data modification?
- *Authentication*: Given the same application logic and environment, what are the threats related to unauthorized data substitution or injection?

Threat scores are relative to the importance of the data and its effect on any business application, not just the one being assessed. An exposure in one application with acceptable losses might cause unacceptable losses in another application. For example, an exposed password for a low-risk application might have minimal consequences, but that same password used in another higher risk application would result in far more severe results. In this case, the password should have been given a higher risk due to its use in a higher risk application. Also, this is an example of poor password management, as the password should not have been used to access different applications of different risk levels. An example risk assessment is provided in §1.3.6 addressing unauthorized access due to cleartext passwords.

1.3.2 Vulnerability Analysis

Vulnerabilities are weaknesses in systems, applications, protocols, practices, or procedures. Systems and applications might have design flaws or programming errors that can be exploited. Hardware devices might have faults that allow unauthorized access. Protocols might have limitations that can be manipulated or abused. Security practices might be insufficient to protect information. Procedures might be deficient or not followed that have an adverse impact on the organization. Table 1.3 provides an example vulnerability risk score, using

Table 1.3 Vulnerability Scores

SCORE	VULNERABILITY LEVEL	SECURITY WEAKNESS ALLOWING ATTACK
5	Very high	Application, system, or network susceptibility with considerable capability to install malware, affect access controls, steal sensitive information, or reuse as an attack platform; also includes substantial human susceptibility for social engineering or various types of phishing attacks
4	High	Application, system, or network susceptibility with substantial capability to install malware, affect access controls, steal sensitive information, or reuse as an attack platform; also includes significant human susceptibility for social engineering or various types of phishing attacks
3	Medium	Application, system, or network susceptibility with significant capability to install malware, affect access controls, steal sensitive information, or reuse as an attack platform; also includes limited human susceptibility for social engineering or various types of phishing attacks
2	Low	Application, system, or network susceptibility with limited capability to install malware, affect access controls, steal sensitive information, or reuse as an attack platform
1	Very low	Application, system, or network susceptibility with negligible capability to install malware, affect access controls, steal sensitive information, or reuse as an attack platform

a simple range of 1 for very low to 5 for very high, consistent with the risk gauge shown in Figure 1.4.

The primary issues in determining vulnerabilities are evaluating whether known vulnerabilities are applicable, and estimating the possibility of unknown weaknesses. Referring to Donald Rumsfeld's discussion on the known and unknown condition [70], knowing what you don't know is different than not knowing what you don't know. Just because a weakness is not known, it does not logically follow that such a weakness does not exist. For example, consider zero-day attacks. In general, an unknown weakness cannot be exploited until someone discovers the vulnerability and develops a corresponding attack; likewise, a specific fix to a zero-day attack cannot be developed and applied until the vulnerability is known, researched, and tested. However a good security program can likely reduce the impact of zero-day exploits.

One of the more daunting tasks for any risk assessment is looking at a blank page to determine what vulnerabilities exist. A good start is to consider the three fundamental information security areas of confidentiality, integrity, and authentication. For the purposes of a risk assessment, the specific source of the vulnerability can be ignored, and vulnerability can be assumed. Consider the following past, present, and future cases. Data damage includes unauthorized modification, substitution, insertion, or deletions.

- *Past incidents*: Historically, has the application data been damaged due to outsider or insider attacks, unauthorized access, inadvertent or malicious misconfigurations, or loss of encryption keys due to improper protection or management? Past poor performance might be an indicator of future problems.
- *Present incidents*: Does the application have any current issues, including unanticipated or unauthorized data damage, unresolved bugs, or outstanding patches? Current poor performance might also be an indicator of future problems.
- *Future incidents*: Based on the past and present performances, future performance can be extrapolated to a reasonable degree of accuracy.

Data damage can include disclosure, modification, substitution, or injection. Disclosure is loss of data confidentiality; modification is loss of data integrity; and substitution or injection is loss of data authentication. Substitution is when existing data are replaced, and injection is when new data are added into an application system or protocol.

- *Confidentiality*: Given an application, its hardware platform, operating system, network interfaces, and communication protocols to customers and other applications, questions about the past, present, and future incidents can be asked.
- *Integrity*: Given the same application and processing environment, similar questions about the past, present, or future incidents regarding data modification can be asked.

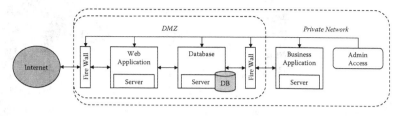

Figure 1.5 Vulnerability examples.

- *Authentication*: Given the same application and processing environment, similar questions about the past, present, or future incidents regarding data substitution can be asked.

As a brief case study, consider the vulnerability example in Figure 1.5 showing a segment of a private network inclusive of a Web application and a database contained within a demilitarized zone (DMZ) consisting of two firewalls and a service application running outside the DMZ. The diagram also depicts administrative access to each of these network components. For the purposes of this case study, we consider the external and internal vulnerabilities.

External vulnerabilities might include weaknesses in the Internet-facing firewall that protects access to the Web application and database server. External scans of the firewall will potentially reveal deficiencies in its patch level that would indicate any outstanding security fixes. Scans will also reveal which ports and protocols are active on the firewall. Discrepancies between firewall configuration management and the actual results of the scan might reveal open ports or improper protocols. However, scans are at a point in time, and so the historical logs can be extrapolated to predict future security status. Further, penetration (pen) testing can reveal if vendor defaults such as passwords have been changed, or if any authentication credentials are weak.

Once the external firewall is breached, then the Web application server vulnerabilities need to be considered, as the Web server can then be infected with malware as part of a botnet or used to attack the database server or the private network. Network servers can likewise be scanned to determine patch levels and active ports and protocols, and pen tested for other weaknesses. The database server can also be scanned and pen tested for any weaknesses in query logic to avoid data dumping. Further, the internal firewall can be scanned to determine any weaknesses that might allow an outsider to attack the private network. Note that if the external and internal firewalls are the same and configured in a similar manner, then the internal firewall might have the same vulnerabilities that allowed penetration of the external firewall.

Once the DMZ is breached, then the business application server vulnerabilities need to be considered, including any logic flaws in the business logic. From a server perspective, scans and pen tests can reveal obvious flaws. However, the business logic also needs to be evaluated for invalid inputs, error handling, and valid outputs. Design flaws, logic errors, software bugs, or misconfigurations can affect the overall security of the business application.

Internal vulnerabilities might include inadequate controls for the business application, weaknesses in the business application server, or weaknesses in the internal firewall. The same weaknesses discussed for outsider attacks equally apply to insiders. The insider might attack the business application, attack the internal firewall to penetrate the DMZ and infect any of the network components, or work in collusion with an outsider attacker.

Another insider weak point might be administrators as bad actors. Administrators require elevated privileges to manage network components; thus authentication and authorization is more important than for regular users. Administrator access should not be ubiquitous; rather it should be restrictive, based on roles and responsibilities. For example, firewall administrators should not have access to Web, database, or business servers, and likewise database administrators should not have access to firewalls. An example risk assessment is provided in §1.3.6 addressing unauthorized access due to cleartext passwords.

1.3.3 Probability Analysis

The purpose of the probability analysis is to tweak the overall risk based on the likelihood of a bad actor perpetrating a successful attack based on the relevant threat and vulnerabilities. Probability is simply a quantitative estimate of an event occurring. That is, given a set of circumstances, the possibility of the event happening can be determined. In some cases, the probability can be calculated. For example, guessing an eight-character password is one chance in the possible password space, which is the character space raised to the eighth power.

Consider the odds for a password consisting of the English alphabet with lowercase, numeric, and uppercase characters.

- For lowercase characters: 26^8 = 208,827,064,576 or about 208 billion (10^{12})
- For lowercase and numeric: 36^8 = 2,821,109,907,456 or about 2 trillion (10^{13})
- For lowercase, uppercase, and numeric: 62^8 = 218,340,105,584,896 or about 218 trillion (10^{15})

The password space also provides a basis to calculate a work factor for password cracking. Assuming an attack capability of a million (10^6) guesses per second, the lowercase password can be determined in less than an hour. However, many passwords are not random characters so the actual search space is much smaller than the possible space. Passwords are often easily remembered patterns, for example Password, pAssword, passw0rd, or pa$$word, such that the search engine can look for more probable occurrences. Keep in mind, the attacker's goal is to find one usable password and not necessarily uncover all of the passwords on the system.

Another method is a dictionary attack, where hash tables of common passwords are precomputed such that the actual attack is the comparison of the stored password hash against the table. Likewise, if the system can be misused to generate chosen passwords, the system can be used against itself. These methods provide a much higher attack rate. Therefore, when considering the probability of any attack, such as password cracking, an overall probability can be assumed. Table 1.2 provides an example threat risk score by using a simple range of 1 for very low to 5 for very high and, alternatively, a percentage value, consistent with the risk gauge shown in Figure 1.4.

The probability analysis can use the range numbers as a multiplier to increase the risk value, or it can use the percentages to decrease the risk; either method works. Percentages allow more granularity, as any value from 1% to 100% works reasonably well. However, for continuity, it is better to use discrete values, as suggested by Table 1.4; otherwise, continuous values are too close together to distinguish between scores.

The probability parameter can alter the affect of the threat or the vulnerability. For example, a high threat or vulnerability can be offset

Table 1.4 Probability Scores

SCORE	PROBABILITY LEVEL	LIKELIHOOD OF SUCCESSFUL ATTACK	PERCENT
5	Very high	Very high probability of occurrence, at least 90% or greater	100%
4	High	High probability of occurrence, roughly 70% to 90%	80%
3	Medium	Medium probability of occurrence, range 50% to 70%	60%
2	Low	Low probability of occurrence, about 30% to 50%	40%
1	Very low	Very low probability of occurrence, less than 30%	20%

due to a low probability or, conversely, a low threat or probability can escalated due to a high probability. Similarly, a high probability can dramatically increase the overall risk if the threat and vulnerability are also high. On the other hand, a low probability can further reduce the risk if the threat and vulnerability are likewise low.

For example, a weak protocol might have an exploitable vulnerability that could be used to usurp an interactive session for committing online fraud. For this scenario, the threat and vulnerability would be rated high. However, the attack requires the adversary to time his interdiction against a known customer using the same Internet Service Provider (ISP) during an online session. But, the probability of an adversary coordinating such a sophisticated attack, however plausible, for each individual customer is unlikely, as the return on investment (ROI) is too low; therefore, the probability might be low.

As another example, a Web application might have a weak enrollment process that is easily exploitable to gain unauthorized access; however, the data are publicly available elsewhere. In this scenario, the threat is relatively low due to the benign nature of the available content. The vulnerability might be medium due to the trivial nature of the enrollment and log-on processes. However, the probability is relatively high due to the straightforward attack of providing an unverified false identity. An example risk assessment is provided in §1.3.6 addressing unauthorized access due to cleartext passwords.

Table 1.5 Impact Scores

SCORE	IMPACT	RESULT OF ATTACK AFFECTING LOSSES
5	Very high	Critical effect on systems, applications, customers, business partners, or compliance issues, resulting in catastrophic (greater than 60% of annual revenue) monetary, productivity, or reputational loss, or legal liabilities
4	High	Major effect on systems, applications, customers, business partners, or compliance issues, resulting in substantial (greater than 10% but less than 60% of annual revenue) monetary, productivity, or reputational loss, or legal liabilities
3	Medium	Important effect on systems, applications, customers, business partners, or compliance issues, resulting in significant (less than 10% of annual revenue) monetary, productivity, or reputational loss, or legal liabilities
2	Low	Minor effect on systems, applications, customers, business partners, or compliance issues, resulting in limited (less than 1% of annual revenue) monetary, productivity, or reputational loss, or legal liabilities
1	Very low	Negligible to no effect on systems, applications, customers, business partners, or compliance issues

1.3.4 Impact Analysis

Impact is the consequence of a realized threat against an application, system, or network. The net effect is often measurable and quantifiable into actual costs. Outcomes might be estimated based on historic fraud metrics or industry research. For example, there are many industry studies that provide an average cost of a data breach. Thus given a cost, c, per customer records and an impact of 1 million stolen records, the overall cost, C, is just $C = c \times 10^6$. As another example, an organization might have its own exact costs associated with customer compensations and reimbursements. However, for the purposes of an impact analysis, the relative severity needs to be merged into the risk assessment. Table 1.5 provides an example impact risk score, using a simple range of 1 for very low to 5 for very high, consistent with the risk gauge shown in Figure 1.4.

As discussed previously, monetary costs might be incurred due to direct loss, indirect productivity loss, reputational damage, or legal liabilities. In general, the impact is relatively independent of the threats, vulnerabilities, and probabilities. Regardless of whether the threat is high or low, the vulnerability is high or low, or the probability is high or low, the impact remains the same. Further, the same impact might result from different threats or vulnerabilities, some of which might have a high probability while others might have a low probability. Simplistically, we can say that the impact is the impact, regardless of whether the attack occurs on a daily basis or if it's one in a million.

Further, it is important to set thresholds such that an impact above some higher level is unacceptable and a result below some lower level is acceptable. Since the higher and lower levels are often not the same, then there is a middle range that requires a more comprehensive analysis to determine trade-offs between losses and gains. For example, using Table 1.5, the very high range might be the upper unacceptable threshold, and the very low range might be the lower acceptable threshold. Thus, anything falling into the high, medium, or low ranges would need to be analyzed for its economic benefits. An example risk assessment is provided in §1.3.6 addressing unauthorized access due to cleartext passwords.

1.3.5 Control Adjustments

As shown in Table 1.1, controls are additional automated processes or manual procedures that can reduce threats, vulnerabilities, probabilities, or impacts. In some cases, a single control might reduce several risk items, whereas sometimes multiple controls might be necessary to affect a single insecurity. As mentioned previously, security controls can be preventive, detective, or recovery types. Security processes and especially procedures added as an after the fact to an existing application environment are often referred to as *compensating controls*.

- Impacts can be reduced by recovery or detective controls.
- Probabilities can be reduced by detective or preventive controls.
- Threats can be reduced by preventive controls.

However, each control must also be evaluated to ensure that it does not create new risks. While a control is intended to reduce a specific risk item, the control itself might introduce its own intrinsic risk or additional unintended risk. For example, as discussed in Chapter 3 (Authentication), consider the vulnerability of storing cleartext passwords within a password verification system. The corresponding threat is unauthorized access to accounts if the password file is stolen. The proposed control to encrypt the password file incurs the inherent problem of securely managing the password encryption key. As discussed in Chapter 7 (Key Management), improper key management might compromise the password encryption key, which results in the same threat, namely unauthorized access to accounts, but due to a different vulnerability, i.e., a compromised key. Thus, while the password encryption control addresses the original problem of cleartext passwords, it introduces the complexity of key management, which basically reintroduces the original threat of unauthorized access to accounts. An alternative control of using a one-way hash to protect passwords within the verification system does not introduce the complexity of key management. Yet, it is also important to recognize that hashing has its own inherent issues such as dictionary attacks for commonly used passwords when salting is not included in the hash algorithm.

Control adjustments are applied to each risk parameter that gets reduced. As mentioned, more than one control might be necessary to address the overall risk. For example, to address the threat of unauthorized access due to cleartext passwords, each phase of the password life cycle needs to be considered, including passwords in storage, passwords in transit, passwords being displayed, and passwords being entered. However, not every risk parameter is necessarily reduced. Again, if the threat is realized, the impact tends to remain unchanged. An example risk assessment is provided in §1.3.6 addressing unauthorized access due to cleartext passwords.

1.3.6 Example Assessment

An example risk assessment is provided to round out the discussion. Two tables are presented for the same example: Table 1.6 uses a probability range 1 to 5, whereas Table 1.7 uses percentages. Otherwise, the two tables are identical, including the threat, the vulnerabilities, the impact, and the controls. The threat is unauthorized access due to the vulnerability of cleartext passwords, both of which are rated very high. Because the attack is easy if passwords are cleartext, the probability is also very high. Further, unlimited access allows massive

Table 1.6   Example Risk Assessment Using Ranges

RATE	THREAT DESCRIPTION	SCORE	VULNERABILITY DESCRIPTION	SCORE	PROBABILITY DESCRIPTION	SCORE	IMPACT DESCRIPTION	SCORE
625	Unauthorized access	5	Cleartext passwords	5	Easy attacks	5	Massive fraud	5
	Stored passwords		Passwords hashed in storage	2	Dictionary attacks	3		
	Transmitted passwords		Passwords encrypted in transit	2	Key management	3		
	Displayed passwords		Passwords masked on display	2	Shoulder surfing	3		
29%	Entered passwords		Passwords captured at entry on each device	3	Malware infection	4		
182.81	Unadjusted threat	5	Adjusted vulnerability	2.25	Adjusted probability	3.25	Unadjusted impact	5

Table 1.7   Example Risk Assessment Using Percentages

RATE	THREAT DESCRIPTION	RATE	VULNERABILITY DESCRIPTION	RATE	PROBABILITY DESCRIPTION	RATE	IMPACT DESCRIPTION	RATE
125	Unauthorized access	5	Cleartext passwords	5	Easy attacks	100%	Massive fraud	5
	Stored passwords		Passwords hashed in storage	2	Dictionary attacks	60%		
	Transmitted passwords		Passwords encrypted in transit	2	Key management	60%		
	Displayed passwords		Passwords masked on display	2	Shoulder surfing	60%		
29%	Entered passwords		Passwords captured at entry on each device	3	Malware infection	80%		
36.56	Unadjusted threat	5	Adjusted vulnerability	2.25	Adjusted probability	65%	Unadjusted impact	5

fraud, so the impact is likewise very high. Table 1.6 shows an intrinsic risk rating of 625 calculated by multiplying the threat score (5), the vulnerability score (5), the probability score (5), and the impact score (5) across the first row.

Control adjustments include stored passwords, transmitted passwords, displayed passwords, and entered passwords. First, consider the adjustments for the vulnerability score. For example, hashing passwords reduces its vulnerability score from a 5 to a 2 for stored passwords. Encrypting passwords during transit reduces its vulnerability from a 5 to a 2. Masking passwords changes its vulnerability score from a 5 to 2 when displayed to avoid shoulder surfing. But a computer infected with malware might still capture passwords during entry, so the vulnerability is lowered from a 5 to a 3. Thus, the adjusted vulnerability is the average 2.25 reduced from an intrinsic score of 5.

Second, consider the adjustments for the probability score. Hashing eliminates cleartext passwords in storage, but it is still susceptible to dictionary attacks, so the probability is reduced from a 5 to only a 3, but no lower. Similarly, encryption eliminates cleartext passwords in transit, but managing cryptographic keys can be problematic, so the probability is reduced from a 5 to only a 3. Masking helps reduce shoulder surfing, but the actual keystroke entry can still be seen, so the probability is lowered from a 5 to a 3. And because there are many types of malware and many ways for a computer to get infected, the probability is reduced, but only to a 4. Thus, the adjusted probability is the average 3.25 reduced from an intrinsic score of 5.

None of the controls affect the original threat, so the threat score remains unadjusted to 5. Also, none of the controls affect the impact, so the impact score remains unadjusted to 5. Table 1.6 shows an adjusted risk rating of 145.25 by multiplying the unadjusted threat score (5), the adjusted vulnerability score (2.25), the adjusted probability (3.25), and the unadjusted impact score (5). The adjust risk is 29% of the intrinsic risk, so the controls provide a 71% risk reduction.

Table 1.7 is a rehash of Table 1.6, where the probability is represented as percentages. The intrinsic risk (125) is the product of the threat (5), vulnerability (5), probability (100%), and impact (5) scores. The adjusted risk (36.56) is the product of the unadjusted threat (5), the adjusted vulnerability (2.25), the adjusted probability (65%), and the unadjusted impact (5). Although the intrinsic and adjusted risk scores differ in Tables 1.6 and 1.7, the process is the same, and the same 71% reduction is shown.

2

CONFIDENTIALITY

We define *confidentiality* as the set of security controls necessary to protect data from unauthorized access during the data life cycle. Figure 2.1 provides a life-cycle framework consisting of data in transit, data in storage, or data in process. Transit occurs when data are transmitted between two points, such as entities A and B. Process occurs when data are resident in the memory of a device. Storage occurs when data are stored on stationary or removable media. The framework is a state-transition diagram that begins at Create and ends at Delete, but as the flow indicates, there really is no "end" to a data element.

A single data element is created into Process A, indicated by the white circle, which might be a manual data entry process, a credit card swipe, or some other input process. While in memory, the data element can be viewed, updated, copied, and eventually deleted. Deletion is indicated by the black circles. The interaction between processes and storage is Read and Write, but each time the data element is copied, its life cycle becomes duplicated, as shown by Copy 1 and Copy 2. For example, when Copy 1 is deleted, its life cycle does not end, as Copy 2 remains. The interaction between processes and transit is Send and Receive. Note that data in transit over networks creates another copy of the data, denoted by Copy 3, which might reside "in the cloud" virtually forever. When data are transmitted to Entity B, all of the same transitions might occur; however, note that Create is not shown for Entity B only to distinguish Entity A as the origin. Entity B might also view, update, copy as shown by Copy 4 and Copy 5, and delete the same data element. Therefore, the total number of instances for any single data element might not be known, discoverable, or manageable. Thus, there may be no "end" to a data element.

Section 2.1 (Data Classification) discusses how information can be organized into categories based on its impact of unauthorized

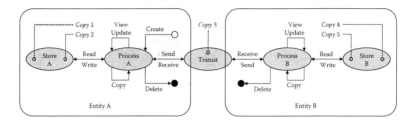

Figure 2.1   Data life-cycle framework.

disclosure due to insider or outsider threats. Table 2.1 provides a grouping of risk-based security levels listed from highest to lowest. This section also discusses the concept of data tagging of other attributes that affect data management.

Section 2.2 (Data States) discusses the applicable security controls when data are in transit (moving from points A to B), when data are being processed in the memory of a computer, and when

Table 2.1   Data Classification Framework

DATA CLASSIFICATION GROUP	SECURITY LEVEL	DESCRIPTION
Cryptography data	Highest	Cryptographic data includes symmetric keys, asymmetric private keys, asymmetric public keys, random number generator (RNG) seeds, salts for hash algorithms, and cryptographic algorithm parameters
Authentication data	Higher	Authentication data includes personal identification numbers (PIN), passwords, one-time passwords (OTP), biometric information, or any other data used to validate an entity's identity
Identification data	High	Identification data includes user ID, name, account numbers, Social Security numbers (SSN), or any other data element that uniquely identifies an entity
Confidential data	Medium	Confidential data includes nonpublic information that has long-term high value to the organization
Proprietary data	Low	Proprietary data includes nonpublic information that has short-term high value or long-term lower value to the organization
Public data	None	Public information includes any data element that is considered openly and widely available information

data are stored on disk drives or removable media. Security includes encryption, access controls, and monitoring.

Section 2.3 (Data Encryption) discusses encryption methods, including session encryption, field encryption, and tokenization. The similarities and differences of cryptography and some aspects of key management are also considered for data in transit.

2.1 Data Classification

Data classification is the practice of assigning information into predefined groups where each group has a common risk and corresponding security controls. This allows common control implementation and documentation that can be audited. The auditor can use a checklist approach to verify that the appropriate data protection controls are in place based on data classification requirements. The U.S. federal government, Department of Defense (DoD), and intelligence agencies have established their own data classification programs addressing national security needs.

For example, the Bell–La Padula (BLP) [10] security model formalizes security levels as consisting of the pair: (clearance, set of categories). Clearances are predefined groups assigned to individuals and objects, such as unclassified, confidential, secret, and top secret groups. Categories are organizational in nature, denoting membership in an organization, division, department, or office. Thus an individual might have a secret clearance and belong to categories A, B, and C, whereas another individual might have top-secret clearance and belong to categories A and C. In general, access is permitted only when the individual's security level is compatible with the object's security level. However, the BLP model does not address data integrity, and the security levels are a bit too rigid for the private sector.

2.1.1 Data Groups

Regarding the security levels, most organizations have similar but not necessarily the same classification groups as do federal governments, much less each other. The similarity is partially due to replication of what seems to work, plus the simple fact that many private sector security professionals have former military backgrounds. In general, too many data classification groups can overly complicate operational controls, and too few groups do not provide a reasonable protection. Any organization has at minimum two groups: public and nonpublic information. Examples of public information might include uniform resource locators (URL) to access Web sites for online services, telephone numbers to call service agents, and physical addresses of retail stores, bank branches, or offices. Nonpublic information is anything else not intended for general public consumption. However, "nonpublic" information is too broad a category to be meaningful, as the source of the information must be considered. At a minimum, organizations have at least three data origins: corporate, employees, and customers.

- Corporate data are information about the organization, such as financial data, intellectual property, strategic plans, policy, practices, procedures, and offices. Some data are accessible by all employees, and some is limited to management, senior management, or specific job roles. Other data are shared with outside groups, such as government agencies, business partners, or service providers. Government agencies might include the Internal Revenue Service (IRS), the Securities and Exchange Commission (SEC), and the Federal Financial Institutions Examination Council (FFIEC), as examples. There is often a difference between raw data and processed data, where the latter have been analyzed, sanitized, or summarized for external consumption.

- Employee data are information about individuals who work for the organization, which includes health-care informatics, salary, bonuses, benefits, and family and contact information. Employees include full-time, part-time, contractors, and consultants. Typically an organization's human resources (HR) department handles much of the employee financial and family data, and benefits can overlap with HR and external health-care providers. Some of the employee data are addressed by privacy laws. Employees also share their employment information such as the employer name, office address, e-mail address, and telephone numbers with friends, family, businesses, and government. Social media networks have also increased employee exposure to outsiders beyond family and friends.

- Customer data are information about companies or individuals who provide revenue to the organization, such as account, transactional, and contact information. Customers are purchasers of goods or services provided by the organization, and can also be employees. Much of the customer data are addressed by privacy laws. Customers typically share some of their data, such as account and contact information, with other providers.

However, not all of the data elements represent the same risk. Risk is often defined as the impact of the vulnerability times the probability of occurrence. For data confidentiality, the related vulnerability is unauthorized disclosure of information, but the impact depends on the sensitivity of each data element. Further, the probability of occurrence is dependent on the controls relating to the data state, whether data in transit versus data in process versus data in storage. Regarding impact, disclosure of sensitive information (or loss of data integrity) can be summarized as follows:

- *Revenue loss*: This may occur when the exploited vulnerability results in direct loss of funds including stealing physical money, illegitimate money transfers, or fraudulent payments such as counterfeit money, checks, credit cards, or debit cards. For example, a disclosed safe combination allows money to be stolen, a disclosed password allows wire transfers, or a disclosed PIN allows fraudulent withdrawals.
- *Resource loss*: This may occur when the exploited vulnerability adversely affects the infrastructure, resulting in loss of services or personnel, resulting in unanticipated costs to recognize, diagnose, monitor, and fix problems. For example, a disclosed password allows routers, firewalls, servers, or other network appliances to be compromised.
- *Reputational loss*: This may occur when the exploitation becomes public knowledge, affecting the status and confidence of the organization. The collateral damage to the organization might include losing new or existing customers, affecting business partners or business deals, or lowering public stock

prices. Such disclosures might be from printed hard copy or electronic formats such as reports, e-mails, or attachments.

- *Legal liability*: This may occur when the exploitation affects customers or business partners who initiate a lawsuit resulting in unanticipated costs in legal fees or hours. The discovery process alone may require hundreds to thousands of hours. Lawsuits sometimes require assistance from outside subject matter experts or other legal firms. And once the case goes to court, there may be additional settlement fees.

Corporations often use the terms *proprietary* and *confidential* data to protect their assets. Proprietary data are then information that has significant value to the corporation but that has limited distribution to employees, and may include distribution to outside groups such as existing or new business partners or government agencies. However, proprietary data tends to be ephemeral, with a shorter shelf life than confidential data. For example, plans for a new application might be proprietary until such time as the application has been announced and publicly released. Conversely, application algorithms or food recipes, which are more valuable for a longer period, might be confidential. Thus proprietary data and confidential data deserve their own classifications.

As discussed in Chapter 3 (Authentication), there is a significant distinction between authentication data and other nonpublic information. In general, unauthorized disclosure of authentication data allows illicit access to corporate data, employee data, or customer data. Therefore, authentication data deserves its own classification. Further, since authentication data are inextricably linked to user identifiers (ID) such as account numbers, user names, nicknames, and similar data, identification data are distinct from other nonpublic information. However, authentication data needs stronger controls than identification data; thus identification data deserves its own classification.

Customer information is not necessarily unique to each organization, as the same individual is likely a customer of more than one service organization. For example, cardholders use the same credit card at multiple merchants; bank customers may have accounts at more than one financial institution; and organizations have many business partners. However, customer information includes identifiers, such as account numbers, and authentication data, such as passwords, so these data elements would be included in identification data and authentication data. Other customer information can be included as confidential data. However, for audit purposes, the ability to "tag" data as customer information regardless of its data classification is beneficial.

As discussed in Chapter 7 (Key Management), cryptography keys must be securely administered throughout their life cycle consisting of key generation, key distribution, key usage, key backup and recovery, key revocation, key termination, and possibly key archive. Therefore, cryptographic keys deserve their own classification.

Table 2.1 presents a list of possible categories. Handling cryptography data with the same controls as authentication data puts keys at risk of compromise. An individual's passwords or PIN must be known by at least the person being authenticated, whereas symmetric and asymmetric private keys should never be known by anyone; otherwise, the key is considered to be compromised. Further, the password or PIN is typically stored using one-way functions to avoid unauthorized disclosure; however, keys must be recoverable and cannot be stored in such a manner, as this would make them useless. While it is true that both authentication data and keys must be encrypted during transmission, this only gives a one-in-three common attribute; thus, again, cryptography data and authentication data must have separate classification groups.

Managing authentication data the same as identification data may not be practical. Identification data are used by applications as the primary search field for employee and customer records and to process customer data. While it is technically possible to store identification data using one-way functions, the one-way result is essentially an alias for the original identifier. For example, if the identifier is an e-mail address or account number and the one-way result is an arbitrary string of alphanumeric characters, the new string becomes a token for the original identifier. Refer to Section 2.3.3 (Data Tokenization) for details. In general, if the identifier without sufficient authentication can be used to perpetrate identity theft or fraud, then it must be protected. Extreme care must be taken to avoid situations where the same data element is reused sometimes as an identifier and other times as authentication data. Regardless, it is prudent to encrypt identification data in transit similar to authentication data and cryptography data.

As discussed previously, many of the controls for confidential data are the same as for cryptography, authentication, and identification data; however, there are significant differences. Attempting to manage all confidential data at higher security levels such as dual control with split knowledge is problematic and overly expensive, yet lowering security controls for cryptographic keys and authentication data to the lowest common denominator puts an organization at significant risk. The control differences between identification data and confidential data are also different, such as monitoring using data loss prevention (DLP), data pattern recognition, and data sanitization methods.

2.1.2 Data Tagging

Data elements have attributes that include a data field name, format, and length. For example, the data field names "Account Number," "Acct Num," or "Card No" might mean the same data field across different systems. The data field format might be "N" for numeric, but the lengths might be different, such as "16" for a credit card number, "19" for the maximum card number length per ISO 7812 [113], or "VAR" for a variable-length field. Maintaining consistency across multiple applications, platforms, operating systems, and programming languages is a constant challenge to developers. Data tagging can be another managed field attribute or an explicit tag such as a database column or an XML field.

Similar to data field attributes and analogous to the BLP categories, data can be "tagged" to reflect its security classification and other associated information. For example, the PCI DSS [190] defines two data types: cardholder data and sensitive authentication data. Cardholder data are defined as Primary Account Number (PAN), Cardholder Name, Service Code, and Expiration Date. Data fields that contain PCI data can be tagged as "PCI" to manage them appropriately. However, data fields that contain the PAN might contain other account numbers that are not within the PCI scope, so tagging a field as "PCI" can be misleading if not managed properly. Likewise, tagging the field as "identification" or "confidential" would not necessarily be sufficient for PCI governance.

Sensitive authentication data (S40) are defined as Full Magnetic Stripe Data, CAV2/CVC2/CVV2/CID, and PIN/PIN Block. Ironically PCI DSS v2.0 mentions passwords in thirty of its requirements and testing procedures, but it does not include passwords in sensitive authentication data, since they are not part of the regular payment system. However, cardholders often log onto online systems to purchase goods and services using their credit cards, so arguably customer passwords should be included in the PCI-sensitive authentication data. Regardless, an authentication data field might contain a wide variety of authentication data elements that might not always relate to PCI, so again the ability to distinguish PCI data from other authentication data elements would be beneficial for PCI governance.

Another interesting data tag might be "privacy" to recognize data elements that fall under international, federal, or state privacy laws. However, since many data fields are applicable to many regulations, multiple tags would be appropriate. For example, an account number is governed by several regulations including privacy laws, PCI (as discussed previously), Gramm–Leach–Bliley Act (GLB), and others. If the individual data fields are appropriately tagged, then resources that transmit, process, or store such data inherit the risk and, correspondingly, the controls to reduce risk. For example, an application that processes PCI data are subject to PCI compliance. Alternatively, attempting to manage tagged resources without tagging data fields is problematic, as changes to inputs or outputs affect the resources.

2.2 Data States

Data has its own unique life cycle: It can be entered, created, distributed, stored, read, written, updated, and deleted. Interestingly, a data element can exist simultaneously in any of these phases. For example, a person's name can be entered into a system and stored into a database; a copy can be sent to a backup system; the name can be viewed remotely and stored locally; and it can be updated. Regardless of where data might be in its life cycle, it occurs in one of three data states: data in transit, data in process, and data in storage. The security issues for each state can be addressed separately.

2.2.1 Data in Transit

Transit occurs when data are transmitted between two points—the sender and the receiver. However, there may be many points in between the originator and the final recipient. For example, if point A is the originator and D is the final recipient, then the flow of message M might be A → B → C → D, where:

- A is the originator to the final receiver D
- A is the initial sender to the intermediate receiver B
- B is the intermediate sender to the intermediate receiver C
- C is the intermediate sender to the final receiver D

For data in transit, confidentiality is possible only (a) when the transmission path can be totally isolated from eavesdropping, such as an infrared or laser beam, or (b) when using encryption on public networks such as the Internet or other telecommunication networks. Encryption has overhead in the form of (a) the extra resources necessary to perform the encryption by the sender and the decryption by the receiver and (b) the additional procedures to manage cryptographic keys over their life cycle. Encryption is a valuable tool that is equally applicable to public and private networks. In general, if there are entities with any type of network access that are not authorized to access the data, then the data should be encrypted. This applies to outsiders and insiders, as even trusted network and systems administrators who have access to resources that transmit, process, or store sensitive information are themselves inevitably vulnerable to bribery or blackmail. For example, a well-known deterrent is to disallow store clerks access to the safe, thereby reducing the risk of insider theft and, just as importantly, outsider robbery. And to continue the analogy, as with any deterrent, risk is not eliminated, as the store clerk still needs access to the cash register, so there remains residual risk of insider theft, outsider robbery, collusion, and physical harm.

2.2.1.1 Encryption Methods

- *Method 1*: This method is often called *end-to-end (E2E) encryption* (see Table 2.2). Message M is encrypted using the symmetric key (K_{AD}) established between A and D, where A encrypts the message and D decrypts the message. The

Table 2.2 E2E Encryption Framework

A	→	B	→	C	→	D
K_{AD}	$K_{AD}(M)$		$K_{AD}(M)$		$K_{AD}(M)$	K_{AD}

intermediaries B and C cannot read the encrypted message because they do not have access to the cryptographic key (K_{AD}). However, this requires that each originator establish and maintain a different key with each final recipient.

2.2.1.2 Encryption Methods 2
- *Method 2*: This method is often called *point-to-point (P2P) encryption* (see Table 2.3). Message M is encrypted using the symmetric key (K_{AB}) established between A and B, where A encrypts the message and B decrypts the message. Message M is reencrypted using the symmetric key (K_{BC}) established between B and C, where B encrypts the message and C decrypts the message. Again, message M is reencrypted using the symmetric key (K_{CD}) established between C and D, where C reencrypts the message and D decrypts the message. There are two schemes for this method designated as 2A and 2B. Method 2A is where each intermediate performs the decrypt and reencrypt as two separate functions where the intermediary can read the message. Method 2B is where the decrypt and reencrypt are combined into a single function called *translation* performed inside a cryptographic hardware module such that the intermediary cannot access the message. Regardless of the scheme, each originator only needs to establish and maintain a cryptographic key with the nearest intermediary.

As discussed in Chapter 3 (Authentication) for possession factors, method 2B is used for ATM and point-of-sale (POS) networks to securely transport the cardholder's PIN from the merchant point of entry to the issuer for verification (see Table 2.4). Participants in debit networks are required

Table 2.3 P2P Encryption Framework

A	→	B	→	C	→	D
K_{AB}	$K_{AB}(M)$	K_{AB} K_{BC}	$K_{BC}(M)$	K_{BC} K_{CD}	$K_{CD}(M)$	K_{CD}

Table 2.4 PIN Encryption Framework

MERCHANT	→	ACQUIRER	→	NETWORK	→	ISSUER
Key A	A(PIN)	Key A	N(PIN)	Key N	I(PIN)	Key I
		Key N		Key I		

to perform PIN translations using approved cryptographic hardware. The major electronic funds transfer (EFT) networks such as STAR, Pulse, and NYCE adopted TR-39 [65] as the security assessment criterion, which is a guideline for X9.8 PIN management [38] and X9.24 key management [42] requirements. Formerly known as TG-3, the TR-39 guideline is the basis for certified TG-3 assessors (CTGA) to perform evaluations of network members.

2.2.1.3 Encryption Methods 3

- *Method 3*: This method is another point-to-point (P2P) encryption scheme using asymmetric cryptography (see Table 2.5). Message M is encrypted using the symmetric key (K_{AD}) randomly generated by A, where A encrypts the symmetric key using D's asymmetric public key (PK_D) and D decrypts the symmetric key using its asymmetric private key (PP_D), which allows D to decrypt the message. As described in method 1, the intermediaries B and C cannot read the encrypted message because they do not have access to the symmetric key (K_{AD}), which cannot be decrypted using D's public key (PK_D). This scheme requires that each originator obtain the public key of each final recipient.

In general, the scheme described in method 3 is included in the Secure Socket Layer (SSL) and Transport Layer Security (TLS) cipher suites [94]. Using asymmetric keys to establish symmetric keys can be accomplished via key transport, as shown in Table 2.5, or via key agreement. Other P2P encryption schemes include Virtual Private Networks (VPN)

Table 2.5 Asymmetric Encryption Framework

A	→	B	→	C	→	D
PK_D K_{AD}	$PK_D(K_{AD})$		$PK_D(K_{AD})$		$PK_D(K_{AD})$	PP_D
	$K_{AD}(M)$		$K_{AD}(M)$		$K_{AD}(M)$	

and VPN/SSL, Internet Protocol Security (IPsec), and link encryption. The key management schemes to securely establish symmetric keys or asymmetric keys are discussed in Chapter 7 (Key Management).

2.2.2 Data in Process

Process occurs when data are resident in the memory of a device. By necessity, data are processed as cleartext (unencrypted data), although this may change in the near future. Homomorphic encryption is a type of cryptography that allows certain computations on the ciphertext that translates back to the cleartext [11]. For example, entity A might encrypt cleartext and send it to entity B for processing without providing the encryption key. Entity B can process the ciphertext without needing to access the cleartext and returns the modified ciphertext to entity A. Entity A can then decrypt the modified ciphertext to recover the modified cleartext. This cryptographic property has been known for several algorithms and functions, but the practicality of the functions is still being researched [221].

Meanwhile, until such time when homomorphic encryption becomes viable or commonplace, cleartext data resides within the memory of the computational device. This includes all of the previously discussed data classifications, including cryptograph keys and authentication data. Therefore, whether measured in days, hours, minutes, seconds, or less, sensitive data can reside as cleartext within memory that might inadvertently be written to disk due to various conditions.

- *Virtual memory* is used by most operating systems as part of its memory management architecture, but virtual memory is actually dedicated disk space. Thus, at any time, almost any memory page might be written to disk, which might include sensitive data. Some operating systems allow memory address ranges to be "pinned" such that the memory space is disallowed to be swapped to disk. Unless sensitive data are restricted to nonvirtual memory, there is always the possibility that it has been copied to disk and might be recoverable.
- *System dumps* are written to disk whenever software has incurred a nonrecoverable error for diagnostics. However,

sensitive data might be included in the system dump. System
administrators who can access system dump files then have
access to the sensitive data.

- *Audit logs* are written to disk and might include sensitive data.
  Logs might be automatically collected into a log management
  system, pulled to a forensics system on an as-needed basis in
  the event of an incident, or left on the source system. The inclu-
  sion of sensitive data might be intentional or inadvertent, but it
  would be accessible by business analysts, security consultants, or
  system administrators. And when the log files are copied from
  the source system to another, the files are also data in transit.

In general, memory is still accessible by system or application
administrators [67]. Only specialized devices such as cryptographic
hardware modules are built with protected memory that is only
accessible by system programs. This creates a security boundary where
only encrypted keys can be imported or exported across the boundary
in and out of the protected memory. Otherwise, sensitive data residing within unprotected memory is still at risk of unauthorized disclosure or modification. This is one of the primary arguments for using
cryptographic hardware modules instead of relying on access controls
to protect cryptographic software modules. Cryptographic modules
are discussed further in Chapter 7 (Key Management).

Other considerations for memory encryption include cryptographic
keys and software. Symmetric keys often reside in memory during
communications sessions. Keys can be temporal, such as customer
browser sessions with SSL [81] or TLS [94], measured in seconds or
minutes. Other session keys might be used for longer periods, such
as employee remote access lasting many hours. Still other sessions,
such as permanent connections for application-to-application connections, might last hours or days, where session keys are changed
periodically using automatic processes. However, if the symmetric
key is used continuously for high-volume traffic, memory encryption
is not an optimal solution, but for connections with sporadic traffic,
memory encryption is a feasible approach. During its use with the
cryptographic algorithm, the key is exposed in memory as cleartext;
however, during idle periods the key would reside as ciphertext.

Applications that rely on proprietary algorithms can be protected by encrypting the software. The software is loaded into memory as ciphertext, decrypted on demand into another memory location to be executed, and then the cleartext version is overwritten when its use is completed. However, similar to cryptographic keys, frequently called software routines make memory encryption infeasible; only infrequent calls to sensitive logic is practicable. Memory encryption for software modules might be reasonable to protect intellectual property based on risk assessment.

2.2.3 Data in Storage

Storage occurs when data are written to stationary or removable media. Stationary storage includes big units such as servers, redundant arrays of independent disks (RAID), or storage area networks (SAN), whereas removable media are smaller units such as universal serial bus (USB) "thumb" drives, compact discs (CD), or digital versatile discs (DVD). Stationary "big units" and removable "small units" have commonalities and differences that affect the types of security controls. Big units reside in data centers or server "closets," where the facility provides some physical security, but small units can be almost anywhere, such as someone's pocket, office, home, lost, or stolen. Small units tend to rely on possession as the primary access control, but big units typically have at least role-based access controls (RBAC) restricting read and write capabilities. Big units store large amounts of data (terabytes or petabytes), and small units store considerably less (gigabytes); however, either can contain millions of records. Small units can be easily and secretly transported, whereas big units tend to be heavier and rather difficult and obvious to move. Big units typically have automatic backup or replication, whereas small units need manual backup and recovery. These characteristics are summarized in Table 2.6.

Data protection methods can be preventive or detective [58]. Preventive measures are proactive to avoid incidents, whereas detective measures are reactive to identify when an incident occurs. Where one control may have a gap, another control can supplement or complement the other.

Table 2.6   Data Storage Framework

SECURITY AREA	STATIONARY "BIG UNITS"	REMOVABLE "SMALL UNITS"
Physical security	Facility	None
Access controls	RBAC	None
Data loss	Tens of millions of records	Millions of records
Device loss	Difficult and overt	Easy and covert
Backup or replication	Automatic procedures	Manual procedures

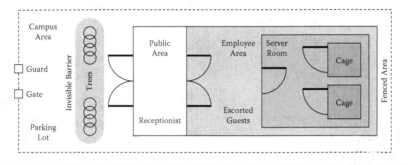

Figure 2.2   Physical security.

- *Physical controls* are preventive measures to reduce the likelihood of stolen devices. These types of controls are primarily perimeter defenses, as shown in Figure 2.2. Campus-level controls might include fences, gated entrances, invisible barriers, and guards. Invisible barriers are basically inconspicuous landscaping such as earth mounds, trees, or rocks. Facility-level controls might include layered access, such as public areas, employee-only areas, dedicated server rooms, and equipment locked in separate cages. Employee-only areas include badges with escorted guests. Server-room-level controls include reinforced locked doors, walls, ceilings, and floors. Cages might provide equipment isolation and separate keyed locks. Higher security areas might include external reinforced rebar walls or double-walled interior walls.
- *Sensor controls* are detective measures to identify unauthorized physical access, as shown in Figure 2.3. External sensors include well-lighted areas for closed-circuit television (CCTV), including entryways, external doors, and loading-dock areas. Internal sensors might include alarmed doors and windows, motion-activated cameras and alarms, and additional CCTV

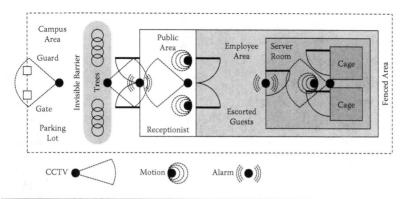

Figure 2.3   Sensor security.

with motion-activated video recording. Higher security areas might include external CCTV covering all walls and roof areas, motion-activated cameras, motion sensors for all externally facing surfaces, audio sensors, and a 24×7 manned security operations center monitoring the video feeds.

- *Logical controls* are preventive measures to reduce the likelihood of stolen data or unauthorized data modification. The primary method is access controls, where entities are authenticated and then authorized to read or write data or to execute programs. Entities can include persons, applications, systems, or groups of entities. Challenges regarding person entities (PE) versus nonperson entities (NPE) are discussed in Chapter 3 (Authentication). Privileges can be managed by groups or individual entities. Role-based authentication controls (RBAC) involve privileges that are allocated based on the role and responsibility of each group, and then entities are assigned to the appropriate groups. Access controls are applicable for physical access such as badge readers or keypads on doors, network log-on, multiuser system log-on, application log-on, and various types of administrator access.

- *Cryptographic controls* are preventive measures to negate the value of stolen data. If the data are encrypted such that it gets stolen, and access to the encryption key is prevented, then the data are useless. Encryption works for any sized data storage. However, the implementation must be carefully designed; otherwise, the encryption can be easily negated. For example, if log-on access to a "big unit" encrypted database automatically decrypts the data for the user to view the information, then a compromised password allows an adversary to access the decrypted data, effectively bypassing the encryption. As another example, if two storage systems A and B use the same encryption key that gets compromised on A but the adversary has physical access to B, then copying the encrypted data from B allows decryption using the compromised key from A. Conversely, encrypting data on a "small unit" using a unique key per device with a discrete and strong password would deter an adversary from unauthorized disclosure.

- *Monitoring controls* are detective measures to identify unauthorized logical access or data leakage. Monitoring can be network or system based. Network monitoring consists of systems sniffing and inspecting data packets. System monitoring might include agents residing on target platforms and reporting to a central server, or it might involve remote inquiries from a central server. Data packets or data files can be analyzed for sensitive data such as Social Security number (SSN) or primary account numbers (PAN) to detect or prevent data leakage. Access to data objects and files can be tracked and reported with real-time alerts.

All of these preventive or detective measures are controls to manage confidentiality for data in storage. Whereas the use of data encryption is essential for data in transit and might be useful for data in process, encryption can be important for data in storage.

2.3 Data Encryption

Data encryption algorithms input the data to be encrypted (called the *cleartext*) and output the result (called the *ciphertext*). And to reverse or repeat the process, the cipher pattern is defined as the encryption key. Symmetric encryption algorithms then have two inputs (the cleartext and the symmetric key) and one output (the ciphertext). When used for decryption, the algorithm still has two inputs (the ciphertext and the symmetric key) and one output (the cleartext). Asymmetric

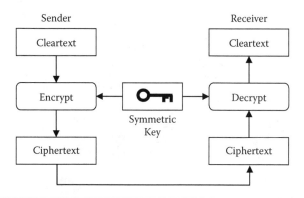

Figure 2.4   Data encryption in transit.

algorithms simply use two different keys: The public key is used for encryption, and the private key is used for decryption.

There are strong algorithms that have been designed and evaluated by cryptographers to be resistant to well-known cryptanalysis attacks. These algorithms typically are selected from an open competition where submissions are evaluated against criteria and each other. The winners are published by government [223] or international (ISO) or national (ANSI) standards. Often the runner-ups are adopted by industry based on the results of the competition. Examples of cryptographic competitions include the data encryption standard (DES) in 1975, the advanced encryption standard (AES) in 2001, and the secure hash algorithm (SHA-3) in 2012. Other algorithms with known vulnerabilities or ones that have not been evaluated (such that the potential weaknesses are unknown) should not be used.

Figure 2.4 shows the relationship between the sender, receiver, and the cryptographic key. This is a simplified version of symmetric encryption discussed in Chapter 3 (Authentication) for cryptography factors. The sender and receiver use the same encryption key, where the sender encrypts the cleartext and transmits the ciphertext, and then the receiver accepts the ciphertext and decrypts it to recover the cleartext. The methods for securely establishing the symmetric key between the sender and the receiver are discussed in Chapter 7 (Key Management).

Figure 2.5 shows the relationship between the system memory and the cryptographic key. Data remains as ciphertext in memory until such time as it is needed. The ciphertext is decrypted, processed, and reencrypted to

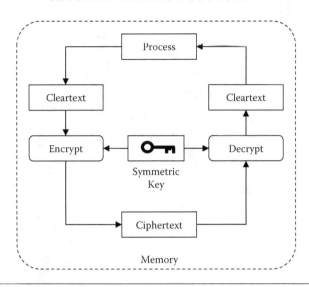

Figure 2.5 Data encryption in process.

protect it in memory. As discussed previously for data-in-process memory, encryption might be feasible for protecting another cryptographic key or a proprietary software module. The cleartext is only vulnerable during its process time. However, if the encryption key is not properly protected, then its compromise will likewise compromise the ciphertext.

Figure 2.6 shows the relationship between the writer, the reader, and the cryptographic key. The reader uses the cryptographic key to decrypt the ciphertext. Typically, the cleartext gets modified, and

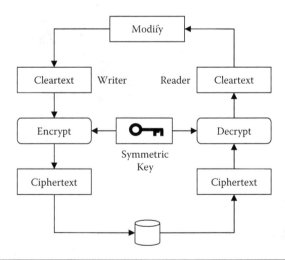

Figure 2.6 Data encryption in storage.

then the writer uses the same key to reencrypt the data. Often the reader and writer are the same entity. For example, an employee reads a record from the database, updates information, and then writes the modified record back to the database. Only ciphertext is stored in the database, and the cleartext is only exposed in computer memory for a short duration. However, the overall security of the encrypted storage is dependent on the protection afforded the key.

Encryption can be applied to individual data fields for data in transit, data in process, or data in storage. Similarly, encryption of all communication messages can be applied within an online session for data in transit or within transaction logs for data in storage. The next sections discuss session encryption versus field encryption as well as another data protection method called *tokenization*. The last section reviews security considerations for data encryption keys.

2.3.1 Session Encryption

Session encryption is when all of the data, i.e., all messages, are encrypted. Security protocols such as Secure Socket Layer (SSL), Transport Layer Security (TLS) [87, 92, 93], and Internet Protocol Security (IPsec) provide session encryption. Another method is link encryption, where both the sender and receiver use a cryptographic hardware device that encrypts outbound traffic and decrypts inbound traffic. To help put things into perspective, Table 2.7 shows how each method fits into the ISO Open Systems Interconnection (OSI) Model [97]. Although the OSI model is becoming unfashionable, it still highlights the differences between the various approaches. This type of encryption is often called a *secured tunnel*.

Table 2.7 OSI Stack

OSI STACK	SECURITY PROTOCOLS	OSI STACK
7 – Application layer		7 – Application layer
6 – Presentation layer		6 – Presentation layer
5 – Session layer	⇐ Virtual Private Network (VPN) ⇒	5 – Session layer
4 – Transport layer	⇐ Secure Socket Layer (SSL) ⇒	4 – Transport layer
	⇐ Transport Layer Security (TLS) ⇒	
3 – Network layer	⇐ Internet Protocol Security (IPsec) ⇒	3 – Network layer
2 – Link layer	⇐ Link encryption ⇒	2 – Link layer
1 – Physical layer		1 – Physical layer

The advantages and disadvantages of using session encryption include the following:

- *Application transparency*: Encryption and key management occur in lower layers such that the application logic does not need to incorporate any relevant controls. Therefore, legacy systems do not need to be modified, licenses for vendor-provided software do not need to be altered, and any changes to the lower encryption schemes are transparent to the applications. Further, any application changes or migrations from one product to another are likewise transparent to the lower layers. However, this dependency of the encryption protocol by applications may inadvertently pose risk, as any security failure in the lower layers is typically undetectable by the application layer.

- *Homogeneous encryption*: This all-or-nothing encryption approach provides overall protection of the traffic, but it also treats each data element within the traffic stream equally. For example, a message consisting of various data elements with different classifications gets encrypted and decrypted at the same time. Thus the sending and receiving end-points have access to all of the data elements. If the message is transporting a cryptographic key, the key is exposed and therefore compromised. If the message contains a password or PIN, the authentication data are exposed and likely compromised. If the message contains identification data, the identifier is exposed. Unfortunately, this approach is noncompliant to various industry standards [38, 191], and therefore may introduce risk to the application environment.

- *Security protocol*: These lower-layer security protocols operate independent of the applications, so management and operational issues—such as exchanging keys, updating configurations, applying software upgrades or modifications, product replacement, or migrations from one scheme to another—do not come into play. However, similar to algorithm evaluations discussed previously, security protocols must also be assessed by industry experts. Security protocols designed and evaluated by industry experts are more reliable than ones developed

Table 2.8 Data Translation

A	⇐ TLS ⇒	B	⇐ TLS ⇒	C	⇐ TLS ⇒	D
Data sender	Encrypted data	Translated data exposed	Encrypted data	Translated data exposed	Encrypted data	Data receiver

by amateurs, including ad hoc cryptography incorporated into application software.

- *Data translation*: Session-layer encryption is point to point, such that data must be translated between each of the termination end points, as shown in Table 2.8. Endpoint A is the data sender and D is the ultimate data receiver. However, there are often intermediaries such as B and C, such that the security tunnel (SSL, TLS, or IPsec) cannot be established between A and D. Thus, when the data are decrypted and reencrypted by each intermediary, the data are temporarily exposed.

These pros and cons make session encryption both flexible and vulnerable at the same time. Secured tunnels are flexible in that many network elements such as firewalls and routers support these protocols: They can be linked together to allow different network topologies to operate autonomously, such that different keys, protocols, and algorithms can be used. But secured tunnels are also vulnerable, in that the encryption and key management is point to point (P2P) and not end to end (E2E).

Therefore, depending on the data classification, the application environment, and the industry segment, a combination of session encryption and field encryption may be necessary. For example, authorization requests are transmitted through secure tunnels, but the PIN is encrypted separately using a PIN encryption key different from the session encryption key; otherwise, the PIN is exposed wherever the encryption tunnel terminates. Exposure of the PIN outside a tamper-resistant security module (TRSM) is noncompliant to industry standards and violates EFT network contractual agreements. Another example is an application log-on request, where the password is encrypted using a password encryption key separate from the session key; otherwise, the password is exposed to unauthorized access.

2.3.2 Field Encryption

Field encryption is when discrete data elements are encrypted, such as a personal identification number (PIN), a password, or primary account number (PAN) [12]. Symmetric algorithms that are block ciphers operate in modes [176]. For example:

- *Electronic Codebook* (ECB) is analogous to code words in a codebook; the input and output of both the cleartext and ciphertext are fixed in size. For example, DES and triple DES algorithms have 64-bit data block sizes, whereas AES has 128-bit data block sizes. If the cleartext to be encrypted is greater than the block size, then the cleartext must be divided into the required block sizes, with each block being individually encrypted. Figure 2.7 provides a graphical representation of ECB.

  One advantage to ECB is that each of the encryptions or decryptions can be performed in parallel, as the output from one has no input to another. Except for the symmetric key, each of the ciphertexts is independent of each other. Also note that the same cleartext encrypted with the same key produces the same ciphertext, which might not be a desirable characteristic. For example, the same PIN used by two different persons would result in the same ciphertext; thus PIN encryption incorporates an XOR with the PIN and PAN prior to encryption, such that the same PIN for two different PANs encrypted with the same key yields different ciphertexts [99].
- *Cipher Block Chaining* (CBC) incorporates feedback of the ciphertext from the previous encryption step to the next one.

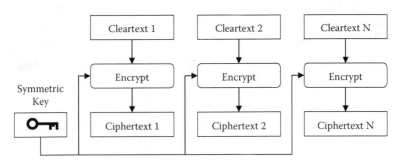

Figure 2.7   Electronic codebook (ECB).

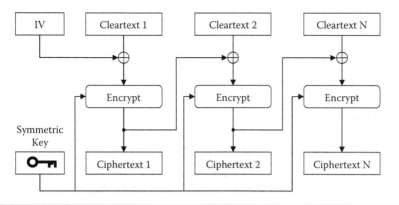

Figure 2.8   Cipher block chaining (CBC).

Since the first encryption step has no previous feedback, another input is used called the *initialization vector* (IV). The inputs are still divided into block sizes: the cleartext for encryption and the ciphertext for decryption. Figure 2.8 provides a graphical representation of CBC.

The IV should be a random number such that it is unpredictable, but it does not necessarily need to be kept secret. The IV is not a cryptographic key per se; it can be reused, known by authorized administrators, and shared among applications, but it must be protected from unauthorized modification or substitution. However, NIST recommends that the IV be changed on each use, such as a one-way function or a transaction reference number.

The ECB and CBC figures are provided as examples, but as this book is not intended to be a dissertation on cryptography or mathematics, no further modes are diagramed. The NIST Special Pub 800-38 suite [176] defines other variants for CBC and several other modes of operation, including cipher feedback (CFB), output feedback (OFB), counter (CTR), cipher-based message authentication code (CMAC), cipher block chaining-message authentication code (CCM), Galois/Counter Mode (GCM), Galois Message Authentication Mode (GMAC), and XEX (XOR Encrypt XOR) tweakable block cipher with ciphertext stealing for the Advanced Encryption Standard (XTS-AES).

The University of California's report to Japan's Cryptography Research and Evaluation Committees (CRYPTREC) provides an evaluation of some seventeen cryptographic modes of operation [13]. The report is organized into three parts addressing (1) Confidentiality Modes, (2) Authenticity Modes, and (3) Authenticated-Encryption Modes. Confidentiality modes include ECB, CBC, CFB, OFB, CTR, and XTS defined by NIST, as discussed previously. Authenticity modes include CBC-MAC [108], CMAC [176], HMAC [174], and GMAC [176]. Authenticated-encryption modes include CCM and GCM defined by NIST, as discussed above. Table 2.9 is the summary evaluation of the cryptography modes and the authenticated-encryption modes from the UC Davis report to CRYPTREC.

In general, ECB is viable as a building block for other schemes but not sufficiently secure to use as a stand-alone encryption method. CBC, CFB, and OFB are resistant to chosen-plaintext attack (CPA) if the IV is random, but not chosen-ciphertext attacks (CCA). CBC is also viable as a building block for other schemes such as CBC message authentication codes (MAC). For each mode, the report discusses in detail its provable security, known attacks, scheme efficiency, usage, robustness, and other topics. One important observation provided by the report is that fashioning a good standard is hard to achieve, both technically and socially, which is the primary reason why standards take years to develop.

2.3.3 Data Tokenization

Tokenization is another data confidentiality method where the original value is substituted for another, and the substitution is used for processing. However *tokenization* is a contemporary term made popular by the PCI DSS [190] as an option for rendering the primary account number (PAN) unreadable when stored. Substitution is actually one of the fundamental cryptographic ciphers along with transposition ciphers and the exclusive OR function. One of the earliest known substitution ciphers was Egyptian hieroglyphics by the priesthood circa 2000 BC. Codes are another substitution method where one word is substituted for another, a technique often used in spy novels, e.g., "ducks" mean "ships" and "eagles" mean "airplanes" in coded messages. The tokenization concept is for a merchant to switch out the PAN for a tokenized value to avoid storing the PAN altogether. The PCI DSS identifies several PAN protection methods.

Table 2.9 UC Davis Report to CRYPTREC

MODE	SUMMARY EVALUATION OF CRYPTOGRAPHY MODES
ECB SP 800-38A	A blockcipher, the mode enciphers messages that are a multiple of n bits by separately enciphering each n-bit piece. The security properties are weak, the method leaking equality of blocks across both block positions and time. Of considerable legacy value, and of value as a building block for other schemes, but the mode does not achieve any generally desirable security goal in its own right and must be used with considerable caution; ECB should not be regarded as a "general-purpose" confidentiality mode.
CBC SP 800-38A	An IV-based encryption scheme, the mode is secure as a probabilistic encryption scheme, achieving indistinguishability from random bits, assuming a random IV. Confidentiality is not achieved if the IV is merely a nonce (random number), nor if it is a nonce enciphered under the same key used by the scheme, as the standard incorrectly suggests to do. Ciphertexts are highly malleable. No chosen-ciphertext attack (CCA) security. Confidentiality is forfeit in the presence of a correct-padding oracle for many padding methods. Encryption inefficient from being inherently serial. Widely used, the mode's privacy-only security properties result in frequent misuse. Can be used as a building block for CBC-MAC algorithms. I can identify no important advantages over CCFB
CFB SP 800-38A	An IV-based encryption scheme, the mode is secure as a probabilistic encryption scheme, achieving indistinguishability from random bits, assuming a random IV. Confidentiality is not achieved if the IV is predictable, nor if it is made by a nonce enciphered under the same key used by the scheme, as the standard incorrectly suggests to do. Ciphertexts are malleable. No CCA-security. Encryption inefficient from being inherently serial. Scheme depends on a parameter s, $1 \le s \le n$, typically $s = 1$ or $s = 8$. Inefficient for needing one blockcipher call to process only s bits. The mode achieves an interesting "self-synchronization" property; insertion or deletion of any number of s-bit characters into the ciphertext only temporarily disrupts correct decryption.
OFB SP 800-38A	An IV-based encryption scheme, the mode is secure as a probabilistic encryption scheme, achieving indistinguishability from random bits, assuming a random IV. Confidentiality is not achieved if the IV is a nonce, although a fixed sequence of IVs (e.g., a counter) does work fine. Ciphertexts are highly malleable. No CCA security. Encryption and decryption inefficient from being inherently serial. Natively encrypts strings of any bit length (no padding needed). I can identify no important advantages over CTR mode.
CTR SP 800-38A	An IV-based encryption scheme, the mode achieves indistinguishability from random bits assuming a nonce IV. As a secure nonce-based scheme, the mode can also be used as a probabilistic encryption scheme, with a random IV. Complete failure of privacy if a nonce gets reused on encryption or decryption. The parallelizability of the mode often makes it faster, in some settings much faster, than other confidentiality modes. An important building block for authenticated-encryption schemes. Overall, usually the best and most modern way to achieve privacy-only encryption.

(Continued)

Table 2.9   UC Davis Report to CRYPTREC (Continued)

MODE	SUMMARY EVALUATION OF CRYPTOGRAPHY MODES
XTS SP 800-38E IEEE 1619	An IV-based encryption scheme, the mode works by applying a tweakable blockcipher (secure as a strong-PRP [pseudo-random-permutation]) to each *n*-bit chunk. For messages with lengths not divisible by *n*, the last two blocks are treated specially. The only allowed use of the mode is for encrypting data on a block-structured storage device. The narrow width of the underlying PRP and the poor treatment of fractional final blocks are problems. More efficient but less desirable than a (wide-block) PRP-secure blockcipher would be.
CCM SP 800-38C	A nonce-based AEAD (authenticated encryption with associated data) scheme that combines CTR mode encryption and the raw CBC-MAC. Inherently serial, limiting speed in some contexts. Provably secure, with good bounds, assuming the underlying blockcipher is a good PRP. Ungainly construction that demonstrably does the job. Simpler to implement than GCM. Can be used as a nonce-based MAC. Widely standardized and used.
GCM SP 800-38D	A nonce-based AEAD scheme that combines CTR-mode encryption and a $GF(2^{128})$-based (Galois field) universal hash function. Good efficiency characteristics for some implementation environments. Good provably secure results assuming minimal tag truncation. Attacks and poor provable-security bounds in the presence of substantial tag truncation. Can be used as a nonce-based MAC, which is then called GMAC. Questionable choice to allow nonces other than 96 bits. Recommend restricting nonces to 96 bits and tags to at least 96 bits. Widely standardized and used.

- *Masking* is the substitution of some PAN digits with a masking character. PCI DSS allows the first six and last four digits unchanged, and the middle six digits masked. The pattern of sixteen digits nnnn nnnn nnnn nnnn would be changed to the pattern nnnn nnmm mmmm nnnn where "n" is any digit 0 to 9, and "m" is some other nondigit alphabetic or special character.

- *Hashing* consists of taking the whole 16-digit PAN as input into a hash algorithm to generate a hash value. Hash algorithms produce a fixed-length output from any length input. For example, MD5 [86] outputs 128 bits, SHA-1 [168] outputs 160 bits, and the SHA-2 [168] family outputs larger hash values.

- *Truncation* is removing some number of leftmost digits from the PAN. However, PCI DSS does not define the minimal number of truncated digits. For example, the last digit of the PAN is a check digit based on the Luhn formula [98], so only truncating the digit does not achieve any protection, as the check digit can be recalculated. Truncating the last two digits only limits guessing the PAN to 1 in 10 possibilities, truncating the last three digits limits guessing to 1 in 100, and so on. Each truncated digit increases entropy by a power of 10.

- *Tokenization* is the partial or whole substitution of the PAN with another value.
- *Encryption* consists of taking all or part of the PAN as the cleartext input into an encryption algorithm with a cryptographic key to generate ciphertext output.

At present there are no standardized tokenization algorithms, but there are several commercially available proprietary ones. At some point in the near future, algorithms will be standardized, but for now this book discusses some of the issues associated with tokenization. Unlike the PIN that is encrypted at the point of entry and remains encrypted during the entire authorization request, the PAN is actually used to route the request from the merchant to the issuer over the payment networks. Further, in addition to authorization, the PAN is also used in the clearing and settlement processes. Tokenization methods might include one or more of the following methods.

- *Random token* is the method of associating a random number to a PAN. Since there is no direct correlation between any token and any PAN, the linkages must be kept in a database. The PAN can be looked up using the token as the search field. The token and PAN pairs need to be protected with confidentiality and integrity, and access to the database needs to have adequate authentication. The token system might be an internal application or an external service provider.
- *Derived token* is the method of generating the token from the PAN using a one-way process such that the PAN cannot be recovered from the token, but given the PAN, the token can be validated. The PAN might still be looked up using the token as the search field if the PAN and token pairs are stored in a database, which might be kept internally or externally.
- *Encrypted PAN token* is the method of generating the token from the PAN using a reversible process such that the PAN is recoverable from the token. The PAN and token pairs would not need to be kept in a database, but the cryptographic key needs to be protected.

Tokenization can be used to help protect data in storage, but its effectiveness is limited to applications that do not need the original data. For example, if the application logic includes parsing of the primary account number (PAN) to determine its customer relationship, the tokenized PAN would not contain sufficient information. Likewise, tokenizing a customer name in one database might prevent searching for the equivalent customer record in another database. The data flows and processing paths need to be carefully analyzed to determine when tokenization can be beneficial.

Unlike a cryptographic one-way function that intentionally prevents recoverability of the original cleartext from the ciphertext, the token and the original data are kept linked somewhere in a "token" database such that applications can retrieve the original data using the token. Therefore, access controls over the token database are paramount. The token database might be managed internally; it might be hosted by an external service provider; and it might even be in the notional cloud. For multitenant environments, the controls additionally need to provide client separation.

2.3.4 Data Encryption Keys

Methods for managing data encryption keys depend largely on the operational environment in which they are used. Cryptographic keys might occur in system memory, within a hardware security module (HSM), or in storage. Cryptographic algorithms might run in memory or within an HSM. Consequently, the cleartext and ciphertext might occur in memory or within an HSM. The relative locations and instances of each component are collectively called the *cryptographic architecture*. As shown in Figures 2.4, 2.5, and 2.6, the cryptographic architectures are similar. For the purposes of comparing hardware and software cryptography with and without key storage, we need only consider data in transit, since it is a more common usage and in general an easier scenario to understood.

Figure 2.9 shows the use of a hardware security module (HSM) without key storage. The ciphertext arrives over a transmission channel and is placed into system memory. An application passes the ciphertext to the HSM. The HSM then inputs the ciphertext and symmetric key into the decryption algorithm and returns the cleartext to system

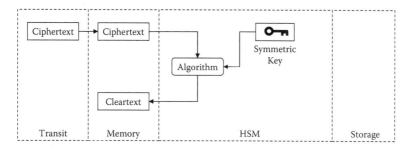

Figure 2.9 Hardware encryption without key storage.

memory. The cryptographic algorithm remains within the security boundary of the HSM, as does the symmetric key. The symmetric key only resides in the HSM. A compromise of the system would compromise the cleartext and potentially allow access to the HSM for using the key, but the key itself would still be protected.

Figure 2.10 shows the use of an HSM with key storage. The ciphertext arrives over a transmission channel and is placed into system memory. The symmetric key is stored encrypted using a key encryption key (KEK). An application passes the ciphertext to the HSM. The encrypted key is fetched and also passed to the HSM, which is sometimes performed by the same application. The HSM first decrypts the symmetric key using the KEK, then decrypts the ciphertext and returns the cleartext to system memory. The cryptographic algorithm remains within the security boundary of the HSM, as does the KEK. The symmetric key only resides in the HSM as cleartext and as ciphertext in storage. Likewise, a compromise of the system would compromise the cleartext, and potentially allow access to the HSM for using the key, but the key itself would still be protected.

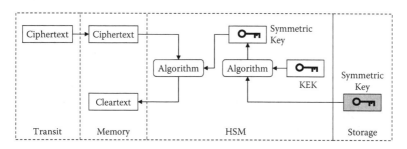

Figure 2.10 Hardware encryption with key storage.

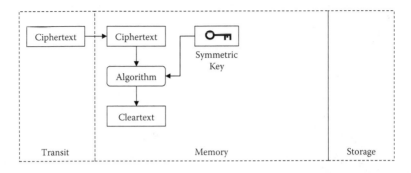

Figure 2.11   Software encryption without key storage.

Figure 2.11 shows the use of software cryptography without key storage. The ciphertext arrives over a transmission channel and is placed into system memory. The cryptographic algorithm and symmetric key likewise reside in memory. The ciphertext is decrypted, and the cleartext remains in memory. A compromise of the system would compromise the cleartext and the symmetric key. Thus, if the system key were used on other systems, those systems would similarly be compromised, as the ciphertext can be decrypted due to the compromised symmetric key.

Figure 2.12 shows the use of software cryptography with key storage. The ciphertext arrives over a transmission channel and is placed into system memory. The symmetric key is stored encrypted using a key encryption key (KEK). The encrypted key is first fetched from storage and decrypted using the KEK; then the ciphertext is decrypted using the recovered symmetric key, and the cleartext remains in memory. A compromise of the system would compromise the cleartext and the KEK, and therefore the symmetric key would be compromised. Thus

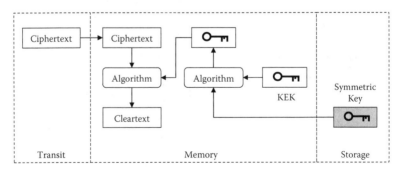

Figure 2.12   Software encryption with key storage.

if the KEK or the symmetric key were used on other systems, those systems would similarly be compromised, as the ciphertext can be decrypted due to the compromised symmetric key. In general, software cryptography, regardless of whether key storage is used, puts cryptographic keys at undue risk.

When physical theft occurs, the missing items and collateral breakage is clear evidence of the illegal incident. However, when data are stolen, its duplication does not leave evidence. Likewise, when a cryptographic key is stolen, its replication leaves no evidence. Further, when the key is used illicitly to decrypt stolen ciphertext, its use is undetectable. Normally the theft of ciphertext is a low-risk issue, but in the unlikely event that the data encryption key has been stolen, the risk is significantly elevated. The ability to detect data theft due to a compromised key is virtually impossible to determine; therefore, the only practical recourse is to protect the cryptographic keys as best as possible.

3
AUTHENTICATION

Authentication is the security discipline for verifying an entity requesting access to system resources or applications. The entity might be a person or a nonperson such as router, firewall, application, database, or other system component. The service providing the verification is called the *verifier* and typically performs this for the system resource or application that is the relying party. There are many authentication methods, but all can be categorized into discrete groups called *authentication factors*. Each factor has advantages and disadvantages, depending on the type of entity and the environment in which it is used—whimsically called the good, the bad, and sometimes the ugly. X9 standards such as X9.117 [60] provide the following definitions:

- *Single-factor authentication*: Authentication of one entity to another using only one authentication technique (note: a credential could contain more than one factor).
- *Mutual authentication*: Process whereby at least two entities each obtain sufficient assurance of the others' identities.
- *Multifactor authentication*: Authentication is the use of two or more independent and different authentication techniques together. The use of multifactor authentication within the scope of this standard means that two or more techniques will be used from the following techniques: something you know, something you possess, and something you are.

The FFIEC Authentication Guideline [7] describes layered security programs as follows:

- *Layered security*: Characterized by the use of different controls at different points in a transaction process so that a weakness in one control is generally compensated for by the strength of a different control. Effective controls include fraud detection and monitoring, dual customer authorization using different access devices, out-of-band verification, threshold limits, Internet address filtering, and appropriate policy and practices.

Authentication is only one aspect of the FFIEC layered security, but it is an important feature. X9.117 [60] categorizes many of the layered controls as "passive authentication" to increase the assurance that the correct user is being authenticated. The primary method is device recognition, whether a personal computer, mobile phone, or landline phone is used. If the device is not recognized, the user can be challenged to provide additional authentication data. This chapter discusses various types of single factors that can be combined for multifactor or mutual authentication.

NIST Special Publication 800-63 (Electronic Authentication Guideline) [181] provides technical guidelines for federal agencies implementing electronic authentication. The recommendation covers remote authentication of users (such as employees, contractors, or private individuals) interacting with government systems over open networks. It defines technical requirements for each of four levels of assurance in the areas of identity proofing, registration, tokens, management processes, authentication protocols, and related assertions.

The X9.117 standard (Secure Remote Access—Mutual Authentication) [60] defines a taxonomy, requirements, operating principles, control objectives, techniques, and technical approaches to enable banks to support secure remote access. Whereas NIST 800-63 defines requirements for assurance levels, X9.117 defines requirements for risk levels that are analogous but not equivalent. Table 3.1 provides a comparison between X9.117 and NIST 800-63.

Note: Since NIST is a government agency, it can specify assurance levels, whereas X9 is an ANSI standards body that can only define requirements within a risk framework that must be interpreted by each financial service organization.

Every authentication method, regardless of its factor type, is susceptible to false-negative and false-positive errors. Historically, these originated as statistical Type I and Type II errors [36]. Type I errors occur when a hypothesis has been incorrectly rejected, that is, the hypothesis is actually correct, but the analysis mistakenly infers that the hypothesis is wrong. Type II errors occur when a

Table 3.1   Comparison of X9.117 and NIST 800-63

X9.117 RISK LEVELS	X9.117 REQUIREMENTS	NIST 800-63 ASSURANCE LEVEL
Risk Level 4 (Highest risk) X9.117 does not define an equivalent Level 4 risk.	X9.117 does not define any requirements for Level 4 risk.	**Level 4** – Level 4 is intended to provide the highest practical remote network authentication assurance. Level 4 authentication is based on proof of possession of a key through a cryptographic protocol. At this level, in-person identity proofing is required.
Risk Level 3 (High risk) Ability to: view or hear customer or individual personal or financial information that is sensitive and whole for more than one individual; or conduct higher financial risk outside of individual customer accounts held at the bank.	Implement strong, multifactor authentication and similar-strength bank service provider authentication for mutual authentication; and confirm the identity of new users and users adding Level 3 features to their account with OOW information or using a multichannel, out-of-band communications channel. Additional (layered) controls are recommended, including techniques that detect anomalous activity.	**Level 3** – Level 3 provides multifactor remote network authentication. At least two authentication factors are required. At this level, identity proofing procedures require verification of identifying materials and information.
Risk Level 2 (Moderate risk) Ability to: view or hear customer or individual personal or financial information that is sensitive and whole for a single individual; administratively add, review, change, or delete customer information; or conduct low financial risk transactions outside a customer's portfolio of accounts held at the bank.	Implement Level 1 authentication with one of the following: KBA information, a second authentication factor or using an out-of-band channel, and similar-strength bank service provider authentication for mutual authentication. Additional (layered) controls are recommended, including passive controls.	**Level 2** – Level 2 provides single-factor remote network authentication. At Level 2, identity-proofing requirements are introduced, requiring presentation of identifying materials or information.

(Continued)

Table 3.1   Comparison of X9.117 and NIST 800-63 (Continued)

X9.117 RISK LEVELS	X9.117 REQUIREMENTS	NIST 800-63 ASSURANCE LEVEL
Risk Level 1 (Low risk) Ability to: view or hear partial customer or individual personal or financial information or nonsensitive; view or hear unmasked historical financial information; administratively add but not review, change, or delete customer or individual personal information; or conduct low financial risk transactions within a customer's portfolio of accounts held at the FI.	Implement single-factor authentication and similar-strength bank service provider authentication for mutual authentication. Additional (layered) controls are recommended, including passive controls.	**Level 1** – Although there is no identity-proofing requirement at this level, the authentication mechanism provides some assurance that the same claimant who participated in previous transactions is accessing the protected transaction or data. Successful authentication requires that the claimant prove through a secure authentication protocol that he or she possesses and controls the token.
Risk Level 0 (No or minimal risk) No ability to: view any customer's or individual's personal or financial information; move money; or administratively change any customer's or individual's personal or financial information.	There are no control requirements for publicly accessible applications that have a risk level of 0.	NIST does not define an equivalent Level 0, although it does recognize publicly accessible, unauthenticated Web sites.

hypothesis has been mistakenly accepted, that is, the hypothesis is actually wrong, but the analysis indicates that the hypothesis is correct. Relating to authentication, a false negative happens when an entity is rejected but should be accepted, and a false positive happens when an entity is accepted but should be rejected. These errors are more commonly known for biometrics, but, for example, a mistyped password can result in a false negative, or a stolen door key can give a false positive.

3.1 Authentication Factors

3.1.1 Single-Factor Authentication

Authentication factors are traditionally categorized into three groups.

- *Knowledge factors*: Something you know. Examples include personal identification numbers (PIN), passwords, and other character strings (e.g., passphrase) that are remembered by an individual.
- *Possession factors*: Something you have. Examples include a myriad of physical objects such as door keys, credit cards, ATM cards, identification cards, employee badges, and even USB tokens.
- *Biometric factors*: Something you are. Examples include fingerprints, voice imprints, facial recognition, iris images, keystrokes, and dynamic signatures.

However, there is an issue with the use of cryptography for authentication. Although key management is addressed in its own chapter (Chapter 7), we state here categorically that since symmetric and asymmetric private keys must be managed such that no individual can know the value of either, keys clearly cannot be knowledge factors. And since keys are obviously not biometric factors, the default classification has been possession factors. However, possession factors are either physical tokens or, sometimes, software objects that have a limited time to live (TTL), whereas cryptographic keys are simple data objects with very special characteristics and controls. And while possession factors are addressed at length in this chapter, to avoid various conundrums, we define cryptography as a fourth authentication factor.

- *Cryptography factors*: Something you control. Examples include message authentication codes (MAC), hash-based message authentication code (HMAC), and digital signatures.

However, it is important to note that cryptography is often used in the design and deployment of the other three factors (knowledge, possession, biometric) to provide additional security controls such as confidentiality, integrity, and arguably nonrepudiation. Thus, the supplemental use of cryptography may provide an additional authentication factor. Each of these security controls are discussed separately in separate sections within this chapter. To fully explore and understand each of these authentication factors, we need to provide a more granular view of the entity being authenticated, and so we offer the following definitions.

- *Person entity* (PE): Individual human that represents oneself and no other entity
- *Nonperson entity* (NPE): Individual nonhuman object (e.g., device, system, application) that represents itself and no other entity

As it turns out, as problematic as person entity (PE) authentication has always been, nonperson entity (NPE) authentication has become a critical issue, particularly when PE authentication partially relies on NPE authentication. Further, cyber security tends to rely on NPE authentication, which presumes an underlying trustworthiness of network devices. The issues for NPE authentication will be addressed in this chapter relative to the factor type.

A basic authentication framework, as shown in Figure 3.1, consists of three functional components: the requester, the verifier, and the relying party. Although many authentication schemes such as Kerberos [8] or biometrics [54] are more complex with additional actions, their functional components are essentially a decomposition of the three presented here and, nonetheless, retrofit into this high-level framework. Further, it is important to note that the verifier may be collocated or embedded within the relying party, but from a functional viewpoint these are fundamentally separate components. Also, depending on the complexity of the application environment, the relying party may consist of many systems and network connections; nevertheless, this simplified framework remains consistent.

The three basic authentication actions provided by this framework (Figure 3.1) include:

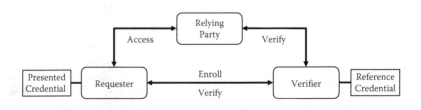

Figure 3.1 Authentication framework.

- *Enrollment*: This action is between the requester and the verifier to establish the reference credential (RC) for subsequent verification and access. For example, a PIN or password is assigned or selected, the employee badge or credit card is issued, or biometric samples are collected to create the template. Enrollment is part of the larger provisioning process whereby information about the individual (PE) is collected and corroborated such that the identity is initially validated. Provisioning is addressed in Section 3.7.
- *Verification*: This action occurs when access is requested. Independent of the authentication scheme, the presented credential (PC) must be provided to the verifier so that it can be verified against the reference credential (RC) established previously by enrollment.
- *Access*: This action occurs between the requester and the relying party to gain access to a network, system, application, or data source. Verification must occur before access is granted, and as discussed previously, access is wholly dependent on verification and the verifier. Also note (as mentioned previously), the relying party might perform verification, but from a functional viewpoint they are fundamentally separate components.

Depending on the authentication scheme, the requester might do any one of the following:

1. Submit the PC to the verifier and then provide the approval response to the relying party as part of the access request, whereby the relying party validates the approval.
2. Submit the access request to the relying party, who then initiates the verification request, but the requester still submits the PC to the verifier, and the relying party only gets the verification result (e.g., approve or deny) from the verifier.
3. Provide the PC to the relying party as part of the access request; the relying party then submits the PC to the verifier and gets the verification result (e.g., approve or deny) from the verifier.

For each scenario, the PC must be protected to ensure that it cannot be replayed by an unauthorized entity and such that it can only have been provided by the legitimate entity or its authorized authentication proxy. Authentication proxies are often used for single sign-on (SSO) solutions where the entity authenticates once to the proxy such that the proxy manages access to multiple relying parties.

This general discussion of authentication factors provides the background for a more in-depth analysis of each type of authentication. In the next few sections, we discuss each authentication factor in more detail, addressing the peculiarities, strengths, and weaknesses of each.

3.1.2 Multifactor Authentication

As noted previously, multifactor authentication is defined [60, 61] as two or more independent and different authentication techniques used together. Both of the qualifiers "independent" and "different" are extremely important for this definition. If two authentication methods share a common element, then they cannot be two factors: hence the "independence" requirement. For example, using the same password for two separate logon screens is not two-factor authentication. Arguably, using two unlike passwords might be perceived as "independent," but the authentication methods are still the same, so they are not different factors. However, unless there are controls in place to enforce password separation, there is no guarantee that the passwords will remain separate: hence the "difference" requirement. Table 3.2 shows the allowable combinations for two, three, and four factors for multifactor authentication.

Table 3.2   Multifactor Combinations for Authentication

MULTIFACTOR	KNOWLEDGE	POSSESSION	BIOMETRIC	CRYPTOGRAPHY
Two factors	Knowledge	Possession	—	—
Two factors	Knowledge	—	Biometric	—
Two factors	Knowledge	—	—	Cryptography
Two factors	—	Possession	Biometric	—
Two factors	—	Possession	—	Cryptography
Two factors	—	—	Biometric	Cryptography
Three factors	Knowledge	Possession	Biometric	—
Three factors	Knowledge	Possession	—	Cryptography
Three factors	Knowledge	—	Biometric	Cryptography
Three factors	—	Possession	Biometric	Cryptography
Four factors	Knowledge	Possession	Biometric	Cryptography

Logically, two-factor is stronger than single-factor, three-factor is stronger than two, and four-factor is the strongest. However, it is not necessarily the case that any two-factor combination is twice as strong as any single-factor, nor is it reasonable to assume that there is a fixed ratio between any multifactor combinations. Further, all single-factor methods are not equivalent, and their overall effectiveness depends on many indefinable and immeasurable attributes such as entropy, schema strength, protocol robustness, and implementation controls. Each of the authentication factors—knowledge, possession, biometric, and cryptography—are discussed individually in Sections 3.2–3.5, respectively.

3.1.3 Multisite Authentication

Multisite authentication is when the same single-factor or multifactor authentication method is employed at one or more sites. When different authentication methods are used, there is no interdependency and, therefore, vulnerabilities are unrelated. But when the same authentication methods are used, a weakness in one site might be exploited at another site. For example, a compromised site yielding passwords might compromise another site if the same passwords are used at both. As another example, a control weakness at one site that gets attacked might be exploitable at another site due to their similarities.

Managing multisite authentication can be problematic when controls are inconsistently applied, such as password length, composition, or number of retries. Storing the same or similar authentication credentials in multiple locations might introduce synchronization problems. Centralized management of multiple authentication systems is not always practical. Dissimilar technologies might have different life cycles, capabilities, or features that need separate tending. For example, passwords can be reset, but biometrics cannot, and hardware tokens often have batteries that might need replacing. Differences in the authentication populations may also affect multisite authentication systems. For example, the authentication rules for employees are characteristically different than for customers.

The issues with multisite authentication are further compounded if some of the sites are not within the control of the same organization. For example, social networks often use single-factor password authentication. However, if the end user has utilized the same password on his employer's system as the social network, and the social network gets compromised, then the employer system becomes at risk for that user despite no changes to the employer system. Since the social network is outside the control of the employer, there is little recourse beyond policy requiring that employees use different passwords for nonemployer systems; however, the policy is not enforceable or auditable.

3.2 Knowledge Factors

Knowledge factors are "something you know" for a person entity (PE) who commits a string of characters to memory and enters the authentication data when presented with a challenge or log-on screen. However, nonperson entities (NPE) such as devices, servers, and applications cannot "remember" anything, so the authentication data must be stored on disk. NPE authentication using passwords is an adaptation of PE authentication that has many pitfalls. Our discussion of knowledge factors will therefore be addressed separately for PE versus NPE; however, there are several security controls common to both.

There is a fundamental assumption that only the authorized entity knows the authentication data, such that an adversary or the verifier does not know it. Further, authentication data must be protected from replay attacks. This also means an adversary must not be able to copy the data and reuse it for unauthorized access. To achieve these goals, there are two fundamental security controls.

1. The requester's authentication data, the presented credential (PC), must be protected during transmission from the requester to the verifier.
2. The verifier's authentication data, the reference credential (RC), must be protected in storage on the verifier.

For data transmission, the only feasible method is encryption, meaning the PC must be encrypted at the requester side and decrypted at the verifier side. This can be achieved by transport-layer encryption such as SSL/TLS or application-layer encryption, where software on the requester's side does the encrypt and similar software on the verifier's side does the decrypt. However, the cryptographic key must itself be protected; otherwise, if the adversary can get access to the key, then the encrypted transmitted data can be decrypted. It is important to recognize that all keys—past, present, and future keys—must be protected; otherwise, if the adversary has recorded the encrypted data, then a compromised key allows the adversary to decrypt and recover the password at a later day. This is especially important if the same key is used for multiple users. For example, if 100 users change their passwords quarterly, a compromised key within that 90-day window would compromise all 100 user passwords.

In addition, if the password-change process employs the same encryption key, then all 100 user passwords would be continuously compromised for as long as the compromised key is used. This raises an important concept that will be discussed further in Chapter 7 (Key Management): the importance of the data life cycle versus the key life cycle. Detection of a compromised password is far easier than the key used to protect the passwords. When the adversary uses the compromised password, the system logs should indicate when actions were taken that can be refuted by the user. Further, if the account is used at odd hours or during vacation periods, detection of misuse is more likely; however, one or two misuses of accounts would tend to indicate isolated incidents of users failing to protect their passwords versus a system-level breach of the password encryption.

Regarding storage of the reference credential (RC), reversible encryption is feasible such that the verifier would decrypt the inbound presented credential (PC), decrypt the stored RC, and compare the two credentials. However, compromise of the RC encryption key would compromise all passwords. Further, even if the encryption key is kept secured, the credentials are exposed in the computer memory of the verifier during comparison, so any malware might capture the credentials. To minimize these risks, the RC is typically stored using a one-way hash function that prevents recovery of the RC from its hashed version. However, hash functions are susceptible to a dictionary attack; thus a salted hash is often used to defeat this attack by adding entropy to the possible hashed RC. Let us take a closer look at dictionary attacks and the use of a salted hash.

The dictionary attack is where the adversary creates a list of all possible passwords and generates a hash of each password, called a rainbow table. The attacker then looks up the hashed RC in the rainbow table to determine the original password. In accordance with Moore's Law, as computing power has continued to increase and disk space continues to become cheaper, generating rainbow tables keeps becoming more feasible. For example, an 8-character password that only allows alphanumeric characters and does recognize uppercase versus lowercase characters is roughly 218 trillion permutations. So the rainbow table would need to contain 436 trillion entries, one for the password and another for the hash, or about 4 petabytes of storage, which is no longer an outrageous amount of storage.

Adding a salt means the data are combined with a fixed value before the hash is computed. Presumably, the adversary, not knowing the salt, would need to generate a rainbow table for each possible salt value, pushing the feasibility of the dictionary attack out of range. However, there are several cautions with this assumption. First, the salt must be handled securely, essentially managing it as equivalent to a cryptographic key; otherwise, if the salt is known, the dictionary attack is again feasible. Second, if the adversary already knows one of the passwords, as is the case for an insider who happens to be one of the authorized users with a legitimate password, the attacker can generate a list of hashes for the one password of every possible salt. This is another type of exhaustive-search attack. Once the salt is determined, the attacker can then generate the rainbow table for all the other passwords. So not only must the salt be kept secure, but it must also be large enough to deter an exhaustive search.

We now look at the good, the bad, and the ugly for person entity (PE) authentication and nonperson entity (NPE) authentication.

3.2.1 Person Entity (PE) Authentication

As discussed previously, person entity (PE) authentication is when an individual remembers the authentication data, the presented credential (PC), and enters it on demand. But all knowledge factors are neither alike nor managed in a similar fashion. Let us begin with the most tightly controlled authentication data, the personal identification number (PIN).

NIST defines a PIN as a password [181] consisting only of decimal digits. This implies that PIN management and password management are the same. However, for financial services, this is not the case. PIN management and security have far more restrictions than do passwords. Many of the original PIN management and security considerations are discussed in the 1970s *PIN Manual*, published by the Interbank Card Association, later to be known as MasterCard [1]. The current PIN management and security requirements and recommendations are defined in ISO 9564 [99] and X9.8 [38] standards.

Essentially, X9.8 is an adaptation of ISO 9564 with a dozen or so ANSI notes providing further restrictions for the U.S. market. Equipment and application manufacturers are incentivized to design their PIN-capable products to be compliant with these standards for economic reasons. To avoid potential liability, merchants, acquirers, and issuers simply do not want to use products that do not meet the minimal interoperable requirements. Further, the card brands (e.g., Visa) have certification programs for PIN entry devices used at point-of-sale (POS) terminals and automated-teller machines (ATM), as does PCI for its PIN Transaction Standards (PTS) [191]. In a nutshell, to keep a PIN secure, there are three fundamental security controls.

1. The PIN must be encrypted at the point of entry.

   This is consistent with the first-knowledge-factor security control; however, this simple requirement has many subsequent implications. PIN entry issues and other authentication data-entry issues are discussed later in this chapter.

2. The PIN must be transmitted encrypted to the issuer for verification.

   This is consistent with the second-knowledge-factor security control; however the nature of PIN encryption and its inherent risks necessitates a third and new key management control.

3. The cryptographic keys used to encrypt the PIN and any associated keys uses to protect the PIN encryption keys must be managed securely.

   We will see that the cryptography and key management controls for PIN used in the financial services industry are far more stringent than for passwords in any other industry. This difference will be highlighted as a control gap for passwords later in this chapter.

An issue when entering a PIN or password is the trustworthiness of the user interface. For example, a PIN is entered using a PIN pad dedicated to that function so it can be immediately encrypted using a cryptographic key. Other data (e.g., dollar amount) is entered using a key pad without encryption. But payment terminals do not have separate pads due to cost restrictions, so the terminal is cognizant of when a PIN is being entered versus other data. If the terminal firmware or software is compromised, it can spoof the user by displaying an "enter PIN" command but keep the key pad in "non-PIN" mode so the entry is not encrypted. The normal operation is for the terminal to put the key pad into "PIN" mode, which activates the PIN entry display and automatically encrypts the entry using the PIN encryption key.

The details of how the PIN is formatted, combined with the card primary account number (PAN), and encrypted are in ISO 9564 [99], and the approved formats for the United States are defined in X9.8 [38]. For the purposes of this discussion, it is sufficient to explain that the PIN and the PAN are combined to create a unique value that is then encrypted so the cryptogram is relatively unique to the PIN and PAN combination. Otherwise, if only the PIN is encrypted, the same cryptogram will result when two individuals have the same PIN. Given a 16-digit card number with the last digit being the Luhn check digit per ISO 7812 [113], there are about 1 quadrillion possible PANs, but given that most PINs are four digits, there are only 10,000 possible PINs, so many individuals must have the same PIN. Thus without the relative uniqueness of the cryptogram per the PIN and PAN combo, an adversary might monitor payment traffic looking for the same cryptogram as his own PIN to determine another's PIN.

An issue when encrypting the PIN or password is the uniqueness and life cycle of the encryption key. For example, PIN encryption keys must be unique per terminal. This compartmentalizes the impact of a compromised PIN encryption key. If a thousand terminals share the same key, and each terminal handles a thousand transactions, and the PIN encryption key is compromised, then 1 million PINs are also compromised. However, if each terminal has a unique key, then the impact is limited to 1,000 transactions and associated PINs.

Regarding the key life cycle, the PIN encryption key must be changed periodically. The adversary always has one cleartext and ciphertext example, its own PIN, and so can always attack the system by an exhaustive key search. This is where the adversary, knowing its own cleartext and capturing a ciphertext from the payment system, can try all possible keys to determine the PIN encryption key. This attack can be especially valuable if many transactions with encrypted PINs have been recorded, because once the key is determined, all other PINs can be decrypted. However, changing the encryption key limits the number of transactions and associated PINs exposed due to a compromised key. The life cycle of the PIN encryption key will differ, depending on the key management scheme. Details regarding the various key management schemes are provided in Chapter 7 (Key Management), but a quick recap of PIN encryption key life cycles per X9.24 [42] is provided here.

- *Fixed transaction key*: This method uses PIN encryption keys that are distributed using physical processes. The PIN encryption key is unique per terminal and tends to be changed annually or earlier if a key compromise is known or suspected.
- *Master key/transaction key*: This method uses a hierarchy of a master key used to encrypt and electronically exchange PIN encryption keys. The PIN encryption key is unique per terminal and exchanged daily or typically every 1,000 transactions, whichever occurs first. The master key might be common or unique per terminal, and tends to be changed annually or earlier if a key compromise is known or suspected.
- *Derived unique key per transaction* (DUKPT): This method uses a hierarchy of a master key at the host system and a derived initial key unique per terminal. The terminal initial key is used to generate a series of PIN encryption keys used once per transaction, such that only unused keys ready for future transactions are in any terminal at any time. The terminal sends a transaction counter along with the encrypted PIN such that the host system can re-create the specific-terminal initial key and regenerate the transaction-specific PIN encryption key.
- *Asymmetric techniques for the distribution of symmetric keys*: This method is essentially the same as the master key/transaction key, except the master key is an asymmetric key pair instead of a symmetric key.

An issue when verifying the PIN or password online is how it is stored at the verifier. The intent for knowledge factors is that only the legitimate user knows the authentication data. Therefore, the reference PIN at the verifier needs to be stored so as not to expose the PIN. This is done by creating and storing a PIN verification value (PVV). The 4-digit PIN is concatenated with part of the account number, encrypted using a PIN verification key, and the resulting ciphertext is decimalized to create a 5-digit PVV. This is a similar process as discussed previously for transporting the encrypted PIN; however, the technical details are sufficiently different such that the encrypted PIN is not the same as the PVV. The PIN and the PAN are combined to create a unique value that is then encrypted and decimalized such that the PVV is relatively unique to the PIN and PAN combination.

Passwords are distinct from PINs in several ways. Passwords are typically composed of alphabetic, numeric, and possibly special characters, whereas a PIN is numeric only. Some password authentication systems support both upper- and lowercase alphabetic characters. Passwords may be used for authentication or access controls, whereas PINs are used for the verification of the identity of a customer within a financial services network. Passwords that are only numeric, such as a 4-digit code to unlock a mobile phone, are not the equivalent of a PIN as defined in X9.8 [38], since they are not managed as a PIN. Passwords may be of almost any arbitrary length, whereas a PIN has a minimum 4-digit length and a maximum 12-digit length. Passwords are managed according to organizational policy and practices, whereas a real PIN is managed in accordance with ANSI or ISO PIN standards. Passwords may be protected by a variety of methods, whereas PINs are encrypted at the point of entry and remain encrypted during transmission to the issuer. Passwords are not typically protected using the same security controls as for PINs. The following is a list of password control gaps:

- *Entry encryption*: Users typically enter passwords via the same keyboard used for all other data inputs, such that key-logger malware can capture passwords.

- *Unique cryptogram*: Some systems still transmit passwords as cleartext, or if they do provide encryption, only the password is encrypted and is thus susceptible to monitoring.
- *Unique key*: Some systems use the same password encryption key for all end users, which makes such systems vulnerable to a single-key compromise.
- *Key life cycle*: Some systems, once having established the password encryption key, rarely change the key, which is vulnerable to an exhaustive key attack.
- *Validation value*: As discussed previously for knowledge factors, most systems use a one-way hash to generate the reference credential (RC), which is vulnerable to a dictionary attack.

Interestingly, there are no current ISO, ANSI, or NIST password standards. FIPS 190 Guideline for Advanced Authentication [171], published in September 1994, includes a section on passwords, and there have been password-management standards in the past. However, they have all been withdrawn for various reasons. FIPS 112 Password Usage [163], published in May 1985 and withdrawn in February 2005, defined ten attributes of an automated password system and specified requirements for each.

1. *Composition* was the set of acceptable characters that may be used in a valid password; the American Standard Code for Information Interchange (ASCII) with its 95-character set was required.
2. *Length range* was the set of acceptable lengths of passwords, expressed as a minimum through a maximum length, consisting of the composition set.
3. *Lifetime* was the maximum acceptable period of time for which a password is valid; the maximum period was one year.
4. *Source* was the set of acceptable entities that can create or select a valid password from among all acceptable passwords, such as a security officer.
5. *Ownership* is the set of individuals who are authorized to use a password, including personal and shared group passwords.
6. *Distribution* is the set of acceptable methods for providing (transporting) a new password to its owner and to all places

where it will be needed in the password system, including an audit log.

7. *Storage* is the set of acceptable methods of storing a valid password during its lifetime, including encryption.

8. *Entry* is the set of acceptable methods by which a password may be entered by a user for authentication or authorization purposes.

9. *Transmission* is the set of acceptable methods for communicating a password from its point of entry to its point of comparison with a stored, valid password, including encryption.

10. *Authentication* period is the maximum acceptable period between any initial authentication process and subsequent reauthentication processes during a single terminal session or during the period data are being accessed; no minimum period was provided.

ANSI X9.26, "Financial Institution Sign-On Authentication for Wholesale Transactions," was last published in 1990 and withdrawn in 1999 due to its intrinsic use of the Data Encryption Standard (DES). DES was defined in FIPS 46, originally published in 1977; its last publication as FIPS 46-3 was 1999, and it was formally withdrawn by NIST in May 2005. Essentially, the DES key length of 56 bits is too short for today's computing power, thanks in part to Moore's Law. Moore's Law is a prediction from Intel cofounder Gordon Moore that the number of transistors on a chip will double approximately every two years. The RSA company sponsored DES Challenges, which demonstrated its weakness when in 1999 a key was exhaustively determined in 22¼ hours, heralding its replacement with alternative algorithms and longer keys. Ironically, ASC X9 decided that passwords were well understood, securely managed, and becoming passé, such that a revised password management standard was not needed.

The Department Of Defense (DoD) Password Management Guideline [68] was issued in April 1985 by the DoD Computer Security Center (CSC), also known as the Green Book. This guideline is part of an information security library called the Rainbow Series, as each book is color-coded. While the Green Book has never been formally withdrawn by the NSA, the whole Rainbow Series is aging. (The Rainbow Series is not to be confused with rainbow tables used for dictionary attacks.) The Green Book notes that the security provided by a password system depends on the passwords being kept secret at all times. Thus, a password is vulnerable to compromise whenever it is used, stored, or even known. In a password-based authentication mechanism, passwords are vulnerable to compromise due to five essential aspects of the password system:

1. A password must be initially assigned to a user when enrolled on the ADP system.
2. A user's password must be changed periodically.
3. The authentication system must maintain a "password database."
4. Users must remember their passwords.
5. Users must enter their passwords into the system at authentication time.

Passwords are often thought of as being used strictly for nonfinancial applications such as e-mail, and PINs were initially designed for high-risk financial transactions such as credit card cash advances or debit card cash withdrawals at ATMs. However, passwords are also used for financial applications such as online banking, online retailers, and online investment services. Up to this point, we have only addressed the protection of the authentication data and not its security strength. PINs are allowed to be four to twelve digits in length per ISO 9564 [99] and X9.8 [38], but most systems still use four digits. Passwords are allowed to be whatever length the organizational policy stipulates, but historically they tend to be eight characters from legacy mainframes.

In general, a longer password is stronger than a shorter password, but of course the overall strength is also dependent on the size of the character set, or its entropy. NIST recognizes [181] that Claude Shannon coined the use of the term *entropy* [2] in information theory. For passwords, entropy basically measures how much information is unknown, or its randomness, so higher entropy equates to a stronger password.

- For example, a 4-digit PIN based on a 10-digit character set tentatively has 10^4 or 10,000 permutations. However, many systems do not support a leading zero, so the more practical number is 9,000 possibilities. Further, if the system disallows certain patterns such as the same digit (1111 or 2222), then the allowable number is even fewer. It is only fair to recognize that ISO 7812 [113] allows up to a 12-digit PIN, which has 10^{12} or 1 trillion permutations.

- As another example, an 8-character password based on a 26-character alphabet and 10-digit character set has 36^8 or 2.8 trillion permutations. And if the system supports upper- and lowercase characters, then the number is 62^8 or 218 trillion passwords. The number is higher if special characters are allowed.

Clearly, the theoretical entropy for passwords is larger than for PINs, and just as obviously, not all passwords have the same entropy depending on what the verification system supports. Further, its entropy also depends on whether the password is randomly generated or selected by the user. Password cracking tools do not need to search for all possible passwords but can focus on the more likely occurrences, such as English words and assorted variations.

NIST defines a password [184] as a secret (typically a character string) that a claimant uses to authenticate its identity, and includes both PIN and passphrase. Passphrases are defined as a relatively long password consisting of a series of words, such as a phrase or a full sentence. However, the special publication notes the following:

> For example, requiring that passwords be long and complex makes it less likely that attackers will guess or crack them, but it also makes the passwords harder for users to remember, and thus more likely to be stored insecurely. This increases the likelihood that users will store their passwords insecurely and expose them to attackers.

Most organizations have security policies requiring periodic password changes such as monthly, quarterly, or annually. The presumption is that the password needs to be changed before it can be guessed. Arguably, a longer password needs to be changed less often than a shorter one; however, most verification systems cannot handle variable password strengths or change periods. Consequently, a fixed password length and rotational period are often implemented.

Another aspect of password management is single-sign-on (SSO) systems. Figure 3.2 shows a SSO framework for discussion. The

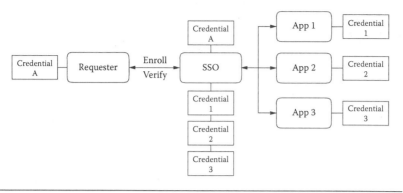

Figure 3.2 SSO framework.

requester enrolls with the SSO system, establishing its password (credential A). Separate alternative credentials are established per each SSO and application pair: (SSO, App 1) = credential 1, (SSO, App 2) = credential 2, and (SSO, App 3) = credential 3.

When access is needed to one of the applications, the requester submits credential A for verification by SSO, and when verified, SSO transparently submits the appropriate alternative credential to the application. The requester to SSO is person entity (PE) authentication, and SSO to the applications is nonperson entity (NPE) authentication, which is discussed in Section 3.2.2. With respect to the authentication framework from Figure 3.1, SSO is the verifier to the requester but also acts a proxy for the requester to the applications. Thus the SSO framework in Figure 3.2 shows each application acting as its own verifier to SSO. However, with a more realistic SSO implementation, each application would rely on other verifiers such as a centralized directory service.

Now that we've discussed person entity (PE) authentication, we can look at the commonalities and differences for NPE authentication.

3.2.2 Nonperson Entity (NPE) Authentication

As discussed previously, NPE authentication is when a system retrieves the authentication data from storage, the presented credential (PC), and submits it to the verifier. But computer systems do not remember anything except what is available on disk, so an NPE password is not really a knowledge factor; it is actually a possession factor.

Because the NPE password must be stored on disk, it is vulnerable to discovery. If the password is stored as unencrypted cleartext, only system access controls prevent it from being copied or viewed and reused to access the target system, the relying party. If the password is stored encrypted, then only system access controls prevent it from being copied and replayed. Further, if the requesting system has a copy of the cryptographic key to decrypt the password, then only system access controls prevent the key from being copied and reused to decrypt the password. And, if the same compromised key was used on multiple systems, then all passwords on each system are susceptible to replay.

Regarding the transmission of the password, the same fundamental security control applies: The password must be protected during transmission from the requester to the verifier. Note that the cryptographic key used to encrypt the password for transmission, call it the *transport password encryption key* (TPEK), needs to be different than the keys used by the requester or the verifier for storage. The TPEK and these latter two cryptographic keys, call them the *requester password encryption key* (RPEK) and the *verifier password encryption key* (VPEK), likewise need to be different. Otherwise, if any of these keys are the same, the stored encrypted password or the transmitted encrypted password can be replayed. Further, if the transmitted encrypted password is the same cryptogram repeated each time, it can also be replayed. Therefore, to avoid replay attacks, the TPEK, the RPEK, and the VPEK need to be different keys, and the transmitted encrypted password needs to include a relatively unique value to change the cryptogram, such as a current time stamp.

Regarding the storage of the reference password, the same fundamental security control applies: The reference password must be protected in storage on the verifier. But the presented password must also be protected in storage on the requester without compromising the transmitted password or the stored reference password. Assuming that file access controls are insufficient to protect cleartext passwords or cryptographic keys for encrypted passwords, we need an alternative solution that meets the following prerequisites.

1. Passwords are invulnerable to replay attacks.
2. Passwords are stored as encrypted objects.

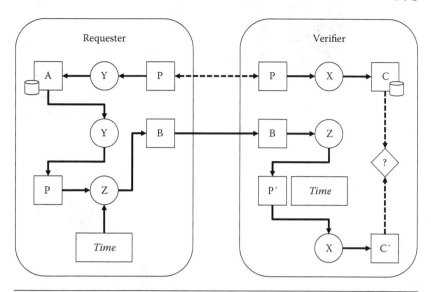

Figure 3.3 Symmetric NPE password solution.

3. Password encryption keys are stored securely.
4. Password encryption keys are changed periodically.
5. Key encryption keys are stored securely.

Figure 3.3 shows a symmetric NPE password solution. The function (X) is a one-way hash; the function (Y) is a symmetric algorithm using key (Y); and the function (Z) is the same symmetric algorithm using key (Z). To establish the password [P], it is hashed using (X) and stored as reference hash [C] on the verifier, and encrypted using (Y) and stored as [A] on the requester. The symmetric key (Y) is either stored on the requester in a system file only accessible by the application or preferably kept secured inside a hardware cryptographic module. Cryptographic modules are discussed in Chapter 7 (Key Management).

For password verification, the requester decrypts [A] using (Y) and reencrypts [P] with a time stamp using (Z) to send token [B] to the verifier. The verifier decrypts token [B] to recover [Z] and checks the time stamp for relevancy. If the token [B] is too old, it is rejected. Otherwise, the presented password [P'] is hashed to create [C'] and matched to the reference hash [C] to verify the password.

Figure 3.4 shows an advanced asymmetric NPE password solution. The function (X) is a keyed hash (HMAC) using key (X); the function (Y) is still a symmetric algorithm using key (Y); but the function

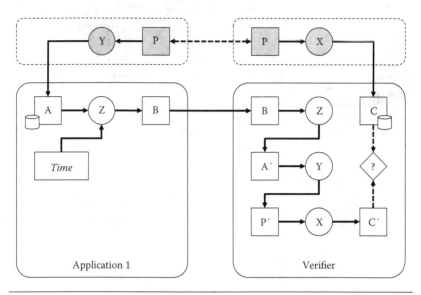

Figure 3.4   Asymmetric NPE password solution.

(Z) is an asymmetric algorithm using the key pair (Z). To establish the password [P], it is hashed using (X) on another system and stored as reference hash [C] on the verifier, and then encrypted using (Y) on another system and stored as [A] on the requester. The encryption key (Y) is not stored on the requester.

For password verification, the requester encrypts [A] with a time stamp using the verifier's public key (Z) to send token [B] to the verifier. The verifier decrypts token [B] using its private key (Z) and checks the time stamp for relevancy. Again, if token [B] is too old, it is rejected. Otherwise, the encrypted password [A′] is decrypted using (Y) to recover the presented password [P′], which is hashed using (X) to create [C′] and matched to the reference hash [C] to verify the password.

As mentioned previously, since an NPE password is actually a possession factor and since biometrics only work for humans, multifactor authentication for NPE can at most be two-factor authentication, as shown in Table 3.3. However, that is not to say that devices cannot be recognized in a fashion analogous to biometrics, and in fact the misnomer "fingerprint" is often used. Some devices have unique identifiers assigned by the manufacturer or the service provider, such as media access control (MAC) addresses or serial numbers used for inventory. Other computing devices, including mobile phones, have relatively unique characteristics based on

Table 3.3 NPE Multifactor Combinations for Authentication

MULTIFACTOR	KNOWLEDGE	PASSWORD	RECOGNITION	CRYPTOGRAPHY
Two factors	not applicable	Password	Recognition	—
Two factors	not applicable	—	Recognition	Cryptography
Two factors	not applicable	Password	—	Cryptography
Three factors	not applicable	Password	Recognition	Cryptography

their operating systems, hardware and software configurations, and application packages. Other devices might have measurable characteristics such as the particle density of a magnetic stripe or the power signature of a field-programmable gate array (FPGA). Device recognition is a valid NPE authentication factor, but similar to biometrics, the device characteristics need to be accurately registered and linked to the PE; otherwise, fraud can still occur. Since device recognition is not an authentication factor such as biometrics and because passwords are actually a possession factor, Table 3.3 is an adjusted version for NPE multifactor combinations.

Devices have identifiers that can be used for recognition, such as MAC addresses, operating system or application version numbers, or other identifiers such as a phone number, International Mobile Equipment Identity (IMEI) number, or Mobile Equipment Identifier (MEID) for mobile phones. However, this information is obtained using communications protocols that typically presume the device is honest. Thus, a fraudulent device can provide false identification information and even simulate being more than one type of device.

3.2.3 Knowledge-Based Authentication (KBA)

Knowledge-based authentication, commonly called KBA, falls under the "something you know" authentication factor. Authentication is based on answers to challenge questions. Answers are based on factoids, information about the requester that is presumably not publicly available. Examples include date of birth, location of birth, credit card number, home address, cell phone number, mother's maiden name, Social Security number (SSN), first pet's name, and numerous other data bits. The working theory is that fraudsters will unlikely know the correct answers.

KBA systems can develop their factoid profiles based on publicly available information, financial transaction services, or customer enrollment processes. Publicly available information can be accessed via Web crawlers to free online databases or fee-based databases. Financial transaction services are typically linked to the KBA system by the service provider. For example, a credit bureau or online banking entity keeps track of financial transactions. Customer enrollment processes include setup of challenge questions by the individual, where customers can select questions from an optional list and provide custom answers. KBA systems have several unique qualities.

- Fraudsters might target their attack to specific individuals such that most or all of the factoids can be discovered using the publicly available resources.
- With the advent of social networks, fraudsters can gather individual specific factoids, such as date of birth, home address, pet's name, or family members' names.
- Individuals can provide incorrect answers to selected challenge questions to avoid fraudsters using public information against them. For example, if the individual's favorite movie genre is thrillers, answering "horror movies" would negate the fraudster's research.

There is also an underlying assumption that each of the factoids are independent of each other; however, this is not necessarily the case. For example, where and when a person is born affects the Social Security number issued to that individual, as before 2010 the Social Security Agency assigned the first three digits of the structured 9-digit number based on zip code. Because of the overall low-security strength of factoids, KBA challenge questions are often used to supplement other controls, thereby leaning toward multifactor authentication.

3.2.4 Zero Knowledge (ZK) Authentication

To complete our discussion on knowledge factors, it is prudent to mention zero knowledge (ZK) authentication methods. Abstractly, a zero knowledge (ZK) proof is an interactive session between a prover (the requester) and a verifier, where the prover convinces the verifier of a statement (with high probability) without revealing any information about how to go about proving that statement. Thus the verifier has "zero knowledge" of the authentication credential, that is, there is no reference credential. Any reliable ZK protocol must have at least the following three attributes.

1. *Completeness*: The verifier always accepts the proof if the fact is true and both the prover and the verifier follow the protocol.
2. *Soundness*: The verifier always rejects the proof if the fact is false, as long as the verifier follows the protocol.
3. *Zero knowledge*: The verifier learns nothing about the fact being proved (except that it is correct) from the prover that could not already be learned without the prover, even if the verifier does not follow the protocol (as long as the prover does). In a zero-knowledge proof, the verifier cannot even later prove the fact to anyone else. (Not all interactive proofs have this property.)

A rudimentary example of a ZK proof is Ali Baba's cave, shown in Figure 3.5. In this scenario, the prover (P) claims to be Ali Baba, and the only evidence is that he knows the secret phrase to open the inner cave. In order to prove he is Ali Baba to the verifier (V) without revealing the secret phrase, he uses a zero-knowledge protocol to convince the verifier that he has access to the inner cave. For this protocol, there are two doors between the inner and outer caves— either one capable of being opened by the secret phrase—divided by a T-shaped wall that not only separates the doors, but also screens them from view. The outer cave also has a curved wall that blocks the view for anyone outside the caves.

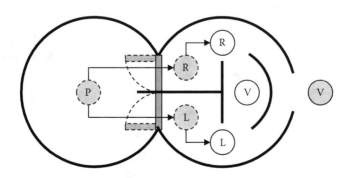

Figure 3.5   Ali Baba's cave.

The ZK protocol consists of the verifier (V) stepping outside the cave so that the prover (P) can position himself either on the right (R) side or the left (L) side behind the T-wall. The verifier then enters the outer cave to challenge the prover to step out from behind the T-wall. There are three possible outcomes.

1. The prover happens to be behind the T-wall on the same side chosen by the verifier, so that the prover can step out on the challenged side without passing through the cave. So the prover either steps out on the right side without opening the cave, or the prover steps out on the left side without opening the cave.

2. The prover is behind the T-wall on the different side chosen by the verifier but cannot open the cave and so steps out on the wrong side. So either the challenger chooses the left side but the prover steps out on the right or the reverse, where the challenger chooses the right side but the prover steps out on the left side.

3. The prover is behind the T-wall on the different side chosen by the verifier, opens the cave, and steps out on the challenged side. So either the prover is on the left side and steps out on the right side, or the prover is on the right side and steps out on the left side.

Unlike password verification, which is a pass-or-fail test, ZK protocols require a series of rounds, where each round increases the probability of authentication. The protocol is repeated until the probability is sufficiently large to satisfy an assurance level. For Ali Baba's Cave, the rounds work as follows:

- *Round 1*: If the prover steps out on the challenged side, there is a 0.5 or 50% chance the prover happened to be standing on the correct side but is not Ali Baba. Otherwise, if the prover steps out on the wrong side, the prover clearly is not Ali Baba, and the protocol is complete.

- *Round 2*: If the prover steps out on the challenged side, then there is another 0.5 chance times the previous 0.5 chance that the prover happened to be standing on the correct side but is not Ali Baba. So there is a 0.25 or 25% chance that the prover is not Ali Baba but, conversely, a 75% chance that the prover is Ali Baba. Otherwise, if the prover steps out on the wrong side, the prover clearly is not Ali Baba, and the protocol is complete.

- *Round 3*: If the prover steps out on the challenged side, then there is another 0.5 chance times the previous 0.25 chance that the prover happened to be standing on the correct side but is not Ali Baba. So there is a 0.125 or 12.5% chance that the prover is not Ali Baba but, conversely, an 87.5% chance that the prover is Ali Baba. Otherwise, if the prover steps out on the wrong side, the prover clearly is not Ali Baba, and the protocol is complete.

- *Round 4*: If the prover steps out on the challenged side, then there is another 0.5 chance times the previous 0.125 chance that the prover happened to be standing on the correct side but is not Ali Baba. So there is a 0.0625 or 6.25% chance that the prover is not Ali Baba but, conversely, a 93.75% chance that the prover is Ali Baba. Otherwise, if the prover steps out on the wrong side, the prover clearly is not Ali Baba, and the protocol is complete.

So after only four rounds, there is a greater than 90% probability that the prover is Ali Baba. The fifth round yields greater than 96%, and the sixth round gives higher than 98%, but the protocol can never achieve 100%, as can password verification. Other ZK protocols tend to be mathematically intensive such that they are only feasible for NPE authentication.

ISO/IEC 9798, "Entity Authentication" [116], Part 5 defines three entity authentication mechanisms using zero-knowledge techniques.

- The first mechanism is said to be based on identities. A trusted accreditation authority provides each claimant with private accreditation information, computed as a function of the claimant's identification data and the accreditation authority's private key.

- The second mechanism is said to be certificate-based using discrete logarithms. Every claimant possesses a public/private key pair for use in this mechanism. Every verifier of a claimant's identity must possess a trusted copy of the claimant's public verification key. The means by which this is achieved is beyond the scope of this standard, but it may be achieved through the distribution of certificates signed by a trusted third party (TTP).

- The third mechanism is said to be certificate-based using an asymmetric encipherment system. Every claimant possesses a public/private key pair for an asymmetric cryptosystem. Every verifier of a claimant's identity must possess a trusted copy of the claimant's public key. The means by which this is achieved is beyond the scope of this standard, but it may be achieved through the distribution of certificates signed by a TTP.

The IETF specification RFC 2945 [89] defines another ZK protocol called the Secure Remote Password (SRP) protocol. Per its abstract:

This mechanism (SRP) is suitable for negotiating secure connections using a user-supplied password, while eliminating the security problems traditionally associated with reusable passwords. This system also performs a secure key exchange in the process of authentication, allowing security layers (privacy and/or integrity protection) to be enabled during the session. Trusted key servers and certificate infrastructures are not required, and clients are not required to store or manage any long-term keys. SRP offers both security and deployment advantages over existing challenge-response techniques, making it an ideal drop-in replacement where secure password authentication is needed.

Regardless of the authentication probability, as the Green Book observes, the security provided by knowledge-factor methods depends on the authentication credential being kept secret at all times. Thus, despite evidence to the contrary that the requester is authenticated, there is always a nonzero probability that the knowledge credential has been compromised and a fraudster has been falsely validated.

3.3 Possession Factors

Possession factors are "something you have," which for a person entity (PE) is a hardware, software, or data object, and for a nonperson entity (NPE) is typically a software or data object. The good, the bad, and the ugly are discussed for each of the object types.

3.3.1 Hardware Objects

Perhaps the simplest hardware object is a door or padlock key. Reportedly the oldest known lock, estimated to be 4,000 years old, was found by archeologists in the Khorsabad Palace ruins near Nineveh, an ancient city across the river from the modern-day city of Mosul, Iraq. The lock's physical shape represents data, the pattern to open the lock. Possession of the key presumably imparts the authority to open the lock and access whatever it is protecting. Hardware keys are typically used for physical security, but it is a possession factor nonetheless. The obvious weakness is that hardware keys can be copied, and much like data objects, an accurate copy is as good as the original. Once the key is physically cut, it can be used many times, so basically it is a write-once and read-many object. Also, much like cryptographic keys, a hardware key can be used to protect other physical keys, and periodically the locks need to be changed with new keys. Key replacement tends to be event-driven, for example after a break-in. But, keys need to be replaced for other events too, such as when a key is lost, when a key holder is terminated for cause, or when an unauthorized access occurs due to an illegal copy of a hardware key.

Another simple hardware object is an electronic hotel room card. The combination is encoded on the card, which is read by the access control system to unlock the door when validated. Hotel keys might be a proximity card or have a magnetic stripe. So the door key is a write-many and read-many object. Much like the hardware key, the room key is anonymous; it does not contain any identifiable data about the guest; that information is retained in the access control and hotel billing systems. But unlike a regular door key, the room key has a relatively short life cycle limited to the stay of the guest, and the hotel will reprogram the room code and card at the request of the guest for a lost key or if the card fails.

A slightly more complex hardware object is an employee badge. Unlike the hotel room card, the badge is not anonymous; it is distinctive in that it provides an identity, for example an employee number. Badges often have an employee photo and displayed name for visual inspection by guards. Badges are typically proximity cards, read by a badge reader, to unlock a door. Hence employee badges are typically

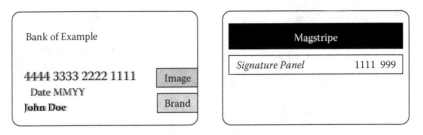

Figure 3.6   Example bank card.

write-once and read-many objects. Employee badges tend toward a longer life cycle, often until the badge physically wears out and a new one is issued, or until the person leaves employment.

Another common hardware object is a bank card, shown in Figure 3.6. The front of the card includes the embossed primary account number (PAN) and the cardholder's name along with the display of the expiration date, the issuer bank name, the associated payment brand (e.g., Visa, MasterCard, American Express), and a hologram (which is sometimes the brand logo). The embossed characters are still sometimes used with imprinter readers, also referred to as knuckle busters, that record the PAN and cardholder name on carbon receipts. The expiration date indicates whether the card is valid, and the hologram indicates whether the card is legitimate, which can be visually validated by a checkout clerk at a merchant location.

The payment card characteristics are defined in a set of ISO-7800 standards.

- ISO-7810 Identification cards – Physical characteristics
- ISO-7811 Identification cards – Recording techniques
- ISO-7812 Identification cards – Numbering system and registration
- ISO-7813 Identification cards – Financial transaction cards

Figure 3.6 also shows the back of the card, which includes the magnetic stripe (magstripe) that contains the cardholder's authentication data encoded in Track 1 and Track 2. Electronic readers embedded into point-of-sale (POS) terminals capture the magstripe for authorization with the issuer bank. Fields are divided by field separation (FS) characters. Both tracks contain the PAN as the most important identifier. Only Track 1 contains the cardholder name. The expiration date displayed on the front of the card is the same as the expiration date encoded in Track 1 and Track 2.

- Track 1: Primary account number FS Cardholder name FS Date FS Discretionary data
- Track 2: Primary account number FS Date FS Discretionary data

The content of the discretionary data are proprietary to each issuer bank; however, they do share some commonalities. One common field is the PIN validation value (PVV), which is a cryptogram derived from the PAN and the PIN using a PIN validation key (PVK). The PVK is used to verify that the cardholder entered PIN, the presented knowledge credential, by regenerating the PVV and comparing it to the reference PVV retained either in the magstripe or stored in the financial database. The PVV is a reference credential analogous to the password hash discussed in the Section 3.2 (Knowledge Factors) discussion. Most cardholders are familiar with entering their PIN when using debit cards, but credit cards also typically use a PIN for cash advance at automated teller machines (ATM) and cash dispensers.

Another common field in the discretionary data are the card security value (CSV). Each of the brands uses a different name: card verification value (CVV) is Visa, card verification code (CVC) is MasterCard, card security code (CSC) is American Express, and card authentication value (CAV) is JCB (originally called Japan Credit Bureau). However the proprietary algorithm is basically the same: The CSV is a cryptogram derived from the PAN, the expiration date, and the card type code (also contained in the discretionary data), which defines how the card can be used. The CSV is used to verify the authenticity of the magstripe data to prevent card skimming and modification.

Figure 3.6 also shows the signature panel on the back of the card. The intention is for the cardholder to sign the back of the card for the sales clerk to validate the cardholder signature on the sales receipt for signature-based transactions, versus PIN-based transactions. There is another similar cryptographically derived CSV imprinted in the signature panel which is used for card-not-present transactions such as mail-order or telephone-order (MOTO) transactions or for online Internet transactions.

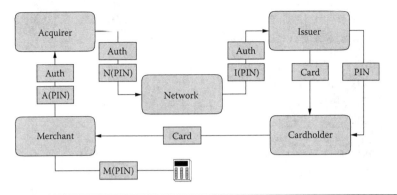

Figure 3.7   Bank card authorization.

Figure 3.7 shows a typical bank card authorization flow, which includes two-factor authentication, i.e., the possession of the card and knowledge of the PIN. To understand the whole scheme, five entities need to be described. There are two financial institutions known as the issuer and the acquirer. The issuer provides financial services to the cardholder, including issuing the bank card. The acquirer provides financial services to the merchant, including acquiring authorization from the issuer. The network provides interbank connections between financial institutions. The cardholder receives the bank card from the issuer for use as payment at the merchant. The merchant accepts the bank card as payment but relies on the acquirer for authorization.

The flow begins when the card and PIN are physically mailed to the cardholder in separate envelopes at different times. The next step is when the cardholder presents the card to the merchant for payment using a debit card that requires PIN authentication. The possession of the card authenticates the cardholder to the merchant. Merchants can enhance authentication by validating the cardholder name against a photo ID. However, the merchant also needs to validate that the cardholder is authorized to use the card, so the merchant must capture the PIN. This is accomplished by having the cardholder enter the PIN into the POS terminal, which immediately encrypts it using a merchant PIN encryption key (M), where the cryptogram is shown as M(PIN).

The merchant sends the authorization request (Auth) with the magstripe data and the PIN to the acquirer; however, the merchant must translate the PIN from the merchant key (M) to the acquirer

key (A) to send the cryptogram A(PIN). Since each merchant manages many terminals and each acquirer manages many merchants, the
keys used by merchants are different than the keys used by acquirers.
Further, the acquirer cannot authorize the cardholder, so the acquirer
sends the authorization request (Auth) and the PIN to the network;
however, the acquirer must also translate the PIN from the acquirer
key (A) to the network key (N) to send the cryptogram N(PIN).
And since the network manages many acquirers and issuers, the keys
used for each are also different. The network sends the authorization
request (Auth) and the PIN to the issuer; however, the network must
translate the PIN from the network key (N) to the issuer key (I) to
send the cryptogram I(PIN).

The issuer validates the cardholder account to authorize the transaction and verifies the PIN, as discussed previously, for knowledge
factors. The PIN authenticates the cardholder to the issuer, and the
magstripe data with its CSV authenticates the presence of the card.
Thus the transaction is authenticated using two-factor authentication:
The PIN is the knowledge factor and the magstripe data indicating
presence of the card is the possession factor. With regard to financial
transactions, card-present transactions are lower risk, whereas card-
not-present transactions are higher risk, since possession of the card
is not known. For example, a cardholder ordering merchandise using
mail order or telephone order (MOTO) or on the Internet provides
the PAN, expiration date, and the CSV from the signature panel, but
without the whole magstripe, the presence of the card is unknown.

These examples are "dumb" hardware tokens that only present
authentication data to a physical reader for verification. Possession of
the token presumably authenticates the token holder by virtue that the
person is holding the token. But for these types of hardware devices,
there is no person-to-token authentication to activate the token, and
there is no token-to-reader authentication to validate the legitimacy of
the reader or the token.

In order for these additional authentication controls to be available,
the device must be "smart," with processing capabilities to transmit,
process, and store information [103]. But this capability should not be
confused with communication protocols for reading and writing data
for contact and contactless integrated circuit chip (ICC) smartcards
[175] or other wireless-proximity cards.

- For person-to-token authentication, the person needs to validate the token, and the token needs to validate the person. Prior to entering an entry code, the person should visually inspect the token for reasonable assurance that it has not been altered or substituted. The token should not perform any actions prior to the correct entry code. Some devices allow limited functions for any user whether or not there is an activation code enabled. For example, many mobile phones allow a user to dial "911" for emergencies; however, it has been reported that some 911 access can bypass the user code [225–227]. Visual inspections can be significantly enhanced if the device has self-tests that can be run periodically or on demand to ensure its firmware and software integrity.

- For token-to-reader authentication, the token needs to validate the reader, and the reader needs to validate the token. Thus, mutual authentication is needed for both NPE directions. Further, one must presume that the communications path, whether it is a physical connection for contact ICC or a wireless connection using radio frequency (RF), is untrustworthy. There are simply too many ways to eavesdrop on wired and wireless communications to assume otherwise. Therefore the token-to-reader authentication protocol must incorporate cryptography to ensure its confidentiality and integrity.

Figure 3.8 shows a smart-token framework that includes a token reader interfacing with the requester system via either a wired or wireless connection. The smart token likewise interfaces with the reader using either a contact or contactless interface. The verifier shares a unique secret credential with the token that is never known by the requester or the reader. The token derives a one-time password (OTP) from the secret and then sends the OTP as the presented credential

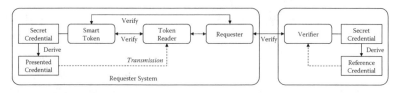

Figure 3.8   Smart-token framework.

to the reader for submission by the requester to the verifier. The verifier similarly derives the reference credential from the same secret to verify the requester.

The presented credential, even though derived from the same secret credential shared with the smart token, does not convey any information to the verifier regarding the person-to-token authentication processes. The verifier might have expectations that the requester will visually inspect the token per a security policy, but there is no evidence of this in the authentication data. More importantly, there is also no evidence that an entry code was used to unlock the token. And even if the token was issued by the verifier with an activation code, there is still the risk that the token was compromised without the requester's knowledge due to a lack of visual inspection. Thus, the use of a token-activation code does not provide a knowledge factor to the verifier; the smart token is still a single factor. This is an important limitation as compared to the PIN being transmitted along with the magstripe to the verifier for financial transactions.

OTP schemes are either unilateral or bilateral protocols. For OTP, unilateral means that the smart token generates the reference credential based on the secret and other public data inferable by the verifier, such as a time stamp. Bilateral means the smart token generates the reference credential based on the secret and other private data provided by the verifier, such as a challenge value. These types of protocols are often described based on the number of messages passed. For unilateral protocols, the authentication scheme is a one-pass method, whereby the requester sends all of the authentication data in a single request message to the verifier. This is akin to the bank card authorization described in Figure 3.7, which is also a one-pass method. Bilateral protocols consist of two or more messages, such as when the verifier sends a challenge message for which the requester returns a response message.

Many smart-token solutions rely on cryptography such as encryption, one-way functions, message authentication codes (MAC), or digital signatures. For example, the verifier might send a random number for the requester to digitally sign or generate some other type of cryptogram. Another example includes authentication protocols that exchange multiple messages between the verifier and the

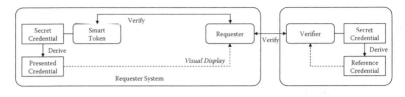

Figure 3.9   Handheld-token framework.

requester or token. These protocols and schemes are discussed further in §3.5 (Cryptography Factors).

Figure 3.9 shows a handheld-token framework where no token reader is used and the token interface is a visual display with the person. The verifier shares a unique secret credential with the token that is never known by the requester. The token derives a one-time-password (OTP) from the secret, and displays the OTP as the presented credential to the requester for submission to the verifier. The token might have a keypad or only a display screen. The verifier similarly derives the reference credential from the same secret to verify the requester.

For tokens with both a display screen and a keypad, the authentication scheme can be a one-pass method where the requester enters a password into the token to display the OTP. Other schemes can be at least a two-pass challenge-and-response method where the verifier sends challenge data that gets entered into the token to display the OTP. For either scenario, the requester then sends the OTP to the verifier, which then validates the password or challenge data. For tokens with only a display screen, the authentication scheme is typically a one-pass method where the token displays the OTP either on rotation or on demand. The requester sends the OTP to the verifier, which then validates the OTP.

Reliance on any hardware token as a possession factor requires that authentication data be presented to the verifier as evidence that the token is present. The authentication data needs to be relatively unique per each request to avoid replay attacks or counterfeit devices. Further, the authentication data must be protected such that its integrity is intact during transmission. Thus, cryptography is often employed as part of the protocol to protect the authentication data.

3.3.2 Data Objects

Data objects are groups of binary bits that are nonexecutable, with an emphasis that the object is only data and not source code that can be compiled into an executable code. Presentment of the data object to the verifier often provides evidence that the requester has been previously verified and remains authenticated. The data object is generated by the verifier and provided to the requester for future reference. Such data objects are known by various other names, including tickets, tokens, credentials, receipts, permits, or even vouchers. Sometimes the term *electronic* is used to distinguish data objects from legacy paper versions.

- An example of a data object used to authenticate a token, and perhaps an unexpected example, is the old reliable magstripe. The merchant's transmission of the magstripe data with its card security value (CSV) authenticates the presence of the card to the issuer. For financial transactions using online authorization, the issuer is, in fact, the verifier.

  Track 1: PAN FS Cardholder name FS Date FS Discretionary data (card type, CSV)
  Track 2: PAN FS Date FS Discretionary data (card type, CSV)

  There is also Track 3, which is defined in ISO 4909 [112] and in X9.1 [37] specifically for bank card usage. However, Track 3 is not widely adopted, and few terminals can read a Track 3 magstripe.

- Examples of authenticated data objects are cookies or flash shared objects (FSO) placed on a user's computer by a Web server. Once the Web server has authenticated the user by another means, typically a log-on ID and password, the Web server sends the cookie to the browser, which places it on the computer. The Web server subsequently can check for the presence of the cookie or FSO to revalidate the user.

When using cookies, precautions must be taken to ensure that the cookie cannot be counterfeited or replayed by a fraudster. Countermeasures against counterfeiting include cryptographic methods such as encryption, message authentication codes (MAC), or digital signatures that can only be created by the Web server that has control of the cryptographic key. Replay can be circumvented by using a time-to-live (TTL) value that limits the validity period of the cookie. The TTL must be protected against modification to avoid an adversary increasing its lifetime. This is necessary, as Web servers using stateless protocols such as Hypertext Transfer Protocol (HTTP) do not inherently manage user sessions.

- Another example is a Security Assertion Markup Language (SAML) object [187, 189]. SAML is a schema using the extensible markup language (XML) [208]. SAML objects are used in other protocols such as simple object access protocol (SOAP) messages [209]. The content of a SAML object might contain identification data, such as a user name or account number, and authentication data such as a password, which is why the SAML object is often encrypted. Further, as evidence that the sender is the authorized entity, the SAML object is often digitally signed.

While this book is not intended as a tutorial on SAML, some description is warranted. Figure 3.10 shows a SAML framework using the SAML terms but mapped to the authentication framework previously presented in Figure 3.1. For our purposes, the SAML user is the requester; the SAML service provider is the relying party; and the SAML identity provider is the verifier. The user enrolls its identity with the identity provider (or IdP in SAML terms), but its access privileges are not necessarily registered with the IdP, as that role may be performed by the SAML service provider (SP). When the request for access is received by the SP, a request is sent to the IdP for identity verification (and possible privileges), and the IdP

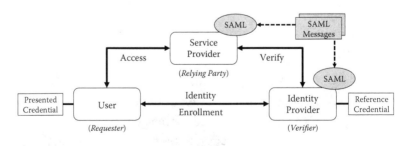

Figure 3.10   SAML framework.

returns a response. Both the SP and the IdP must use interoperable SAML software.

The primary purpose of SAML is Internet (or Web) single sign-on (SSO), which is expandable to many application environments and extensible to many other organizations to achieve federated identity. The expandability of SAML is that one IdP can service many SPs. Thus an organization can implement a standards-based common access-control method, which arguably can eliminate proprietary solutions. The extensibility of SAML is that an SP with another organization can rely on the IdP of another. However, the practicality of federated identity between organizations tends to be limited to business partners with unambiguous service agreements and assigned liabilities. Looking beyond the technology, there are obvious business risks and potential legal issues when one organization asserts the user identity to another organization. There are also risk differences between an IdP asserting the identity of an employee versus a customer to another organization SP. For example, logging onto a social media network is not the same as logging into an online banking application. One must be careful to not allow an unintentional authentication "step up" from a lower assurance level to a higher one.

3.3.3 Software Objects

Software objects are executable code. The object originates as source code that gets compiled into software that can be executed by an operating system. For person-entity (PE) authentication, the code might run on an end-user device, which might be a desktop, a laptop, a notebook, a tablet computer, mobile phone, smartcard, or some other smart token. The code might be an applet dynamically downloaded and executed in the computer or mobile browser, downloaded and installed by the user, or preinstalled by the device provider or manufacturer. For nonperson-entity (NPE) authentication, the code might be installed on another server, a network device such as a router or firewall, or some other network appliance. The purpose of the code is to enable functionality between the requester (the client) and the verifier (the server) for end-entity or device authentication.

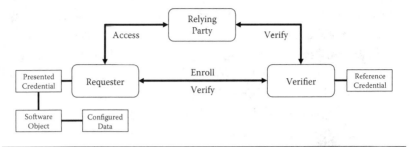

Figure 3.11   Software-object framework.

Figure 3.11 provides a software-object framework. Publicly available software, or generic software, might incorporate configuration
data to customize interoperability or personalize entity authentication with the verifier. Proprietary software that functions with the
verifier by design might still incorporate configuration data to personalize entity authentication. The enrollment process might include
installation of the software object and the configuration data. Note
that the configuration data are actually another type of data object,
as discussed previously. The software object interacts with the verifier and possibly the relying party as part of the overall application
environment.

The verifier or relying party is dependent on the existence of the
software object on the end-user device, which was either preinstalled
as part of an initialization or enrollment process or downloaded as
part of the access process. The following are the likely person-entity
(PE) scenarios:

- *Static preinstallation by the device manufacturer.* In this scenario, the software object is part of the device configuration
  such as a computer or mobile device. The software object is
  static from the viewpoint that, once installed, it resides on the
  device, ready for execution. The software object is generic in
  the sense that it can potentially interoperate with any verifier
  or relying party; hence the verifier might additionally down-
  load and install one or more configuration data objects for
  customization or personalization during enrollment.
- *Static preinstallation by the requester from a third-party source.*
  In this scenario, the user has downloaded the software object
  from another source such as a freeware site, software site, or

mobile store. The software object is still generic, so the verifier might need to customize or personalize it per one or more configuration data objects.

- *Static preinstallation by the verifier during enrollment.* In this scenario, the software object might be proprietary, developed by the verifier, or it might be generic and customized or personalized per one or more configuration data objects. Again, the software object is static. Once installed, it resides on the device, ready for execution. Whether proprietary or generic, the verifier must also manage the software life cycle and provide updates and modifications to the device.

- *Dynamic installation and execution by the verifier during access.* In this scenario, the software object is downloaded to the device as needed, such as an applet that runs on a computer or mobile browser. The applet does not reside on the device, so the software life cycle relevant to the device is simplified, as it always gets the latest applet.

Software life cycle can be an ugly situation. Software objects with fixed vulnerabilities or enhanced authentication protocols can be difficult to distribute to thousands or millions of devices. For all static preinstallations, the verifier must address the software life cycle, and for manufacturers or other third-party sources, this can be very challenging. The following are the likely nonperson-entity (NPE) scenarios:

- *Static preinstallation by the device manufacturer.* In this scenario, the software object is part of the operating system, utilities, or software package provide by the platform vendor. Installation might be customized per software parameters or configuration data objects, but personalization is atypical, as one NPE server is typically treated like any other.

- *Static preinstallation by the requester from a third-party source.* In this scenario, the software object is a solution purchased from a third-party software vendor. Again, customization might via software parameters or configuration data objects might be used, but not personalization.

- *Static preinstallation by the verifier during enrollment.* In this scenario, the software object is an in-house-developed solution.

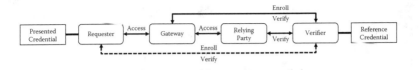

Figure 3.12 Gateway framework.

Dynamic installations are uncommon, as NPE authentication does not typically employ browsers. However, there are scenarios where a gateway server sits between end-user computers (requester), and a Web server (relying party) acts as the requester to the relying party and as the relying party to the requester. NPE authentication is normally used for the gateway server, but since it emulates the client browser, dynamic installation might be used. Figure 3.12 shows a gateway framework where both the requester indirect access and the gateway direct access to the relying party require authentication. However, the verifier might not be cognizant of the requester as opposed to the gateway.

A common authentication method for software objects is one-time password (OTP). Similar to OTP discussed for hardware tokens, the software object supports either a unilateral or bilateral OTP protocol with the verifier. Software objects installed on end-user computers are often called "soft" or "software" tokens. Similar to a handheld device, the soft token might display the OTP for entry by the end user into an online menu. Another method is a graphical display whereby a keyboard is shown on the screen for entry of a password (knowledge factor) by the end user using a mouse or touch screen in such a manner that the screen coordinates are random for each use. Alternatively, similar to a smartcard, the soft token might interact directly with the verifier using an online protocol. There are numerous ways a software object might provide authentication.

Care must be taken when developing proprietary authentication schemes and protocols. Design flaws and coding errors are easy to make and difficult to identify. Commercially available software is often notorious for vulnerabilities and zero-day attacks that require constant updates and modifications, so likewise it follows that any software development suffers from similar issues. Authentication protocols tend to be even more difficult to design and implement. Source-code reviews and software assurance is an important discipline that is beyond the scope of this book.

Care must also be taken when using publicly available third-party software, especially free open-source software (FOSS). It has been argued that defects may be found and fixed more quickly in open-source projects than in closed-source projects. Independent third-party software analysis or certification programs exist. However, any authentication software objects must be tested and undergo internal quality assurance. Software parameters can be misconfigured, introducing vulnerabilities. Another important aspect is an exact coding of security protocols and cryptographic algorithms; otherwise, an inaccurate implementation has weaknesses that can be exploited [58].

Another important principle for software objects is ensuring their integrity and authenticity. The end-user device should not install any downloaded software objects without first checking its legitimacy. Further, the device should regularly recheck the software object's legitimacy. This can be done using a variety of cryptography methods, but the most common is code signing, where the manufacturer has digitally signed the software object using an asymmetric private key [218–220]. The device can validate the digital signature using the corresponding public key embedded in a digital certificate. However, the certificate validity dates must be managed carefully, as an expired certificate will cause the code sign verification to fail even though the signature might be valid if the code was signed before the expiration date. Digital signatures do not inherently indicate when something was signed. For this reason, a trusted time stamp [55] is a superior cryptographic method. Integrity and authenticity methods are discussed further in Section 3.5 (Cryptography Factors).

An extremely important principle for software objects is never to hardcode an unencrypted cryptographic symmetric or asymmetric private key. This is a simple rule that should never, ever be violated. The confidentiality of keys cannot be achieved in software objects. It is extremely difficult to keep source code secured to the extent that no copies have ever been lost, misplaced, or viewed by unauthorized personnel. Software objects can be copied infinitely, and executable code can be inspected or scanned for cleartext keys. Asymmetric public keys are not confidential; however, their integrity and authenticity must be protected. Key management is discussed further in Section 3.5 (Cryptography Factors).

3.3.4 One-Time Passwords (OTP)

One-time-password (OTP) methods were discussed previously in Section 3.3.1 (Hardware Objects) for smart tokens (see Figure 3.8) and handheld tokens (see Figure 3.9) and in software objects (see Figure 3.11). As mentioned, OTP schemes are either unilateral (one-pass) or multilateral (multipass) protocols, referring to the number of messages. The basic strengths of an OTP scheme include the following:

- The OTP is pseudo-random such that it cannot be predicted. It cannot be truly random; otherwise, the verifier could not synchronize with the requester and verify the OTP.
- The OTP is valid only for a limited time period such that it cannot be replayed. Otherwise, the OTP could be copied and reused by an adversary.
- The OTP is relatively unique to each requester. Otherwise, if it is not distinctive to each user, the verifier would be unable to distinguish one OTP from another.

OTP schemes typically use a secret credential distributed to the requester and the verifier and a one-way function to generate the presented credential and the reference credential. Unilateral protocols often include a time mechanism for the requester and verifier to synchronize their answers. For example, inputting the secret credential and a time stamp into a one-way function yields a relatively unique and deterministic (or pseudo-random) OTP. The secret credential associates the OTP to the requester, and the time stamp links the OTP to the valid time period. Inputting both into a one-way function creates the pseudo-random OTP. Bilateral protocols often incorporate the challenge issued by the verifier, which in fact can be a random number, to generate a relatively unique OTP. The OTP one-way function might be a cryptographic hash algorithm, an encryption algorithm, a digital signature algorithm, or some other proprietary algorithm. Hash, encryption, and digital signature algorithms are discussed further in Section 3.5 (Cryptography Factors).

3.4 Biometric Factors

Biometric factors are "something you are," which is only applicable for person entities (PE). A biometric factor is a measurable biological or behavioral characteristic that distinguishes one person from another. Biological characteristics include a wide range of traits including fingerprints, iris scans, voice patterns, and facial features. Behavioral characteristics include dynamic signatures, keystroke dynamics, and even gait recognition. Biometrics are unusual in that they offer two distinct types of authentication that other factors do not: verification versus identification.

- Biometric verification, also called one-to-one or "1-1" authentication, is similar to typical authentication, where a claimed identity is presented for verification. The claimed identity is used to fetch a specific biometric template from a database, which is then matched to the live biometric sample to verify the identity. See Figure 3.13 for biometric verification.
- Biometric identification, also called one-to-many or "1-N" authentication, is unique, where the live biometric sample is matched against all of the biometric templates in the database to determine the identity. See Figure 3.14 for biometric identification.

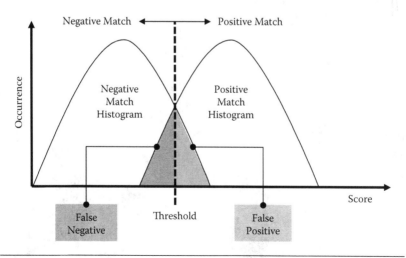

Figure 3.13 Biometric verification.

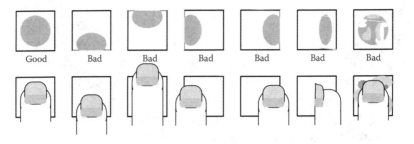

Figure 3.14 Biometric identification.

For either verification or identification to work, there must be a biometric template to compare with the PE live sample. The biometric template is generated and linked to the PE identity during enrollment within the biometric authentication system [120–121, 124–132].

- Biometric enrollment consists of collecting live samples from the PE to generate the biometric template and establishing a link to the PE identity. See Figure 3.15 for biometric enrollment.

The most important aspect of any biometrics authentication is to recognize that biometric data are public information. People leave fingerprints and DNA wherever they go [6]. Faces can be photographed and captured on surveillance cameras. Voice can be overheard and recorded. Therefore, authentication cannot rely on the secrecy of biometric data, since it is not private; it is public. Thus, biometrics must rely on the integrity and authenticity of its data, and might be encrypted for privacy reasons. X9.84 [54] and ISO 21188 [110] require security mechanisms to maintain the integrity of data between any two components as well as mutual authentication between the source and

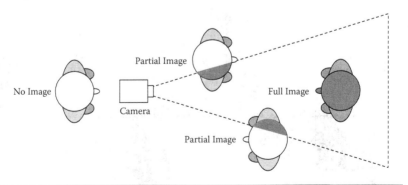

Figure 3.15 Biometric enrollment.

destination of data. Both standards also recognize that mechanisms may be in place to ensure the confidentiality of the biometric data between any two components and within any component. Biometric data includes live samples, templates, and matching results. Each principal biometric process (enrollment, verification, and identification) has its own characteristics, strengths, and vulnerabilities that are discussed separately, independent of the technology. In addition, each biometric technology [122] has its own applicability and restrictions.

3.4.1 Biometric Technology

Each biometric technology operates under a common assumption that it is unique per person. However, since this cannot feasibly be tested for every person on the planet, this an unprovable hypothesis. For the most part, there is enough empirical and statistical evidence that this is true for many biometrics such that the technologies are sufficiently reliable. However, for any biometric technology there are four possible comparison outcomes.

- Positive match is when the sample and template are very similar.
- Negative match is when the sample and template are very dissimilar.
- False positive is when the sample and template are somewhat similar but are not a match.
- False negative is when the sample and template are somewhat dissimilar but are a match.

Figure 3.16 shows two histograms, one for negative matches and the other for positive matches that have been drawn to emphasize the false negatives and the false positives [123, 146]. The shape of the curves will differ for each biometric technology, but the negative and positive curves will always overlap. In general, scores that fall to the

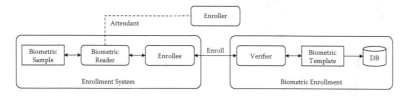

Figure 3.16 Biometric histograms.

right of the threshold are positive matches, and ones that fall to the left of the threshold are negative matches. However, there are two dispute areas. Scores that fall to the right of the threshold but under the negative-match curve are false positives. Likewise, scores that fall to the left of the threshold but under the positive-match curve are false negatives. The threshold can be adjusted to decrease one of the false scores, but the corresponding result is the increase of the other score.

Fingerprints [147] are probably the most well known and widely used technology, primarily due to its incorporation by law enforcements since the 1890s. Latent fingerprints were collected at crime scenes and visually matched to fingerprints collected from criminals. Modern fingerprints are captured and compared electronically for verification, and latent fingerprints are collected and converted to electronic format for identification. There are criminal databases such as the Automated Fingerprint Identification System (AFIS) or the Integrated Automated Fingerprint Identification System (IAFIS) and other databases used by professional organizations.

Authentication systems employ fingerprint readers, which require the physical placement of the finger onto a flat surface. However, the relative placement of the finger can adversely affect the sample. Figure 3.17 shows examples of one good and several bad samples. Placing the finger off center or turning the finger only provides a partial read. A dirty or defective reader can also prevent a good read from occurring. Fingerprint readers tend to not work well in unsanitary or unattended environments, or where hands are covered in gloves.

Fingerprint patterns of ridges and valleys are typically sorted into left- and right-oriented loops, whorls, and arches. This allows large databases to be sorted into "bins" for faster lookup. The binning process can incur errors if the sample is misinterpreted. Hence a biometric sample interpreted as a right whorl might not be found in the

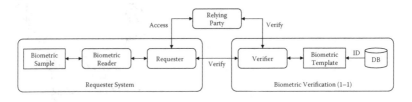

Figure 3.17   Finger-reader placement.

database if the biometric template is categorized as a left loop and stored in a different database bin.

Face images can be captured, analyzed, and compared for identification or verification. Facial identification systems are often covert, used by law enforcement for antiterrorism at airports and other travel depots, and even by private organizations such as casinos in Las Vegas for fraudsters. Facial recognition systems are limited by the quality of the biometric template, whose "enrollment" might be involuntary, and by the value of the live samples based on the environment. The environmental conditions include the condition of the camera, lighting, angles, and traffic patterns. See Figure 3.18 for examples of camera-view placement. As another example, a poor photo would be difficult to match to a partial facial image. Further, facial recognition is often used to identify a potential match or candidates list and not necessarily a confirmation of identity.

Images of the iris, the colored portion of the eye surrounding the pupil, are often confused with images of the retina, which depict the structure of blood vessels on the interior back of the eye. Unlike retinal images, where the camera is placed inches from the eye, iris images can be reliably captured several feet away. The richness of iris images gives them the highest data amount over any other technology. Further, there does not appear to be any correlation between an individual's left or right iris, much less between twins, siblings, or other family members. Iris image capture suffers from similar

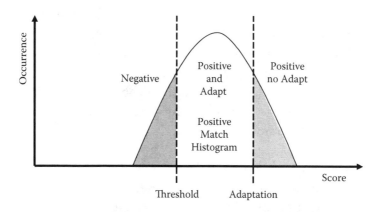

Figure 3.18 Camera-view placement.

environmental limitations as do facial images, but also must deal with reflections from eyeglasses and contact lenses.

An interesting attribute of iris technology is how the template and samples are encoded. The images are encoded as bit maps, whereby the comparison is an exclusive or (XOR) operation. A perfect match results in all zeroes, so that the closer the match, the fewer "1" bits appear in the result. The simple XOR operation is very fast, such that biometric identification using large databases is very feasible.

Voice patterns can be used for biometric authentication, both verification and identification, and for recognition, which is not a type of authentication. Voice recognition is when the utterance is processed for comprehension. The simplest example is recognition of decimal digits. When a customer is asked to speak their credit card number, the phrase for each digit is recognized and captured. Other examples include simple responses such as "yes" and "no" and other one-word commands. Yet the recognition of the digits, responses, or commands does not authenticate the speaker. The analysis software uses different phonics for each language (e.g., English, Spanish, or French) but is agnostic to individuals such that it performs the same syllable evaluation regardless of the end user. Thus voice recognition is not a biometric authentication factor. An advantage of voice recognition includes its use on the existing telephony and emerging mobile infrastructures. One of its disadvantages, however, is casual eavesdropping on the information spoken by the legitimate end user.

Voice biometrics for authentication does distinguish individuals and can be implemented using static or dynamic phrases. A static phrase is when the same phrase is used repeatedly by multiple individuals. For example, in the movie *Sneakers*, the phrase "my voice is my passport verify me" is used for authentication. The same phrase was used by all employees, and the phrase was presumably unchanged for weeks, months, or years. A dynamic phrase is when individual words are strung together in a random fashion as a challenge. For example, after capturing the ten numeric digits, the challenge could be a string of random numbers that the speaker would repeat. Voice authentication is dependent on the quality of the microphone and suffers degradation from background noises.

Dynamic signatures are based on the capture and analysis of pen movements similar to handwritten signatures [161]. The magnitude

and direction of each pen stroke, the vectors, are collected, analyzed, and processed to create a biometric authentication factor.
Dynamic signatures are often confused with the graphical image
of a handwritten signature, or with digital signatures, which are a
cryptographic process. Further confusion exists due to some commercial products that combine the graphical image linked with
the cryptographic digital signature, which again is not a biometric
dynamic signature. One last note regarding confusion is the difference between dynamic signatures versus electronic signatures.
Electronic signatures, also called e-signatures, are legally defined
as an electronic sound, symbol, or process attached to or logically
associated with a contract or other record, and executed or adopted
by a person with the intent to sign the record. Thus a dynamic signature can be used as an e-signature, but not all e-signatures are
dynamic signatures. E-signatures are discussed further in §3.6.4
(Electronic Signatures).

There are many other biometric technologies, but of course the
ultimate is deoxyribonucleic acid (DNA) identification. Just like any
other biometric, there must be a template to match against the sample;
otherwise, the DNA results are anonymous. And just like any other
biometric, the template identity must be accurate; otherwise, a false
identity is matched to the sample. Further, just like any other biometric, samples can be surreptitiously collected and misused [217]. The
controls necessary to rely on biometric authentication are discussed in
the next few sections for enrollment, verification, and identification.

3.4.2 Biometric Enrollment

The X9.84 [54] biometric security standard defines enrollment and
distinguishes between the initial enrollment and subsequent reenrollment. The difference is that for the initial enrollment, the person entity
(PE) must be authenticated to reliably establish the link between the
biometric template and the assigned identifier, whereas for succeeding
reenrollments the link is already established. Reenrollment usually
occurs to update the biometric data due to aging or changes in the
technology, or to add new biometric data, such as another fingerprint
or voice recording.

- *Enrollment*: The process of collecting biometric samples from a person and the subsequent generation and storage of biometric reference templates associated with that person.
- *Initial enrollment*: The process of enrolling an individual's biometric data for the first time, such that the individual must provide a nonbiometric means of authentication such as a password or ID in order to establish or confirm an identity.
- *Reenrollment*: The process of enrolling an individual's biometric data where the same or other biometric data has been enrolled at least once.

Figure 3.15 shows the biometric enrollment process. The requester must be physically present at a biometric reader to capture one or more biometric samples. The samples are processed to create the biometric template, which is then stored in a database and linked to an identifier. Processing might occur on the requester system or the verifier system. The identifier might be a person's name, Social Security number (SSN), account number, or some other value. The link between the template and the identifier is critical to establish and maintain throughout its life cycle, so cryptographic processes such as MAC, HMAC, or digital signature are important. These algorithms are discussed further in Section 3.5 (Cryptography Factors).

Enrollment is [154] usually an attended activity with an enroller and the enrollee. The enroller is authenticated and authorized to perform the enrollment, and the enrollee is authenticated and authorized to be enrolled into the authentication system. The claimed identity of the enrollee needs to be properly verified using collateral material, such as photo identification. Some biometric enrollments have an additional step to check the database for existing templates to protect against fraudulent enrollments. For example, it is illegal to have more than one drivers license from any state with the Department of Motor Vehicles (DMV). Depending on the purpose of reenrollment, the existing biometrics might be used for authentication, or they might be updated or replaced using fresh live samples, and collateral material might also be used to reverify the enrollee.

3.4.3 Biometric Verification

Verification is a 1-to-1 authentication [148–160] where the requester presents a claimed identity along with the live biometric sample. The claimed identity (ID) is used to fetch a single biometric template from the database for matching. If the wrong identifier is provided, then the wrong template will be used for comparison, so the result will be a negative match. However, if the linked identifier is modified by an adversary to another template, then the resulting positive match will yield a fraudulent identity. This is not the same as a false positive, which is an inherent error characteristic of biometrics; rather, this is an overt attack on the biometric authentication system. Thus, establishing and maintaining integrity controls within the database are critically important.

Another attack is the substitution or modification of the template during its transmission from the database to the verifier. The verifier needs to validate the integrity and authenticity of the template, i.e., that the template originated from a legitimate source. Similarly, another attack is the substitution or modification of the live sample from the reader and requester to the verifier. Likewise, the verifier needs to validate the integrity and authenticity of the sample. A final attack is the substitution or modification of the matching results from the verifier to the relying party, such that the relying party needs to validate the integrity and authenticity of the matching results. Again, transmission of the sample or the template can also be encrypted to protect the privacy of the requester, but since biometric data are not secret, its encryption is not necessarily a security control to protect the authentication system.

Some biometric technologies support adaptation, which has the original authentication threshold, and another adaptation threshold, as shown in Figure 3.19. Adaptation occurs when the match result, or

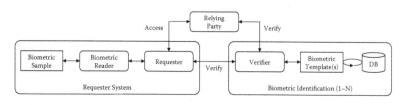

Figure 3.19 Biometric adaptation.

the score, is high enough for a positive match, but low enough that the biometric template can be updated for a better subsequent match. If the score is above the adaptation threshold, the result is a positive match but no update is performed. If the score is above the authentication threshold but below the adaptation threshold, the result is a positive match and the biometric template is updated. If the score is below the authentication threshold, the result is a negative match but no update is performed.

3.4.4 Biometric Identification

Identification is a 1-to-N authentication where no identifier is provided by the requester and the live sample is used to search the database for a candidates list. Match results with high scores above the authentication threshold are included in the list, whereas templates with low scores are not. The list is typically provided to the relying party for further inspection. Identification has the same dependency on the linkage between the identifier and the template as verification. Thus establishing and maintaining integrity controls within the database are critically important. Identification also has the same transmission vulnerabilities as verification. Therefore each component needs to validate the integrity and authenticity of the templates, sample, matching results, and candidates list.

In addition to establishing and maintaining integrity controls within the database, access controls are also important to prevent unauthorized access. The number of templates (N) searched within the database varies, depending on implementations. As discussed previously for fingerprint technology, when databases are sorted into bins, it is possible for the wrong bin to be chosen such that no matches are found, generating an empty candidates list. For some implementations, the size of N can be rather small, often called one-to-few, such as a small group of templates stored on a smartcard.

Smartcards or other peripheral devices that provide biometrics offer an interesting challenge. The device might only provide storage, in which case the template is exported to the matcher. Alternatively, the device might include the matching process, in which case the live sample is imported to the device. Another scenario is that the entire biometric system, including the reader, the matching process, and template storage, is onboard the device, in which case the device itself provides the integrity controls.

3.5 Cryptography Factors

Cryptography factors are "something you control" for a person entity (PE) or a nonperson entity (NPE) that employs one or more cryptographic algorithms, keys, schema, and protocols. While it can be argued that keys are data objects and cryptographic functions are software objects that run on hardware objects, the necessary controls to maintain security of cryptographic keys over their life cycle is better addressed by recognizing cryptography as a separate authentication factor.

A basic understanding of cryptography is necessary to discuss authentication factors. Cryptography is organized into two primary methods: symmetric or asymmetric algorithms. Symmetric algorithms use one key, whereas asymmetric algorithms use two keys. Symmetric keys are random numbers that are also called *secret keys*. Asymmetric keys are mathematically related numbers where one key is kept private and the other key is made public. Hence asymmetric cryptography is also called *public key cryptography*. Asymmetric private keys are managed confidentially using the same controls as symmetric secret keys. Asymmetric public keys are managed very differently in order to maintain their integrity and authenticity. We define several terms for this discussion.

- *Cleartext* is unencrypted data, typically a message in human readable format.
- *Ciphertext* is encrypted data, appears as random values, and is not human-comprehendible.
- *Random* is a value that has an equal probability of occurring as any other value of the same size. For example, a random three-digit number means any number between 100 and 999. Any number smaller than 100 is not a three-digit number. Another example is any random number less than 1,000 which would be any number from 0 to 999. Generating a true random number requires a source of entropy such that the chance of choosing the same number twice is an independent

event equal to the probability of the first event times the probability of the second event. So choosing a number less than 10 in the set of whole numbers from 0 through 999 has a probability of 0.1 (or 10%), and choosing the same number twice has a probability of $0.01 \times 0.01 = 0.0001$ or one hundredth percent.

- *Pseudo-random* is a value generated using a deterministic function based on an input commonly called a seed, where the output number has a statistically smooth probability distribution. The same input always produces the same output. This is important when the same pseudo-random number needs to be generated either at different times or by different entities.

- *Hash* is a value generated using a hash function, which is a one-way function that takes an arbitrary input string (s) and generates a fixed-length output. Uppercase H denotes the function, and lowercase h symbolizes the output. A secure cryptographic hash has three significant attributes. Given an output h, it is infeasible to find an input string (s) such that $h = H(s)$, also known as pre-image resistance. Given an input string (s1), it is infeasible to find another string (s2) such that $s1 \neq s2$ and $H(s1) = H(s2)$, also known as second pre-image resistance. And in general, it is infeasible to find two different input strings s1 and s2 such that $H(s1) = H(s2)$, also known as collision resistance.

An overview of symmetric and asymmetric cryptography is provided for both confidentiality and integrity mechanisms, namely encryption, message authentication (MAC), and digital signatures.

3.5.1 Symmetric Cryptography

Figure 3.20 shows how the same key is used by two different entities, the sender (Alice) and the receiver (Bob), such that the snooper (Sam) cannot read the message. Alice inputs the cleartext message and the symmetric key into the encryption algorithm, which generates the cryptogram or ciphertext. Alice then sends the ciphertext (C) to Bob. Bob inputs the ciphertext and the same symmetric key into the decryption algorithm to recover the cleartext message. Sam might be able to

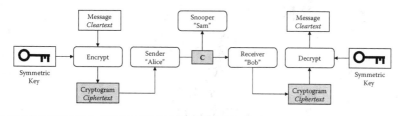

Figure 3.20 Symmetric encryption.

eavesdrop on the ciphertext, but without the symmetric key he would not be able to decrypt it and read the cleartext message. Alice and Bob must use the same symmetric key and algorithms for the encryption and decryption to work properly. The trick is how Alice and Bob established the symmetric key in the first place without Sam snooping a copy of the key. Key management is discussed in Chapter 7.

Encryption provides confidentiality of the message, but cannot by itself ensure its integrity. Sam might intercept and modify the ciphertext such that Bob would not be able to read the decrypted message; or if the original message was not human-comprehendible, Bob might not recognize that the ciphertext had been altered. In either case, Sam would still not know the original message, but then again, neither would Bob.

Figure 3.21 shows how a similar key is used by Alice and Bob to provide integrity of the message. Alice inputs the cleartext message and the symmetric key into the encryption algorithm, which generates the ciphertext. Alice sends the original cleartext message (M) and a partial piece of the ciphertext, also called a message authentication code (MAC) [108], to Bob. Bob inputs the cleartext message and the symmetric key into the encryption algorithm, which generates the ciphertext and compares it to the MAC received with the message. If the MAC matches the same partial piece of the ciphertext, Bob knows that neither the message nor the MAC has

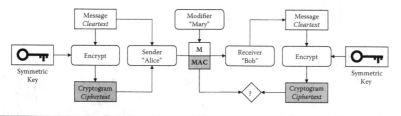

Figure 3.21 Symmetric integrity.

been altered. This is call MAC verification. Otherwise, if Mary modified either the message or the MAC, then the MAC verification would fail.

Since Bob can verify the MAC, the integrity of the message is preserved. And, since only Alice and Bob have the symmetric key, and Bob knows he did not send the message to himself, Bob can authenticate that the message came from Alice. However, the integrity and authenticity is not provable to a third party, so the message does not have nonrepudiation. For example, if Alice or Bob denied sending the message and ended up in court, a judge would conclude that either party could have generated the MAC, since both have access to the same symmetric key. Therefore, the MAC by itself is repudiatable.

3.5.2 Asymmetric Cryptography

Figure 3.22 shows how an asymmetric key pair, namely Bob's public and private keys, is used to encrypt data. Alice inputs the cleartext data and Bob's public key into the encryption algorithm, which generates the ciphertext. Alice then sends the ciphertext (C) to Bob. Bob inputs the ciphertext and his private key into the decryption algorithm to recover the cleartext data. The ciphertext encrypted by the public key can only be decrypted by the private key. Sam cannot decrypt the ciphertext because only Bob controls the private key. Further, since asymmetric algorithms are computationally more intense than symmetric algorithms, typically the "data" encrypted by the sender using a public key are actually a random symmetric key transported to the receiver for subsequent use as a symmetric encryption key. Sam might intercept and substitute the ciphertext by reusing Bob's public key and masquerade as Alice unbeknownst to Alice or Bob.

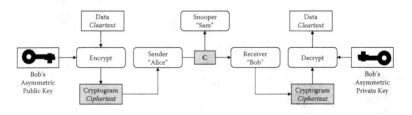

Figure 3.22   Asymmetric encryption.

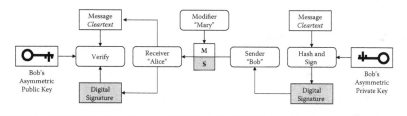

Figure 3.23 Asymmetric signature.

An obvious question is whether there is any reason for Bob to use his private key such that anyone with his public key can read his message. Figure 3.23 shows the fundamental process for asymmetric digital signatures. Bob first inputs his cleartext message into a hash algorithm that generates a hash value (or "hash"), also called a *message digest*. The hash is a smaller mathematical representation of the larger message whose reduced size is compatible with asymmetric algorithm modularity. Bob then inputs the hash and his private key into the signature algorithm to generate the digital signature. Bob sends the message (M) and the digital signature (S) to Alice. Alice inputs the cleartext message (M), the digital signature (S), and Bob's public key into the verification algorithm to verify the message.

Since Alice can verify the digital signature, the integrity of the message is preserved. And, since Bob's public key mathematically corresponds to Bob's private key, the message is authenticated. Further, since only Bob controls the private key, the integrity and authenticity is provable to third parties and, thus, is arguably a significant component for nonrepudiation. There are many other cryptographic, operational, and legal controls necessary for nonrepudiation, which are discussed in Chapter 5 (Nonrepudiation).

3.5.3 Cryptographic Authentication

Entity authentication is essentially proving control of a cryptographic key by generating ciphertext that is verifiable by another entity. The requester generates the ciphertext and the verifier validates the ciphertext. This can be achieved in a variety of ways using symmetric or asymmetric methods.

Encryption can be used to demonstrate that the requester controls an encryption key shared with the verifier. Refer to Figure 3.20. The requester and verifier might synchronize the cleartext such that when the requester sends the ciphertext, the verifier can decrypt and validate it. The cleartext could be a static password that is shared by both the requester and verifier, which is changed periodically. It can also be a dynamic value such as a time stamp that renews for each authentication. The cleartext might also be a one-time password (OTP), but the OTP scheme must be independent of the encryption scheme. Alternatively, the verifier might send random cleartext as a challenge to the requester for encryption. The requester might encrypt and return the challenge cleartext or modified cleartext based on a conversion algorithm. For example, the verifier sends a random number to which the requester adds a predetermined number before encryption. The verifier can also send the challenge encrypted for the requester to decrypt, modify, reencrypt, and then send back to the verifier.

Regardless of the cleartext schemes discussed here, the authentication is only valid if the encryption keys are unique per requester. Otherwise, the verifier cannot rely on the distinctiveness of any key if more than one requester uses the same encryption key. Thus the verifier needs to manage a different encryption key for each requester. For large requester populations, the verifier may need to manage thousands or millions of keys. While this may seem like a large number of keys, it is actually not all that onerous when one considers today's databases containing millions to billions of records measured in petabytes, which is over a quadrillion ($10^{15} \approx 2^{50}$) bytes. However, there are key management schemes such as Derived Unique Key Per Transaction (DUKPT) that allow a verifier to interoperate with numerous end points, each with a unique PIN encryption key, using only a single master key. For details, refer to Chapter 7 (Key Management).

Message Authentication Code (MAC) [108] can be used to demonstrate that the requester controls a MAC key shared with the verifier. Refer to Figure 3.21. Similar to encryption, the requester and verifier might synchronize the cleartext, or the verifier might send a challenge to the requester. The requester generates the MAC from the cleartext and sends it to the verifier for validation. Again, the authentication is only valid if the MAC keys are unique per requester; otherwise, the verifier cannot distinguish one MAC generated by one requester from another. Thus, similar to encryption, the verifier needs to manage a different MAC key per requester. Unlike DUKPT, where the end points use the unique key to encrypt the PIN entered by the cardholder, there is no scheme defined for MAC keys.

Since the cleartext cannot be derived from the MAC, the requester may need to send the cleartext to the verifier for validation. If the cleartext is sensitive data such as a password or other challenge-based responses, then the cleartext needs to be encrypted. However, different cryptographic keys must be used to separate the ciphertext results from the MAC algorithm and the encryption algorithm. Otherwise, too much information about the key might be revealed for cryptanalysis. Figure 3.24 provides a flow diagram of a combined MAC and encryption example.

The requester (Alice) inputs the cleartext message into both the MAC algorithm and the encryption algorithm, along with the associated key. The resulting ciphertexts, the encrypted message (C) and the MAC, are transmitted from the requester (Alice) to the verifier (Bob). Bob first inputs the encrypted message (C) and the encryption key into the decryption algorithm to recover the cleartext message. Bob then inputs the cleartext message and the MAC key into the MAC algorithm to regenerate the ciphertext for comparison to the received MAC sent by Alice. If the MAC verifies, then Bob confirms that neither the transmitted MAC nor the encrypted message (C) have been altered. If the encrypted message or the MAC had been modified, the MAC validation would have failed.

Similar to a MAC, a Hashed Message Authentication Code (HMAC) [174] can be used to demonstrate that the requester controls a MAC key shared with the verifier. The HMAC algorithm, also called a *keyed hash*, employs a hash algorithm as its primary function

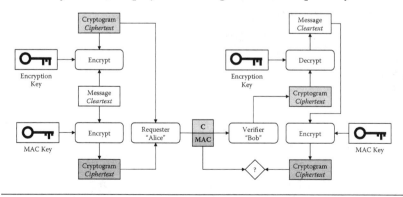

Figure 3.24 Combined MAC and encryption example.

instead of encryption, along with a symmetric key that gets combined with the cleartext message. HMAC verification is the same process as for MAC. And as with a MAC, authentication is only valid if the HMAC keys are unique per requester, so the verifier needs to manage a different HMAC key per requester. And similar to using MAC and encryption, the HMAC can be combined with encryption to transmit the encrypted message and the HMAC. HMAC verification with encryption is the same processes as for MAC with encryption.

Digital Signature can be used to demonstrate that the requester exclusively controls an asymmetric private key. Refer to Figure 3.23. The requester and verifier might synchronize the cleartext, or the verifier might send a challenge to the requester. The requester generates the digital signature from the cleartext using its private key and sends it to the verifier for validation. The verifier uses the requester's public key to validate the digital signature. The uniqueness of the asymmetric key pair per requester satisfies the validity of the authentication; however, the verifier must still manage the different public keys. If public key certificates are used, the certificates can be stored in the verifier's database without undue security controls, or the requester can send the certificate along with the signed message. The verifier needs to validate the certificate before using the public key. Certificate validation is discussed in Chapter 7 (Key Management).

3.5.4 Cryptographic Protocols

The cryptographic authentication schemas discussed here need to be implemented in a protocol with defined messages and error handling. ISO/IEC 9798 Entity Authentication [116] is a multipart standard that defines seventeen mechanisms: six using symmetric key cryptography, seven using digital signatures, and four using cryptographic check functions.

- ISO/IEC 9798 Part 2: Symmetric-key Cryptography
  1. 9798-2-1 One-pass unilateral authentication
  2. 9798-2-2 Two-pass unilateral authentication
  3. 9798-2-3 Two-pass mutual authentication
  4. 9798-2-4 Three-pass mutual authentication
  5. 9798-2-5 Four-pass with TTP

6. 9798-2-6 Five-pass with TTP
- ISO/IEC 9798 Part 3: Digital Signatures
  1. 9798-3-1 One-pass unilateral authentication
  2. 9798-3-2 Two-pass unilateral authentication
  3. 9798-3-3 Two-pass mutual authentication
  4. 9798-3-4 Three-pass mutual authentication
  5. 9798-3-5 Two-pass parallel mutual authentication
  6. 9798-3-6 Five-pass mutual authentication with TTP, initiated by A
  7. 9798-3-7 Five-pass mutual authentication with TTP, initiated by B
- ISO/IEC 9798 Part 4: Cryptographic Check Functions
  1. 9798-4-1 One-pass unilateral authentication
  2. 9798-4-2 Two-pass unilateral authentication
  3. 9798-4-3 Two-pass mutual authentication
  4. 9798-4-4 Three-pass mutual authentication

The ISO/IEC 9798 standard defines unilateral authentication as when only one of the two entities is authenticated by use of the mechanism, which is really single factor, and not to be confused with the OTP unilateral protocols mentioned previously. As is true with any protocol, especially those addressing or incorporating security mechanisms, there are always cryptographic transitions [9], and recent analysis [4, 5] has determined that the mechanisms have several weaknesses, and so revisions are likely to be published. The standard also includes mechanisms that rely on a trusted third party (TTP). What is also true is that TTPs are not necessarily without problems. For example, there were several certification authorities (CA) that were publicly compromised in 2011, and there have been other historical cases where the TTP is no longer operational [212–216].

FIPS 196 [172] adapts ISO/IEC 9798 Part 3, second mechanism Two-pass unilateral authentication and ISO/IEC 9798 Part 3, fourth mechanism Three-pass mutual authentication for federal departments and agencies that use public key–based authentication systems to protect unclassified information. For the sake of brevity, only the two methods defined in FIPS 196 are described herein and are shown in Figure 3.25. Both ISO/IEC 9798 and FIPS 196 use the term claimant versus requester, defined as an entity that is or represents a

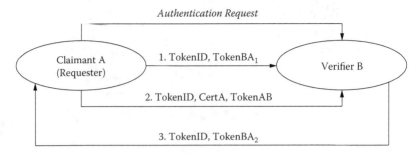

Figure 3.25   FIPS 196 entity authentication.

principal for the purposes of authentication. But the term also implies that the requester provides an identity for its authentication request, whereas when we address biometrics, this is not always the case.

Figure 3.25 shows four messages, but the initial authentication request is optional and not considered part of the authentication protocol. The first method adapted from ISO/IEC 9798-3-2 (two-pass unilateral) only encompasses messages (1) and (2), whereas the second method adapted from ISO/IEC 9798-3-4 (three-pass mutual authentication) relies on all three messages (1), (2), and (3). Both authentication methods are a bilateral challenge-and-response protocol. The data fields in the messages are referred to as "tokens," not to be confused with the hardware tokens discussed in this chapter. In single-factor authentication,

1. The verifier (B) sends $TokenBA_1$ to (A) with an optional TokenID that provides a unique reference to avoid ambiguity. The $TokenBA_1$ nomenclature means that the token is generated by B and sent to A, and the subscript 1 distinguishes the first BA token from the second one. $TokenBA_1$ represents a challenge from B to A consisting of a random number (R_B).
2. The claimant (A) returns TokenAB to (B) with its X.509 public key certificate (CertA) and another optional TokenID. TokenAB consists of a digital signature over the random numbers (R_B) and (R_A) and optionally the identity of the verifier (B), along with the random number (R_A). The verifier (B) authenticates the claimant (A) by validating the digital signature in TokenAB using the public key provided in CertA.

As noted previously for data objects as possession factors, the Security Assertion Markup Language (SAML) supports a myriad of authentication methods inclusive of knowledge, possession, biometric, and cryptography factors. Digital signatures are the primary cryptographic method, and numerous public key management schemes are supported. Encrypted content is also supported. Extended Markup Language (XML) digital signatures [211] and encryption [210] are referenced by SAML. This book is not intended as a guideline on SAML, but more information is available online at the OASIS Security Services (SAML) Technology Committee site at https://www.oasis-open.org.

3.6 Signature Synonyms

The term *signature* originates from the Latin word *sigare*, meaning "to sign." The partial evolution from paper-and-ink handwritten signatures to computer-based "signatures" includes legal, technology, and market issues. One of the earliest known scribal signatures circa 3100 BC is from the Shøven Collection of Sumerian pictographic scripts. The autograph by the scribe Gar Ama is on the back of the clay tablet, the front of which is a lexical list of forty-one titles and professions (Figure 3.26).

Regarding handwritten signatures, technology has evolved from clay tablets, to papyrus, to paper, and eventually to computers and graphical user interfaces (GUI). But technology has also evolved into cryptography for digital signatures and into biometrics for dynamic signatures, and the user interface (UI) has graduated to the user experience (UX). As new laws and regulations are published, the interpretation of what constitutes a legally binding signature changes. The adoption of technology and legal effects is often driven by market trends or advocacy by one group over another.

Figure 3.26   Sumerian signature.

Figure 3.27   John's digitized signature.

3.6.1 Handwritten Signatures

Probably one of the most famous signatures in U.S. history is John Hancock's on the Declaration of Independence, shown in Figure 3.27, a digitized version. Pen-and-ink signatures are considered to have two fundamental characteristics: provenance and intention. The presence of the inked signature presumes provenance of the document; it is the original document, not a copy, and not a fake. The inked signature also proves intent by the signatory to abide by the terms and conditions of the document—the agreement.

Further, the physical attributes of the paper, the chemical characteristics of the ink, and the interaction between the two offer both visual and tactile feedback. There is also a permanence of the paper that is not afforded by digital data. Modern-day business practices rarely allow all parties to be physically present and to have everyone sign all duplicates, so everyone has an "original" copy. For example, often one party can fax an unsigned document for signature by another; the second party faxes the signed document back to the first party; and the first party faxes a countersigned document back to the second party. Business practices such as these actually create many interim documents. However, when purchasing large-ticketed items such as an automobile or a house, all parties are required to be physically present to sign all "original" documents.

3.6.2 Dynamic Signatures

As discussed previously, dynamic signatures are a type of biometric technology. Typically an electronic stylus or touch-sensitive device is used to measure and capture vector information about the hand movements. Since biometric algorithms are vendor proprietary, Figure 3.28 shows how a notional dynamic signature might operate using John Hancock's signature. Each letter is measured for distance, angles, and speed, which are compared to the biometric template such that if the

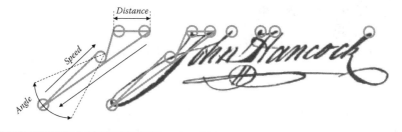

Figure 3.28 John's dynamic signature.

live sample is within threshold tolerances, the signature is considered a match. Note that the dynamic signature shown in Figure 3.28 is not the same as the digitized signature shown in Figure 3.27.

The dynamic signature technology works for any sequence of letters, as long as the template and sample are the same doodle. An actual autograph is not a prerequisite, and in fact the signature could be any fictitious name. Thus, the scrawl still provides authentication, but the scribble itself does not necessarily provide identity. If the dynamic signature is intended to be reused as a digitized signature, then policy needs to state the requirement that users must sign their legal name.

3.6.3 Digital Signatures

As discussed previously, an asymmetric key pair can be used to generate or verify a digital signature, where the private key owner uses it to generate the signature, and the relying party uses the owner's public key to verify the signature. Figure 3.29 shows the digital signature

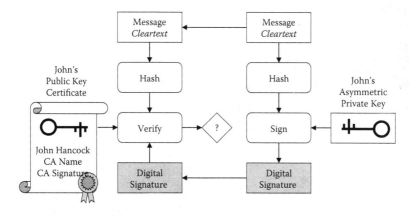

Figure 3.29 John's digital signature.

process in more detail than previously shown in Figure 3.23. To generate the digital signature, John first inputs the cleartext into the hash algorithm, which outputs a hash value, and then inputs the hash value and the asymmetric private key into the signature (sign) algorithm, which outputs the digital signature.

To verify the signature, the relying party inputs the cleartext into the hash algorithm to recalculate the hash value, and then inputs the hash value, the asymmetric public key, and the digital signature into the verify algorithm, which outputs essentially a yes or no answer. Many illustrations of digital signatures describe using the public key to decrypt the digital signature, which recovers the hash and then compare it to the recalculated hash; however, this is only true if the digital signature algorithm is reversible, such as RSA [43]. Other digital signature algorithms are irreversible, such as DSA [170] or ECDSA [47], whose verification process mathematically differs. In order for the relying party to trust John's public key, John's public key certificate, also called a *digital certificate*, must be validated. Certificate validation is discussed in Chapter 7 (Key Management).

3.6.4 Electronic Signatures

Electronic signatures are often confused with digital signatures and are somewhat misunderstood. In 1996, the United Nations Commission on International Trade Law (UNCITRAL) Model Law on Electronic Commerce was published. This influenced several bodies of law. In 1999, the United States in the Uniform Electronic Transactions Act (UETA) released by the National Conference of Commissioners on Uniform State Laws (NCCUSL) defined "electronic signature" as an electronic sound, symbol, or process, attached to or logically associated with a contract or other record and executed or adopted by a person with the intent to sign the record. This is consistent with the European Union (EU) Directive on Electronic Signatures published in 1999.

For example, when a person installs software on a computer, there is typically a popup menu presenting an end-user license agreement (EULA). The user is expected to read the agreement and then click on an "agree" button before the software is installed. The mouse click on the button is a form of an electronic signature. When the user clicks on the button, the installation wizard captures the event.

Another example is when a cardholder chooses an option from an ATM menu such as cash withdrawal and enters the PIN. The act of touching the screen or buttons and using the PIN pad constitutes an electronic signature signifying the cardholder's intent to conduct the financial transaction.

Any of the authentication factors can be interpreted as an overt action indicating intent to "sign" the record if the authentication process is linked to an application process. When using biometrics for authentication, the act of providing a live sample via the biometric reader can be interpreted as an overt action that represents an electronic signature. Placing a finger on the reader, speaking into a microphone, or looking into the camera are all actions by the user signifying intent. When the user accesses its private key to generate a digital signature, or its symmetric key to generate a MAC, HMAC, or encrypt authentication data, these actions likewise signify intent. Thus a digital signature can be applied as an electronic signature, but clearly not all electronic signatures are digital signatures.

3.7 Provisioning

As mentioned previously when discussing enrollment as part of the authentication framework, provisioning is the process whereby information about the individual (PE) is collected and corroborated such that the identity is initially validated. Here we stress the difference between authentication and identification, the former being based on internal processes under control of the organization, whereas the latter is a dependency on external processes outside control of the organization. This book offers the following definitions:

- *Authentication* is an internal process of verifying an individual based on an assigned identifier, such as an employee number, and authentication credentials based on the enrollment action.
- *Identification* is the process of validating an individual based on identity credentials issued by an external agency that are beyond the control of the organization.

The definition differences are subtle in that similar words are used to describe similar processes. The problem is exasperated by the fact that the terms are sometimes used to mean different things. For example, when biometrics [54] is used for one-to-one (1-to-1) authentication where the requester presents a live biometric sample with a claimed identifier and the sample is matched against the biometric template associated with that identifier, it is called *verification*. But, when biometrics are used for one-to-many (1-to-N) authentication where the requester only provides the live biometric sample that is used to scan the template database and determine the identifier, it is called *identification*. Consider what identity credentials are created during an individual's lifetime prior and possibly subsequently to enrollment.

Personal information in the United States begins in the form of a birth certificate. Table 3.4 shows the information contained in a

Table 3.4   Birth Certificate

ENTITY	CONTACT DATA	MEDICAL DATA	AUTHENTICATION DATA
Child information	• Birthplace – city, county, state • Name – last, middle, first • Sex – male or female • Birth type – single, twin, triplet • Birth date – year, month, day	—	—
Mother information	• Maiden name – last, middle, first • Birthplace – state • Mailing address – street, city, state, zip • Residence – city, county, state	• Color or race • Age	—
Father information	• Name – last, middle, first • Birthplace – state	• Color or race • Age	—

Document information	• Certificate number
	• Attendant's address Year, month, day
		—	• Attendant's information
			  • Signature
			  • Signature date
			• Registrar information
			  • Signature
			  • Signature date

Table 3.5 Social Security Card

ENTITY	CONTACT DATA	FINANCIAL DATA
Citizen information	• Name – first, middle initial, last • Address – street, city, state, zip	• Social Security number (SSN)

typical state-issued birth certificate, which is a rather complex document consisting of numerous data elements. The majority of the data elements can be considered contact information (names, addresses). Color, race, and age are realistically medical information relative to actuarial science. Signatures and dates are authentication information attesting to the validity of the document.

Some time after birth and before the child becomes a teenager, the parents typically registers for the child's Social Security number, which is issued as a Social Security card. Table 3.5 shows the information issued by the Social Security Administration, which is a relatively simple document consisting of a few data elements. The Social Security number (SSN) is financial data for federal tax purposes. The remainder of the data are contact information (name, address).

During the child's growth, pediatrician and/or physician visits are inevitable, which results in the creation of medical records. Table 3.6 shows typical information collected by a health-care service provider. The majority of data elements can be considered contact information

Table 3.6 Medical Records

ENTITY	CONTACT DATA	MEDICAL DATA	FINANCIAL DATA
Patient information	• Name • Address • Phone number • Birth date	• Age • Symptom • Prescription	• SSN
Guardian information	• Name • Address • Phone number	—	• SSN • Account number • Amount
Insurance information	• Name • Type of coverage	—	• Group number • Account number
Physician information	• Organization • Name • Address • Phone number	• Diagnostic code	—

Table 3.7 Driver's License

ENTITY	CONTACT DATA	AUTHENTICATION DATA
Driver's information	• Name • Driver's license number • Date of birth	• Height • Weight • Eye color • Photo
DMV information	• State name • Date of issuance • Expiration date • Class of license	• Holograph • Watermark • State logo

(names, addresses). Medical data includes those items that provide health-care information. Financial data includes payment information.

One of the big events in a teenager's life is getting a driver's license. Table 3.7 shows the information provided in a typical state-issued drivers license.

Later in life, school records become important. Table 3.8 shows the information provided in a typical school transcript. Many of the data elements are contact information (names, addresses), and the rest comprise scholastic information (student ID, grade-point average).

Another data source is financial transactions. Table 3.9 shows the information provided in a typical payment transaction with a merchant. BIN is the Bank Identification Number and is the first six digits of the primary account number (PAN); CVV is the Card Verification

Table 3.8 College Transcript

ENTITY	CONTACT DATA	SCHOLASTIC DATA	FINANCIAL DATA
Student information	• Name • Address • Telephone number • e-mail address	• Admissions application • Test scores • Academic coursework • Grades • Transcripts • Major field of study • Dates of attendance • Student ID number	• Primary account number • Expiration date • Amount • Balance due
Institution information	• University name • Address	—	• Bank name • Account number • Tax ID

Table 3.9 Merchant Transaction Record

ENTITY	CONTACT DATA	FINANCIAL DATA	AUTHENTICATION DATA
Consumer information	• Name	• Primary account number • Expiration date • Amount	• Signature
Merchant information	• Name • Address • Phone number • URL	• Bank name • Account number • Tax ID	—
Bank information	• BIN	• Card type • Discretionary data	• CVV

Value. Contact data identifies the consumer and bank as entities; the financial data are used to process the payment transaction; and the authentication data are used to verify the consumer and the bank card.

For provisioning to validate the individual's identity, the assurance level of each identification credential must be evaluated for its accuracy and validity before it can be used in the validation process. For example, a bad agent may present a counterfeit birth certificate, driver's license, and a merchant receipt (e.g., paid utility bill) as evidence. Since the names match, the age seems correct, the eye color and height are correct, and the current addresses match, the provisioner might conclude the proffered identity information is correct and therefore enable enrollment for subsequent authentication. On the other hand, the forgery of three credentials, one of these being a government-issued document (a driver's license) with anticounterfeiting features (e.g., hologram, watermark, and state logo), is not an inexpensive feat, so the adversary's gain must be compared to his fraud investment as part of risk management. If the adversary can net a profit, obtain confidential information, damage reputation, or achieve other goals, then the identity fraud is likely, whereas if the investment costs are too high, the likelihood of fraud is much lower.

However, this one-dimensional approach has an inherent risk in that a zero-profit identity fraud might be used as a vector for a higher-profit fraud attack. For example, a fraudster might join a merchant site for sales information, and then use that relationship to make a layaway purchase, and then use that more trusted relationship to get a credit line for larger purchases that will never be paid. The merchant has little recourse to collect the bad debt when it discovers the person does not exist. This vectored fraud attack is more difficult to detect when it occurs across multiple organizations.

Thus the reliance on documents that are easily counterfeited should only be used for low-risk enrollments, and enrollments for higher risk applications cannot necessarily rely on previous enrollments. For example, a high-risk enrollment may require criminal and legal background checks in addition to forgery-resistant identification documents. However, such actions are subject to local laws, as for example in some countries background checks for financial stability are against the law. Another consideration is the temporal nature of identify information. Financial stability and no criminal records might be the case during the hiring process, but things can go wrong, so depending on the risk, a refresh of the identification might be necessary. For example, government agencies may require periodic background updates; athletic groups may require intermittent drug tests; and law enforcement may run occasional fingerprint checks.

Table 3.10 provides a simple approach for high-, medium-, and low-risk application environments. Organizations will need to determine the appropriate trade-offs for employees versus customer inconvenience, the relative costs and delays of background checks, and the risk granularity of the applications. For example, an organization may have a "no risk" environment; they may not have a "low" risk environment; or conversely they may have both a "high" and "very high" risk environment.

Most organizations have risk assessment processes that might be adaptable to address Table 3.10 for provisioning. It is also important to note that acceptance of an identification credential does not necessarily need to be done in person; rather, virtual environments with high-definition scanners, including mobile devices, are now prevalent. From a technology perspective, mobile devices today convey a much higher pixel rate than their older fax machine cousins, which have been used for ages to transmit copies of passports, drivers licenses, and other legal documentation.

Table 3.10 Identity Risk Framework

RISK LEVEL	INITIAL IDENTIFICATION	SUBSEQUENT IDENTIFICATION
High risk	Background checks • Job history and references • Last three years IRS returns • Check all three credit bureaus • Criminal AFIS fingerprints • Lawsuit check • Drug test **and** Identity credentials • Government-issued ID with photo and biometric (e.g., fingerprint, iris) **or** • Federal-issued ID with photo (e.g., passport) • State-issued ID with photo (e.g., driver's license)	Minimal financial and criminal background checks **and** Identity credentials • Government-issued ID with photo and biometric (e.g., fingerprint, iris) **or** • Federal-issued ID with photo (e.g., passport) **or** • State-issued ID with photo (e.g., driver's license)
Medium risk	Minimal financial and criminal background checks **and** Identity credentials • Government-issued ID with photo and biometric (e.g., fingerprint, iris) **or** • Federal-issued ID with photo (e.g., passport) • State-issued ID with photo (e.g., driver's license)	Minimal financial and criminal background checks
Low risk	Identity credentials • Government-issued ID with at least photo (e.g., passport, driver's license) **or** • Birth certificate • Photo documentation (e.g., school yearbook) • Merchant receipt with current address	None

4

INTEGRITY

Data integrity is defined as those security controls to detect data modification or substitution due to unauthorized access. Notice the definition does not address prevention, as it is infeasible to stop active attacks or avoid inactive actions. For data in storage, access controls might be circumvented, systems might be hacked to gain root admin access, or authorized users might be socially engineered to give up passwords. For data in process, software bugs might inadvertently change data, or a system infected with malware might alter data. For data in transit, there are many environmental factors that might corrupt data such as power fluctuations, electromagnetic interference (EMI) or even bad weather for wireless communications, and transmission factors that can cause data loss such as a failed network component, power failure, or network congestion.

This definition is different than many others, which often deal with accuracy and consistency, as these are operational controls suitable for applications or databases. Data input controls are basically validation rules to ensure the syntax and semantics. Syntax rules include data types such as numeric (N), alphabetic (A), alphanumeric (AN), special characters (S), and the like. Syntax can also include data formats such as length, dates (yyyy/mm/dd), times (hh:mm:ss), telephone numbers (nnn-nnn-nnnn), and others. Also refer to §2.1.2 (Data Tagging) in Chapter 2 (Confidentiality). Semantic rules might include reconciling age with date of birth, zip code with street, city, and state address, eligibility with business logic, and the like. However, these are not security controls.

Whereas the Bell–La Padula (BLP) [10] security model is based on confidentiality for military systems, the Clark-Wilson [71] security model is focused on data integrity for commercial systems. Their paper postulates well-formed transactions and appropriate separation of duties such that the integrity of each data item, including software objects, and therefore that of the whole system is maintained. This is achievable by using transformation procedures that only change data items from one valid state to another and by integrity verification procedures used for validation before and after data transformations. This book focuses on the integrity verification procedure, namely the integrity check value (ICV).

4.1 Integrity Check Value (ICV) Description

An integrity check value (ICV) is a special data element derived from one or more data elements using an integrity check (IC) algorithm that is relatively unique to those data elements. In this case, relatively unique means that the same ICV can be derived from multiple dissimilar data elements. This is unavoidable because the length of the ICV output is much smaller than the input. Consider in Figure 4.1 an IC algorithm shown as a mapping from the set of all input strings of any arbitrary length to the set of all fixed-length ICV output strings, as shown in Figure 4.1. The set of ICV outputs consists of all possible data strings of an N-bit fixed length. However, the set of inputs consists of all possible data strings of all possible lengths: 1-bit, ..., N-1, N, N+1, ..., N+M bit strings, where N is the length of the ICV and M is some large, practical upper limit. Theoretically, M is infinite with no upper bound; however, in reality any IC algorithm implementation typically has some constraint due to buffer size or memory limitations.

So clearly the same output ICV can be generated from multiple inputs since there are far many more inputs than outputs. When more than one input yields the same output, it is called a *collision*, where a good IC algorithm distributes the collisions evenly. For example,

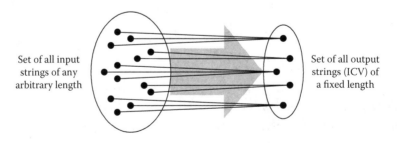

Set of all input strings of any arbitrary length

Set of all output strings (ICV) of a fixed length

Figure 4.1   Integrity check algorithm mapping.

an extremely bad algorithm might map all inputs to a single output, which is basically useless. Further, a good IC algorithm yields dissimilar ICV with large differences for inputs that are similar with small differences, such that a small change in the original data gives a big change in the ICV. For example, if an original message (M) yields a particular ICV, then changing a single character in M should generate a completely different ICV. The next two sections discuss how ICVs can be composed and where they can be used.

4.1.1 ICV Composition

An integrity check value (ICV) is derived from one or more data elements using an integrity check (IC) algorithm such that ICV = IC (Data). Thus an ICV can be calculated for one data element, a group of data elements such as a message, or a whole database. Further, multiple ICVs can be used, and not every data element might have an ICV, as demonstrated in Figure 4.2. For example, ICV-1 is derived from Data-1 and ICV-3 is from Data-3. The data elements Data-2 and Data-4 do not have individual ICVs.

The data structure (a) consists of the three data elements (Data-1, Data-2, and Data-3) and the two integrity check values ICV-1 and ICV-3. In this example, ICV-a1 is calculated over data structure (a); however, the inputs are only Data-1, Data-2, and Data-3. The two other check values ICV-1 and ICV-3 are not included in the computation of ICV-a1. Conversely, ICV-a2 is calculated over the whole data structure (a) inclusive of the three data elements and the two ICVs.

The data structure (b) consists of the four data elements (Data-1, Data-2, Data-3, and Data-4) and the two integrity check values ICV-1 and ICV-3. In this example, ICV-b is calculated over the whole data structure (b), inclusive of the four data elements and the two ICVs. While these two examples may seem overly complex, Figure 4.3 shows the Track 2 magstripe, introduced in Chapter 3 (Authentication) for

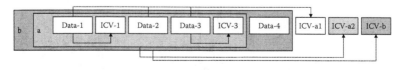

Figure 4.2 ICV compositional options.

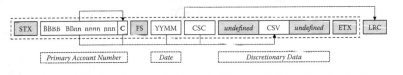

Figure 4.3   Track 2 magstripe.

credit cards and debit cards, which includes three different types of ICV over various data elements.

The Track 2 magstripe is encoded in a 5-bit character scheme, consisting of four data bits (0000 to 1111) and one parity bit. Odd parity is used, such that the total number of 1 bits in the preceding four data bits is an odd number, as shown in Table 4.1. Arguably, the parity bit could be considered another type of ICV, but for the purposes of this discussion, the parity bits will be disregarded. Thus, the magstripe data elements can be analyzed independent of the encoding scheme. The data content of the Track 2 magstripe consists of four data fields: the primary account number (PAN), the expiration date, the card service code (CSC), and the discretionary data. The expiration date is a 4-digit value representing the year (YY) and month (MM). The CSC is a 3-digit value signifying usage such as international for purchase, ATM, or cash advance. Within the discretionary data, there

Table 4.1   Magstripe Character Parity Bit

USAGE	CHARACTER	ASCII	BINARY	PARITY BIT	PARITY
Number	0	30	0000	1	1-odd
Number	1	31	0001	0	1-odd
Number	2	32	0010	0	1-odd
Number	3	33	0011	1	3-odd
Number	4	34	0100	0	1-odd
Number	5	35	0101	1	3-odd
Number	6	36	0110	1	3-odd
Number	7	37	0111	0	3-odd
Number	8	38	1000	0	1-odd
Number	9	39	1001	1	3-odd
—	:	3A	1010	1	3-odd
STX	;	3B	1011	0	3-odd
—	<	3C	1100	1	3-odd
FS	=	3D	1101	0	3-odd
—	>	3E	1110	0	3-odd
ETX	?	3F	1111	1	5-odd

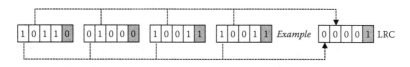

Figure 4.4 Magstripe LRC and parity bits.

is a 3-digit card security value (CSV), but the remainder of the data are proprietary, so for the purposes of this book, the rest is marked as "undefined." There are also several field separators (FS), including the start sentinel (STX) and end sentinel (ETX) fields. Overall, there are three distinct integrity check values in the Track 2 magstripe.

- Across the overall magstripe is a longitudinal redundancy check (LRC). Each of its four bits is an odd parity bit for all of the corresponding character parity bits. Thus the first bit of the LRC forces odd parity for all of the first-character bits; the second LRC bit forces odd parity for all of the second-character bits; and the third and fourth LRC bits force odd parity for the third-character and fourth-character bits, respectively. As shown in Figure 4.4, the LRC also has its own character parity bit of its four LRC bits.
- Traversing three of the magstripe data fields is the card security value (CSV). The primary account number (PAN), the expiration date, and the card service code (CSC) are the data inputs into the CSV algorithm. These three fields are combined and encrypted using a dedicated cryptographic key; the resulting ciphertext is then sorted and "decimalized" to create a string of sixteen digits; and the first three digits are used as the CSV. The CSV algorithm is proprietary but is published in the operating rules for the major brands, including MasterCard and Visa.
- Within the PAN is a check value (C) based on the Luhn formula in ISO 7812 [113]. It is a single decimal value whose original purpose was to avoid sales clerks from transposing digits when manually keying in the account number. The Luhn formula can be defined in various mathematical expressions, but it can be quickly calculated as shown in Table 4.2.

Table 4.2 Example of Luhn Formula

2	1	2	1	2	1	2	1	2	1	2	1	2	1	2	1	2	1	2	C
0	0	0	0	4	9	9	9	9	9	9	8	7	6	5	4	3	2	1	4
0	0	0	0	8	9	18	9	18	9	18	8	14	6	10	4	6	2	2	—
0	0	0	0	8	7	6	5	4	3	2	0	5	1	2	6	2	4	6	**4**

Since the CSV is derived using a cryptographic key, it cannot be generated by anyone else who does not have access to the key. Thus any changes to the PAN, the date, or the CSC negates the validity of the CSV, and it cannot be regenerated without the key. Conversely, since the LRC and the Luhn check-digit algorithms do not incorporate a cryptographic key, anyone can change data and regenerate new values that will verify. For example, the LRC and Luhn check digit can be regenerated if a PAN digit is changed, but the CSV would not verify. However, any changes in the discretionary data would not be detected in the Luhn check digit or the CSV, and the LRC can be regenerated. Therefore, the LRC and Luhn check digit only provide integrity to the extent of an inadvertent data change and not an adversarial attack.

However, the CSV only provides integrity over some of the magstripe but not all of it. Further, because the CSV algorithm relies on a symmetric key, both the generator of the CSV and the verifier of the CSV must use the same key. For card authorization when the issuer generates and verifies the CSV, the key can essentially reside in one location. But when the issuer outsources card issuance to a service provider, it must share the CSV key with the provider. Also, when the issuer allows card authorization by other service providers, called *stand-in processing*, it must likewise share the CSV key. As a general risk-assessment rule, the more parties that share a key, the greater is the risk of a key compromise.

The magstripe character set for Track 2 is shown in Table 4.1, which maps to the ASCII character set 30 ("0") to 3F ("?"). The digits 0 to 9, the start sentinel (STX), the end sentinel (ETX), and the field separator (FS) are encoded in the magstripe. The parity bit for each character is shown along with the odd-parity calculations for one, three, and five odd bits. The LRC calculation is shown in Figure 4.4 using four example characters. As noted previously, each character has its own odd-parity bit, and the LRC reflects odd parity for each position of the four data bits. The first bit for each character affects the first bit of the LRC; the second bit of each character affects the second bit of the LRC, and so on. In this example, the LRC is computed to be 0000, so its parity bit is a 1 for odd parity.

Similar to the parity bits and the LRC shown in Figure 4.4, the Luhn check digit shown in Table 4.2 is also determinable by anyone with access to the data and the algorithm. As mentioned previously, the Luhn formula was designed to catch transposed digits and avoid a store clerk from entering the wrong account number. It is not a computationally intense algorithm, and in fact with a bit of practice it can be calculated in one's head without using a calculator or paper and pencil.

Table 4.2 contains twenty columns to allow the maximum 19-digit account number as defined in ISO 7812 [113]. The first row contains the alternating multipliers 2 and 1. Enter the PAN right-justified with leading zeros into the second row per the 16-digit 4999999876543214 example. Multiply each PAN digit by the multiplier and enter the results into the third row. So $2 \times 4 = 8$, $1 \times 9 = 9$, $2 \times 9 = 18$, and so on. Skip the last column and copy the first nonzero digit in the third row to the same cell in the fourth row. Beginning with the first nonzero cell in the fourth row, add each individual digit in the next cell in the third row, subtract 10 if greater than 9 from the subtotal, and enter the result into same cell in the fourth row, as shown in Figure 4.5. Double-digit numbers in the third row are treated as individual numbers, so 18 is 1 and 8, and 14 is 1 and 4.

So, $8 + 9 = 17 - 10 \Rightarrow 7$, and $7 + 1 + 8 = 16 - 10 \Rightarrow 6$, and so on until $4 + 2 = 6$. Take the last digit (6) and subtract it from 10, so $10 - 6 = 4$, which is the check-digit value. This will work for any major branded card and most private label cards. However, as demonstrated, anyone can calculate the Luhn check digit, and being only a single digit, there are only ten possible values.

Figure 4.5   Luhn formula addition.

4.1.2 Integrity Check Points

Essentially, an integrity control enables the detection of unauthorized modification or substitution, but it does not ensure its accuracy. For example, if the wrong date of birth is entered into the system, when it is read and viewed, its integrity can be validated in that it has not been fraudulently altered, but the birthday date is still wrong. Data integrity is achieved by using an integrity check value (ICV) that is associated with one or more data elements. Figure 4.6 reconsiders the data life cycle introduced in Chapter 2 (Confidentiality). The life cycle is a state-transition diagram consisting of data in transit, data in storage, and data in process. Two entities A and B are shown to demonstrate data in transit.

Figure 4.6 shows the integrity points within each data state where an integrity check value (ICV) is generated, stored, or validated.

- *ICV generation*: An ICV is generated when the data are created, updated, copied, or sent. When the data are first created, its integrity is initially established by generating the ICV for one or more data elements. When data are updated, the ICV must be regenerated. When data are copied, a new ICV must be generated for the copy, as even though the data content might be the same, the metadata changes, such as the file path, creation date, and modification date. When the data are sent to another party, the ICV must be generated for the data in transit.
- *ICV storage*: An ICV is stored when the data are written to storage.

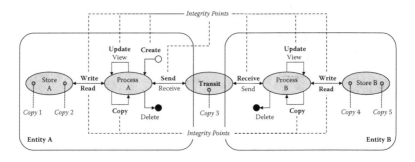

Figure 4.6   Data life-cycle framework.

- *ICV validation*: An ICV is validated when the data are read from storage, prior to its viewing, updating, copying, or sending. The ICV is also validated when data in transit is received from another party.

For the purposes of maintaining data integrity, each transition between the life-cycle stages incorporates ICV generation, storage, or validation. Table 4.3 provides a summary of the ICV actions for each transition and the relative data states. When a data element is read from storage, its ICV is validated to ensure its integrity. When a data element is written to storage, its ICV is regenerated and stored along with the data element. Optionally, the ICV can be regenerated for each update, copy, or when a new data element is created such that is it always ready for storage; otherwise, the regeneration can occur immediately prior to its storage.

During transmission, an ICV is freshly generated by the sender (A) and validated by the receiver (B). This is necessary for two primary reasons. First, the ICV generation methods and parameters might be particular to entity A and unavailable to entity B; so for the sake of interoperability, one or more new ICVs are generated. Secondly, the transit stage will have its own protocols and message structures such that an ICV is generated over the whole message or message parts. In summary, integrity check value (ICV) can be used for data in transit, data in process, and data in storage. The next sections discuss ICV uses for each of the data states and various ICV methods.

Table 4.3 ICV Actions

		ICV ACTIONS		
TRANSITION	RELATIVE DATA STATES	GENERATION	STORAGE	VALIDATION
Read	Store A ⇒ Process A	—	—	Validation
Write	Process A ⇒ Store A	Generation	Storage	—
Update	Within Process A	*optional*	—	—
Copy	Within Process A	*optional*	—	—
Create	Within Process A	*optional*	—	—
Send	Process A ⇒ Transit	Generation	—	—
Receive	Transit ⇒ Process B	—	—	Validation

4.2 Data Integrity States

As discussed in Chapter 2 (Confidentiality) and described in Figure 4.6, data has its own unique life cycle, but it can ultimately be addressed in one of three data states: data in transit, data in process, and data in storage. The data-integrity security issues for each state can be addressed separately.

4.2.1 Data in Transit

For data in transit, refer to Figure 4.7. The sender generates an ICV from the cleartext and then transmits both objects (the ICV and cleartext) to the receiver over the transmit media. Upon initial receipt of the ICV and cleartext from the transmit media, the receiver does not know if either object is unaltered. There is always the chance that data has become corrupted due to transmission media errors, but such communication protocols typically have error-detection and -correction algorithms, so the integrity question is whether an adversary has modified or substituted either object in transit. Hence the receiver's objects are denoted with an asterisk (*) or a hash (#) as ICV*, ICV#, or cleartext#, indicating a potential difference from the sender's ICV and cleartext objects.

The receiver generates an ICV# from the cleartext# and compares the newly generated ICV# to the ICV* received over the transmit media. If the generated ICV# matches the received ICV*, then the receiver knows there is a very high probability that the received ICV*

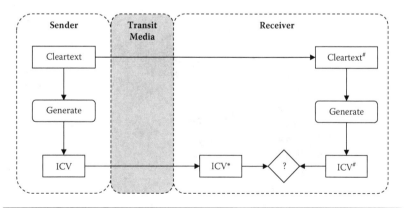

Figure 4.7 Data integrity in transit.

matches the sent ICV and the received cleartext# matches the sent cleartext based on the presumptions that only the sender and receiver can generate the ICV. Given A as the ICV algorithm, then logically both ICV = A (cleartext) = ICV* and ICV# = A (cleartext#) are true, and the following consequences are also true.

- If cleartext = cleartext# (the received and sent messages are the same) and ICV = ICV* (the received and sent ICV are the same), then ICV* = ICV# must also be true.
- If cleartext = cleartext# and ICV ≠ ICV*, then ICV* ≠ ICV# has a high probability of being true, but there is a small nonzero probability that ICV* = ICV#, although this is highly unlikely.
- If cleartext ≠ cleartext# and ICV = ICV*, then ICV* ≠ ICV# has a high probability of being true, but there is a small nonzero probability that ICV* = ICV#, although this is highly unlikely.
- If cleartext ≠ cleartext# and ICV ≠ ICV*, then ICV* ≠ ICV# has a high probability of being true, but there is a small non-zero probability that ICV* = ICV*, although this is highly unlikely.

However, if any other party can generate a legitimate ICV, then it is possible for the cleartext and ICV to be intercepted and for the cleartext to be altered or substituted unbeknownst and undetectable to the receiver. Further, an adversary can also generate and send cleartext with a legitimate ICV such that the receiver will presume that the cleartext originated from the genuine sender. Thus an authentication mechanism must be included in the transmission protocol or within the ICV algorithm itself.

4.2.2 Data in Process

For data in process, refer to Figure 4.8. The system startup sequence might read the cleartext and ICV from storage for use within memory, such as a routing table or customer records, update the cleartext as needed in memory, and occasionally write the cleartext to storage. During memory usage, if the integrity of the cleartext needs to be ensured, the system can validate the ICV periodically, such as before a transaction is routed or a customer record is processed. There is always the chance that data has become corrupted

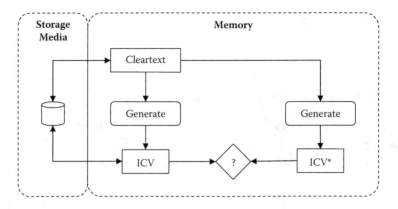

Figure 4.8 Data integrity in process.

within the system by a software bug, malware, another misbehaving application, or a logic error. For this discussion, the temporary objects are denoted with an asterisk (*) as ICV* and cleartext*, indicating a potential difference between the current and previous versions in memory.

The system generates an ICV* from the cleartext and compares the newly generated ICV* to the existing ICV retained in memory. If the generated ICV* matches the retained ICV, then the system knows there is a very high probability that the cleartext is whole and sound. Given A as the ICV algorithm, then logically ICV = A (cleartext) = ICV* is true.

- If ICV = ICV*, then the cleartext is unaltered.
- If ICV ≠ ICV*, then the cleartext is altered.

However, if any entity such as another application [192], malware, or other software process can generate a legitimate ICV, then it is possible for the cleartext and ICV to be altered unbeknownst and undetectable to the system. Nonetheless, implementing integrity schemes for data in process is rather unusual, as most applications rely on system controls to maintain data integrity within memory. Much more common are integrity controls for data in transit followed by data in storage.

4.2.3 Data in Storage

For data in storage, refer to Figure 4.9. The writer generates an ICV from the cleartext and then writes both the cleartext and the ICV to

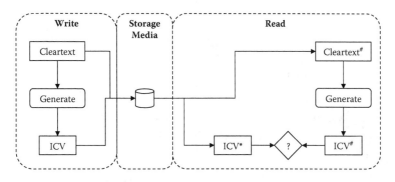

Figure 4.9 Data integrity in storage.

the storage media. Upon initial read of the ICV and cleartext from the storage media, the reader does not know if either object is unaltered. There is always the chance that data has become corrupted due to storage media errors, but read-and-write protocols typically have error-detection and -correction algorithms, so the integrity question is whether an adversary has modified or substituted either object in storage. Hence, the reader's objects are denoted with an asterisk (*) as ICV* and cleartext*, indicating a potential difference between the writer's ICV and cleartext objects.

The reader generates an $ICV^{\#}$ from the $cleartext^{\#}$ and compares the newly generated $ICV^{\#}$ to the ICV^{*} read from the storage media. If the generated $ICV^{\#}$ matches the read ICV^{*}, then the reader knows there is a very high probability that the read ICV^{*} matches the written ICV and the read $cleartext^{\#}$ matches the written cleartext, based on the presumptions that only the writer and reader can generate the ICV. The same rules and consequences apply equally as discussed for data in transit. Given A as the ICV algorithm, then logically both ICV = A (cleartext) = ICV^{*} and $ICV^{\#}$ = A ($cleartext^{\#}$) are true, and the following consequences are also true.

- If cleartext = $cleartext^{\#}$ (the read and written messages are the same) and ICV = ICV^{*} (the read and written ICV are the same), then ICV^{*} = $ICV^{\#}$ must be true.
- If cleartext ≠ $cleartext^{\#}$ and ICV ≠ ICV^{*}, then ICV^{*} ≠ $ICV^{\#}$ has a high probability of being true, but there is a small nonzero probability that ICV^{*} = $ICV^{\#}$ due to a collision, although it is highly unlikely.

- If cleartext ≠ cleartext# and ICV = ICV*, then ICV* ≠ ICV# has a high probability of being true, but there is a small nonzero probability that ICV* = ICV# due to a collision, although it is highly unlikely.

- If cleartext ≠ cleartext# and ICV ≠ ICV*, then ICV* ≠ ICV# has a high probability of being true, but there is a small non-zero probability that ICV* = ICV# due to a collision, although it is highly unlikely.

In general, if any other party can generate a legitimate ICV, then is it possible for an adversary to read the original cleartext and ICV written to the storage media, alter or substitute the original, and rewrite it to the storage media unbeknownst and undetectable to the reader. It is important to note that the reader might not be the writer, so consequently the reader is wholly dependent on the integrity controls. For example, many file systems track the modification date; however, this metadata about the file is based on the reliance of the system clock, which can be adjusted by an unscrupulous administrator.

Another technology often touted as an integrity control is the write-once-read-many (WORM) drive. The argument is that integrity is preserved, as information is only able to be written once to a hard drive, and thereafter is only accessible in read-only mode. However, there is a false assumption in this line of reasoning. Information read from the drive must be displayed to the user, and the software interfaces themselves are vulnerable to data alteration or substitution. For example, an inventory record of twenty units can be written to storage, but when the record is read, the intermediate software layer displays fifteen units, although the true record is still twenty units. Thus without some verifiable ICV mechanism, the WORM technology does not provide a reliable integrity-assurance level.

4.3 Integrity Check Methods

There are many integrity check methods in existence, each being applicable in their appropriate roles, but they are not necessarily interchangeable. Some are stronger than others. For the purposes of this book, the methods discussed here are characterized as being either strong or weak, defined as the following:

- *Weaker integrity methods* can detect inadvertent data corruption due to transmission errors or environmental factors, but these can be circumvented by an adversary.
- *Stronger integrity methods* can detect inadvertent data corruption and adversarial data modification or substitution with a high degree of probability.

This book cannot possibly address every integrity check method, as there are hundreds if not thousands in use in telecommunication systems, wireless transmissions, file-sharing protocols, security schemes, and application messaging. The following methods were chosen to represent the more common weaker ones versus the more frequently used stronger ones.

4.3.1 Longitudinal Redundancy Check (LRC)

An example of a message error-detection method is the longitudinal redundancy check (LRC), defined in ISO 1155 [95] and as shown in Figure 4.10. Each of the bytes of the cleartext are added to each other, and using the logical AND operator with hexadecimal FF, the intermediate sums are kept within a byte for the range of 0 to 255. The final summation is then adjusted using the logical XOR operator with hexadecimal FF, and a final 1 is added with one last AND to keep the LRC within a byte range.

Table 4.4 shows the bit-wise operations for logical AND (•) and exclusive OR (XOR, ⊕). The logical AND operator outputs a 1 only if both input bits are 1; otherwise, the output is a 0. The logical XOR

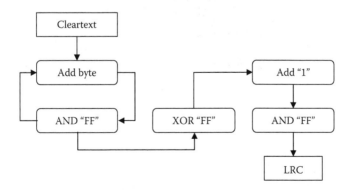

Figure 4.10   Longitudinal redundancy check (LRC).

Table 4.4 Logical Operators

BIT-WISE OPERATIONS	LOGICAL AND	LOGICAL XOR
	$0 \bullet 0 = 0$	$0 \oplus 0 = 1$
	$0 \bullet 1 = 0$	$0 \oplus 1 = 0$
	$1 \bullet 0 = 0$	$1 \oplus 0 = 0$
	$1 \bullet 1 = 1$	$1 \oplus 1 = 1$

operator outputs a 1 if both inputs are the same 0 or 1 values, and it outputs a 0 if the inputs differ.

The LRC is a weak integrity method, as it cannot detect an attack. Given access to the cleartext and knowledge of the algorithm, an adversary can modify or substitute the cleartext and generate a new LRC unbeknownst to any relying party such as a receiver, a reader, or application, as discussed previously.

4.3.2 Cyclic Redundancy Check (CRC)

Another example of an error-detection code is a cyclic redundancy check (CRC), attributed to William Wesley Peterson [14] and based on polynomial long division. The message is used as the dividend, and a generator polynomial is used as the divisor. The resulting quotient is discarded, and the remainder is used as the CRC. Polynomial long division is analogous to regular long division with numbers. As an example, let's divide $x^2 - 9x - 10$ by $x + 1$ as shown in Table 4.5.

- Multiplying x by the divisor $x + 1$ gives $x^2 + x$, which subtracted from $x^2 - 9x$ yields $-10x$.
- The leftover -10 is brought down to create $-10x - 10$.
- Multiplying -10 by the divisor $x + 1$ gives $-10x - 10$, which subtracted from $-10x - 10$ yields 0.

In this example, the quotient is $x - 10$ and the remainder is 0.

Table 4.5 Polynomial Long Division

Table 4.6 CRC Calculation

1.	Message with 3 bits padding	11010011101100 000
2.	Divisor left justified	1011
3.	XOR 4 bits	01100011101100 000
4.	Shift divisor to next 1 bit	1011
5.	XOR 4 bits	00111011101100 000
6.	Shift divisor to next 1 bit	1011
7.	XOR 4 bits	00010111101100 000
8.	Shift divisor to next 1 bit	1011
9.	XOR 4 bits	00000001101100 000
10.	Shift divisor to next 1 bit	1011
11.	XOR 4 bits	00000000110100 000
12.	Shift divisor to next 1 bit	1011
13.	XOR 4 bits	00000000011000 000
14.	Shift divisor to next 1 bit	1011
15.	XOR 4 bits	00000000001110 000
16.	Shift divisor to next 1 bit	1011
17.	XOR 4 bits	00000000000101 000
18.	Shift divisor to next 1 bit	101 1
19.	Remainder 3 bits is the CRC	00000000000000 100

CRC calculations are actually performed using the binary numbers 0 and 1 and the XOR operator, where polynomials are represented using coefficients of only 0 and 1. Thus the polynomial divisor $x^3 + x +1$ is represented by the binary string 1011, where $1x^3 + 0x^2 + 1x^1 + 1x^0 = x^3 + x +1$. Given the message 11010011101100 as the dividend and 1011 as the divisor, the division is shown in Table 4.6.

In this example for Table 4.6, the generator polynomial $x^3 + x +1$ encoded as the binary string 1011 is XOR multiple times with the message string. Refer to Table 4.4 for the XOR operator. To set up the table, both the message string (1) and the generator string (2) are left-justified, and note that the message string is also padded on the right with an initial CRC of three binary zeroes. The message fragment 1101 is XOR with the generator 1011, which yields 0110 (3). The generator string is then shifted right to the first remaining 1 bit in the message string (4). In this case, the leading zero of the message string marked in gray is skipped. The next message fragment 1100 is XOR with the generator 1011, which gives 0111 (5). Now the message string has two leading zeros marked in gray, and the generator is shifted to the next 1 bit in the message string (6). This process is repeated until the entire message string bits are changed to zero marked in gray (19), and the 3-bit CRC has a final value of 100.

In this simple example, our 4-bit generator string 1011 represents the polynomial $x^3 + x + 1$ of order 3, i.e., x raised to the third power, so our 3-bit CRC string 100 would be considered a CRC-3, but the more commonly used polynomial lengths are CRC-8, CRC-16, CRC-32, and CRC-64. It is worthwhile to note that the polynomial encoding can be accomplished using other schemes and that there are many implementations, although too many for discussion here. There are also numerous technical specifications and standards defining a wide variety of different CRC algorithms used for cabled devices, wireless, and broadband telecommunications, but again, there are far too many to list here.

Regardless, the CRC is a weak integrity method, as it cannot detect an attack. Given access to the cleartext and knowledge of the algorithm, an adversary can modify or substitute the cleartext and regenerate a new CRC unbeknownst to any relying party such as a receiver, a reader, or application, as discussed previously. There are much better integrity check value algorithms to detect adversarial attacks.

4.3.3 Hash and Message Digest

Cryptographic hashes, also called message digests, by themselves are a relatively weak integrity method in that they cannot detect an attack. Given access to the cleartext, an adversary can modify or substitute the cleartext undetectable to any relying party. However, hashes do not actually employ a cryptographic key, but we include them here because hashes are fundamental building blocks for other methods. At a minimum, a good hash function must demonstrate the properties of first pre-image resistance, second pre-image resistance, and collision resistance, which are summarized in Table 4.7.

Table 4.7 Summary of Hash Properties

HASH PROPERTIES	FUNCTION	INPUT	INPUT	OUTPUT
Pre-image resistance	H	Find c	—	h
Second pre-image resistance	H	c1	Find c2	h
Collision resistance	H	Find c1	Find c2	h

- *Pre-image resistance*: Given a hash function H and an output hash value h, it should be hard to find any cleartext c such that h = H(c). That is, there is sufficient information loss by the one-way function H such that, given h, it is infeasible to find a corresponding c. Since many different cleartext of varying length can generate the same hash value, it is important for the hash function to be pre-image resistant.
- *Second pre-image resistance*: Given a hash function H and an input cleartext c1, it should be hard to find another input c2 such that c1 ≠ c2 but H(c1) = h = H(c2).
- *Collision resistance*: Given a hash function H, it should be hard to find any two cleartext c1 and c2 such that H(c1) = h = H(c2). The pair (c1, c2) is called a hash collision. The length of the hash value, measured in binary bits, must be sufficiently long to avoid the phenomenon called the birthday paradox.

The birthday paradox can be explained as follows. Given a roomful of individuals, the question is how many must be present before two share the same birthday date. Since there are 365 days in a year (ignoring February 29 occurring every four years), clearly if there are 366 individuals present, then at least two must share the same birthday. However, only fifty-seven individuals need be present for a 99% probability that two share a birthday, and only twenty-three individuals are needed for a 50% chance.

Hash algorithms such as MD4 [85], MD5 [86], and the SHA family [168] operate differently. To avoid an endless dissertation on hash functions, we discuss them generically, as shown in Figure 4.11. For any hash algorithm, the input can be of any length, but the output is always of fixed length. For example, MD4 and MD5 provide 128-bit

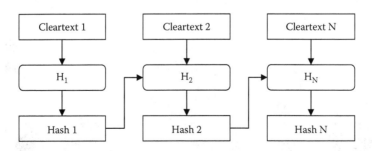

Figure 4.11 General hash algorithm.

values; the SHA-1 hash has a 160-bit output; and the SHA-2 suite of hash algorithms includes 224-bit, 256-bit, 384-bit, and 512-bit outputs. NIST announced the final winner of the five-year SHA-3 competition in October 2012 as Keccak (pronounced "catch-ack"), which provides 224-bit, 256-bit, 384-bit, and 512-bit outputs, which are the same size as SHA-2 but with an altogether different algorithm.

The cleartext must first be divided into the data block size required by the hash algorithm. For example, SHA-1 uses a 512-bit block size, so an input of 1025 bits would be divided into three blocks, where the third block is padded to the prerequisite 512 bits. So the actual input is 512 + 512 + 512 = 1536 bits in length. Each block is then processed according to the algorithm rules, where the intermediate prehash output of each block is also included in the input of the next block. So cleartext 1 is processed per the hash (H) rules of H_1, cleartext 2 and prehash 1 are processed per the hash rules of H_2, and so on. The final cleartext N and the final prehash N − 1 (in this case N − 1 = 2) are processed by the hash rules H_N to generate the final hash output hash N, whose length matches one of the outputs discussed here.

Hashes, also called *message digests* or sometimes *fingerprints* (not to be confused with biometrics), are a relatively weak integrity method in that they cannot detect an attack. Given access to the cleartext, an adversary can modify or substitute the cleartext and regenerate a new hash that is undetectable to any relying party. However, a cryptographic key can be used with a hash to make it strong, called a hashed message authentication code (HMAC), which should not be confused with a message authentication code MAC.

4.3.4 Message Authentication Code (MAC)

Message authentication codes (MAC) are strong integrity methods. MAC methods employ a symmetric key such that, when an adversary changes the cleartext, the corresponding MAC cannot be updated, thus allowing the relying party to detect the change. This is not a preventive method as such, in that the MAC cannot stop an adversary from changing the cleartext, but it is a deterrent to the extent that such attacks are less likely because of the attack being discovered.

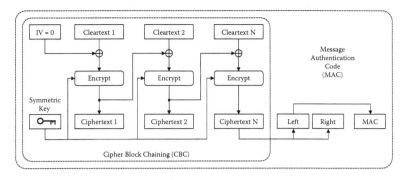

Figure 4.12   Message authentication code (MAC).

The MAC algorithm [108] and [115] shown in Figure 4.12 is based on the Cipher Block Chaining (CBC) mode for symmetric encryption algorithms discussed in Chapter 2 (Confidentiality). Irrespective of the underlying symmetric encryption algorithm, CBC encryption has three inputs: the cleartext, an initialization vector (IV), and a symmetric encryption key. For the MAC algorithm, the IV is always set to zero and the CBC encryption proceeds as normal. The ciphertext output is used to generate the MAC.

The cleartext must first be divided into the data block size required by the encryption algorithm. For example, data encryption standard (DES) and triple DES (3DES) algorithms have a 64-bit block size, and AES has a 128-bit block size. Each block is then encrypted using the symmetric key, where the ciphertext output from one block is XOR with the input of the next block. Normally, for CBC encryption, the final ciphertext is the concatenation of all the outputs (ciphertext 1, ciphertext 2, ..., ciphertext N), but for the MAC algorithm, only the final ciphertext output is used. The final ciphertext N is divided into left and right parts, where the left part is used as the MAC. The length of the MAC depends on the specific algorithm chosen.

Because the MAC employs a symmetric key with the CBC encryption algorithm, both parties must share the same cryptographic key to generate and verify the MAC. Therefore, if the sender generates the MAC and the receiver verifies the MAC, the receiver is ensured both data integrity and authentication of the message (the cleartext). The authentication is achievable because the receiver presumably knows that he did not send the message to himself. However, the authentication is not provable to a third party; either the sender or receiver can generate the MAC, and therefore the MAC cannot provide nonrepudiation.

4.3.5 Hashed Message Authentication Code (HMAC)

Hashed message authentication codes (HMAC) are strong integrity methods. HMAC methods employ a symmetric key with a hash algorithm such that when an adversary changes the cleartext, the HMAC cannot be updated, thus allowing the relying party to detect the change. The HMAC is not a preventive method in that it cannot stop an adversary from changing the cleartext, but nonetheless it is a deterrent to the extent that such attacks are less likely because of the attack being discovered.

The HMAC algorithm [174] shown in Figure 4.13 is based on any hash algorithm. First, the key is XOR with two fixed data patterns used for padding the input (iPAD) and the output (oPAD), which creates two internal keys (K1 and K2). Next, the cleartext and K1 are hashed to create a message extract (MX), and then MX and K2 are hashed to create the HMAC. The hash operates the same as described in §4.3.3 (Hash and Message Digest).

Because HMAC uses a symmetric key with a hash algorithm, both parties must share the same cryptographic key to generate and verify the HMAC. Therefore, if the sender generates the HMAC and the receiver verifies the HMAC, the receiver is ensured of both data integrity and authentication of the message (the cleartext). The

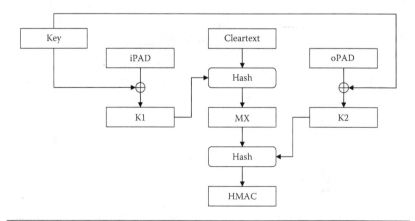

Figure 4.13   Hashed message authentication code (HMAC).

authentication is achievable because the receiver presumably knows that he did not send the message to himself. However, the authentication is not provable to a third party; either the sender or receiver can generate the HMAC, and therefore the HMAC cannot provide nonrepudiation.

It is interesting to note that the SSL [81] protocol refers to MAC, but it actually employs an HMAC for data integrity along with data encryption. When the client places a Hypertext Transfer Protocol [88] Secure (HTTPS) request, the server sends its digital certificate for the client to encrypt a random master secret using the server public key, which the server can decrypt using its private key. Both sides then derive a common encryption key and HMAC key. SSL does not actually use a digital signature for data integrity; rather, the digital signature is used for authentication when the client has its own certificate. As part of the SSL handshake, the client digitally signs a challenge using its private key that the server can verify using the client public key contained in its digital certificate.

4.3.6 Digital Signature

Digital signatures are strong integrity methods that employ an asymmetric key pair with a hash algorithm such that when the adversary changes the cleartext, the digital signature cannot be updated, thus allowing the relying party to detect the change. The asymmetric key pair components, consisting of a public key and a private, are used in a very exact way, as discussed in §3.5.2 (Asymmetric Cryptography) in Chapter 3 (Authentication) and shown again in Figure 4.14. In general, the owner of the key pair uses the private key to generate the digital

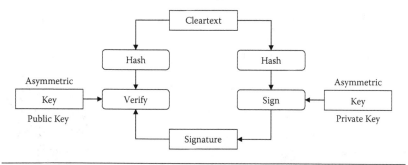

Figure 4.14   Digital signature.

signature, and the relying party uses the owner's public key to verify the digital signature. The details vary, based on the digital signature algorithm, but first we generically describe the sign and verify processes.

To generate the digital signature, the cleartext is first hashed to create a relatively unique digital object that mathematically corresponds to the cleartext. The asymmetric private key is then applied to the hash value to create the digital signature. It is important to recognize that although the hash is an intermediate step, it is the cleartext being digitally signed, not the hash. Therefore, using the phrase "signs the hash" is erroneous; rather, phrases like "signs the data" or "signs the message" are more appropriate and accurate. Further, the importance of the hash properties discussed in §4.3.3 are reemphasized for digital signatures; the first pre-image, the second pre-image, and collision resistance are the security cornerstones of digital signatures.

To verify the digital signature, three elements are necessary: the original cleartext, the digital signature, and the corresponding public key. First, the cleartext is rehashed to re-create the hash value. Note that the original hash is not available to the verifier, so the newly recreated hash may not match the original hash, which is not known until the signature is verified. The rehash, the public key, and the signature are used in different manners for verification, depending on the specific digital signature algorithm

- *RSA*: The Rivest-Shamir-Adleman (RSA) signature algorithm [43] is probably the most well known, and its signature operation is actually the inverse of its data encryption. Because RSA is reversible, data encrypted with the public key can only be decrypted with the associated private key. For digital signatures, the hash is encrypted using the private key to generate the signature such that the corresponding public key is used to decrypt the signature and recover the hash. Thus, the verification is a simple comparison of the recovered hash to the re-created hash.

- *DSA*: The digital signature algorithm (DSA) developed by NIST [170] is an irreversible algorithm in that it cannot be used for encryption. This is by design, as it can be used for data integrity and authentication, without the ability to misuse it for data confidentiality. For the DSA, the signature itself is actually a pair of numbers designated (r, s), where both components r and s are used to compute a verification value v such that if v = r, then the signature verifies.

- *ECDSA*: The elliptic curve digital signature algorithm (ECDSA) [47] is an elliptic curve analog of the digital signature algorithm (DSA). For the ECDSA, the signature is likewise composed of a pair of numbers (r, s) that are used to compute and confirm that v = r for signature verification.

Regardless of the algorithm, it is always a good idea for the signer to validate the digital signature prior to its usage. If an invalid signature is inadvertently generated by the signer due to a system glitch, programming bug, or other acts of god, in some cases it can be used by an adversary to determine information about the private key, possibly even deriving the private key itself. In addition to the various standards that define the hash and digital signature algorithms, further reading on general cryptography and background mathematics may be of interest, such as the *Handbook of Applied Cryptography* [15], also known as the HAC or *Applied Cryptography* [16].

Unlike MAC and HMAC, digital signatures use an asymmetric key pair, where the verifier only needs the signer's public key and the signer maintains explicit control over the associated private key. Verification of the signature provides data integrity and authentication, and since only the signer can generate the signature, the integrity and authentication controls are provable to a third party; hence the signature also supports nonrepudiation. However, this claim is stated with several caveats.

The nonrepudiation is dependent on many cryptographic, operational, and legal issues, including the uniqueness of the asymmetric key pair, key management controls over the private key, access controls over usage of the private key, the contractual relationship between the signer and the verifier, and the signer's intent of generating the digital signature. Controls for managing asymmetric private keys and managing digital certificates are discussed in Chapter 7 (Key Management), and issues surrounding nonrepudiation are discussed in Chapter 5 (Nonrepudiation).

The integrity is also dependent on the trustworthiness of the signer. When exchanging messages, the verifier has the reasonable expectation that the signer will not modify any of the cleartext at a later date, honoring an implicit or explicit agreement. However, if the data originator changes the cleartext and adjusts any relevant time stamps, the integrity is forfeited. For this reason, time-stamp authorities (TSA) can issue time-stamp tokens (TST), as described in Section 4.3.7.

4.3.7 Time-Stamp Token (TST)

Trusted time stamps are strong integrity methods that employ cryptographic functions that bind an integrity check value (ICV) to a verifiable time stamp. Historically, paper and ink was the primary and authoritative method with fundamental physical and chemical characteristics that provided an acceptable degree of integrity and authenticity. Beginning in the 1950s with the introduction of business computers, paper documentation was converted to electronic formats by armies of data-entry operators. Slowly, paper has devolved as the secondary means for documentation, although it has taken over half a century with multiple generations of users and technology. Data now originates in electronic format where paper copies can be printed, scanned, processed, edited, and reprinted into anything needed. Electronic data can be stored almost indefinitely, duplicated infinitely, distributed to anyone, and posted in the cloud such that they survive in perpetuity [17].

To better understand the untrustworthiness of time, consider the two scenarios—date alternation and data alternation—shown in Figure 4.15. The time line shows seven different increasing times (T) marked t–5, t–3, t–1, t, t+1, t+3, and t+5. The cleartext boxes are positioned to the time line per their creation time but linked to their associated published time.

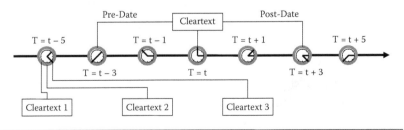

Figure 4.15   Untrustwothy time line.

1. *Date alternation*: These scenarios are shown in the top line. At time (t), the cleartext is published with a digital signature and time stamp (t). Any relying party can verify the legitimate signature and thereby interpret the time stamp as the publication date.

   a. *Pre-date scenario*: For this scenario, the signer discovers a situation where an earlier publication date is financially advantageous. At time (t), the cleartext is republished with a digital signature and time stamp (t–3). Any relying party can verify the signature, as a new signature remains legitimate; however, the falsified time stamp is interpreted as the valid publication date, enabling the fraud.

   b. *Post-date scenario*: For this scenario, the signer discovers a situation where a later publication date is financially advantageous. At time (t), the cleartext is republished with a digital signature and time stamp (t+3). Any relying party can verify the signature, as a new signature remains legitimate; however, the altered time stamp is interpreted as the valid publication date, enabling the fraud.

2. *Data alternation*: This scenario is shown in the bottom line. At time (t–5), the original cleartext (1) is signed and published with time stamp (t–5). For this scenario, the signer discovers a situation where modification of the cleartext is financially advantageous. At time (t–1), the altered cleartext (2) is re-signed and published with time stamp (t–5). At another later time (t+1), the cleartext (3) is altered again, re-signed, and published with time stamp (t–5).

The keystone of trusted time stamps are aligned clocks beginning with the International Timing Authority (ITA) Bureau International des Poids et Mesures (BIPM) located in France. Aligned clocks are not the same as synchronized clocks. Synchronizing clocks means adjusting their settings so two or more clocks measure the same time, whereas aligning clocks means evaluating and documenting the differences. National Measurement Institutes (NMI) align their clocks to the ITA. For the United States, the two NMI are the National Institute of Standards and Technology (NIST) and the U.S. Naval Observatory (USNO). NIST operates the atomic clock in Boulder,

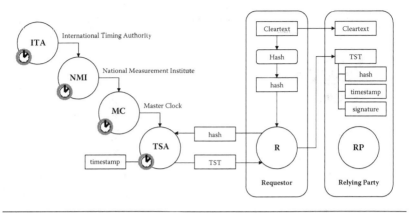

Figure 4.16 Time-stamp authority.

Colorado, and the USNO operates the Global Positioning Satellites (GPS) system. Many organizations operate Master Clocks (MC) that align to various NMI and operate independent Time Stamp Authorities (TSA) (Figure 4.16) [55].

Requesters generate a regular hash, as discussed in §4.3.3, from the cleartext and submit a request to a TSA. The TSA generates a time-stamp token (TST) by cryptographically binding the hash with a time stamp from a clock aligned to a master clock (MC). There are several cryptographic bindings defined in X9.95 [55], and for this discussion, the digital signature method [90] is referenced. The TSA returns the signed TST to the requester. Note that the TSA never has access to the original cleartext; it only has access to the hash, such that it remains independent of the requester.

Requesters can then provide the original cleartext and the TST to any relying party. The relying party first regenerates the hash from the cleartext and compares it with the hash in the TST to confirm that the cleartext and TST correspond to each other. The relying party then verifies the TSA signature, as discussed in §4.3.6. Once the signature is verified, the relying party then knows that the time stamp is valid. Thus, the TST validates the data integrity of the cleartext to a reliable point in time. This information security control is sometimes call *data integrity plus* (integrity+) or *data reliability*.

Requesters can also use trusted time stamps to enhance digital signatures for nonrepudiation. For this process, the requester first signs the cleartext with its asymmetric private key and then hashes the signed cleartext, that is the cleartext and the digital signature, which is submitted to the TSA. Thus, the TST not only validates the data integrity of the signed document, but it also links the requester's digital signature to the TSA time stamp. Therefore, trusted time stamps can prove when a document was signed, which significantly enhances digital signatures for nonrepudiation. Controls for managing asymmetric private keys and managing digital certificates are discussed in Chapter 7 (Key Management), and issues surrounding nonrepudiation are discussed in Chapter 5 (Nonrepudiation).

5
Nonrepudiation

Nonrepudiation is the set of controls necessary to prevent repudiation, which is the refusal by one party to acknowledge an agreement claimed by another party. For example, *anticipatory repudiation*, also called an *anticipatory breach*, is a term in the law of contracts that describes a declaration by the promising party to a contract that he or she does not intend to live up to his or her obligations under the contract. Thus, the set of controls to prevent repudiation includes both data integrity and entity authentication. However, dispute resolution between two parties invariably involves a third party such as an arbitrator or judge. Therefore, nonrepudiation requires that both data integrity and authenticity be equally provable to a third party. In Chapter 4 (Integrity), we looked at several methods.

- *Message authentication codes* (MAC): This integrity method uses a symmetric key. Both parties must share the same cryptographic key to generate and verify the MAC; therefore, authentication and integrity are not provable to a third party.
- *Hashed message authentication codes* (HMAC): This integrity method also uses a symmetric key. Both parties must share the same cryptographic key to generate and verify the HMAC; therefore, authentication and integrity are not provable to a third party.
- *Digital signatures*: This integrity method employs an asymmetric key pair, where the signature is generated using the public key and the signature is verified using the private key; therefore, authentication and integrity are provable to a third party.
- *Time-stamp tokens* (TST): This integrity method employs cryptographic techniques managed by an independent third party, including digital signatures or hash chains; therefore, authentication and integrity are provable to a third party.

In Chapter 7 (Key Management), we note that neither MAC nor HMAC can achieve nonrepudiation, as the control over the symmetric key cannot readily be distinguished between the generators versus the verifiers of the ICV. Only digital signatures or time-stamp tokens (TST) can provide nonrepudiation services.

In Chapter 3 (Authentication), we noted that, for symmetric methods, the integrity and authentication are not provable to a third party, so the message cannot have nonrepudiation. For asymmetric methods, the integrity and authenticity is provable to third parties; however, there are many other cryptography, operational, and legal controls necessary, which are discussed in this chapter.

We now look at the cryptographic, operational, and legal considerations for nonrepudiation services from the viewpoint of the registration authority (RA), certification authority (CA), subject, and relying party. Cryptographic considerations, as discussed in Chapter 7 (Key Management), include controls of the asymmetric keys over the management life cycle. Operational considerations, as discussed in Chapter 3 (Authentication), include information security controls over personnel and system resources. Legal considerations include dispute resolution and evidentiary rules for testimony and expert witnesses.

5.1 Technical Considerations

From the viewpoint of the relying party, as discussed in Chapter 7 (Key Management) on public key infrastructure (PKI), consider the logical connections between the subject digital signature, the subject certificate, the certificate chain, and the various certificate authorities (CA). If the relying party is to recognize the subject's claim toward nonrepudiation, there needs to be some indicator signifying that the subject digital signature warrants it. We will look at each aspect of the nonrepudiation components.

First, consider the digital signature itself. The signature is the result of the subject applying its asymmetric private key to the hash generated from the message. The structure and format of the signature is a string of binary bits (0 and 1) with no inherent information signifying any intent by the signer as to its purpose or assurances. The signed message might contain some overt indication of nonrepudiation, or the application environment might include some covert representation of nonrepudiation. However, there are no common message formats or standards for nonrepudiation.

Second, consider the subject certificate. As mentioned in Chapter 7 (Key Management), the X.509 [80] key usage extension defines its nonrepudiation (nonRepudiation) bit as follows:

> The nonRepudiation bit is asserted when the subject public key is used to verify digital signatures, other than signatures on certificates (bit 5) and CRLs (bit 6), used to provide a non-repudiation service that protects against the signing entity falsely denying some action. In the case of later conflict, a reliable third party may determine the authenticity of the signed data. (Note that recent editions of X.509 have renamed the nonRepudiation bit to contentCommitment.)

Setting the nonRepudiation flag in the certificate does not automatically achieve nonrepudiation for the asymmetric key pair or subsequent digital signatures. Rather, the subject needs to implement the appropriate cryptographic, operational, and legal controls to achieve nonrepudiation. Further, there are no cryptographic, operational, and legal requirements mandating the setting of the X.509 nonRepudiation bit. The PKI Assessment Guideline (PAG) [33], published by the American Bar Association (ABA) Information Security Committee (ISC), discussed in Chapter 7 (Key Management), offers its own opinion of the nonRepudiation bit.

> A considerable debate exists as to the effectiveness of the nonrepudiation bit in accomplishing the goal of indicating that a subscriber cannot falsely deny some action, such as digitally signing a message. Although an accurate summary of the debate is beyond the scope of the PAG, the debate is based on several factors. First, there is no general agreement as to what can be communicated by setting or clearing a single bit. A bit can only be set to TRUE or FALSE, and therefore cannot capture the nuances common in policies and contractual responsibilities. Second, preventing a person from false denial of an action in theory can occur only after the party seeking to bind the subscriber to an action has initiated and prevailed in a litigation or other dispute resolution proceeding, all appeals are exhausted, and the judgment has been executed upon. Preventing repudiation depends on the effectiveness of the dispute resolution process that can back up the use of certificates. Third, people

differ as to what was intended by the adoption of the bit by the drafters of X.509. Under one view, for instance, the non-repudiation bit may mean no more than the fact that the CA offers a non-repudiation service to assist in preventing repudiation. Under another view, setting the non-repudiation bit means no more than the fact that the private key corresponding to the public key in the certificate is not the subject of key escrow.

Further, the key usage bits in the certificate are typically set by the CA based on the type of certificate requested by the subject. The certificate signing request (CSR) [202] contains the subject distinguished name and the subject public key, including its related information. Additional attributes can be requested by the subject; however, none of the public key cryptography standards (PKCS) specify the key usage attribute. Moreover, most CA systems employ certificate profiles that predefine the static certificate fields, including the key usage bits and extended key usage object identifiers (OID).

Third, consider the certificate chain and the associated CA. The absence or presence of the nonRepudiation bit, or for that matter any key usage bit or extended key usage OID in the subject certificate, has no correlation to the CA certificates. Per the X.509 [80] standard, the CA certificate has its own key usage bits for signing certificates (keyCertSign) and CLR (cRLSign), and typically does not use the digital signature (digitalSignature) or nonrepudiation (nonRepudiation) bits.

Fourth, there is no industry "nonrepudiation" program. For example, the CA/Browser Forum (CABF), which promotes the Webtrust for CA auditing standard, also developed the complementary Extended Validation (EV) SSL certificate standard [35]. The CA/Browser Forum membership consists of either an issuing CA, a root CA, or a browser software vendor. The primary purposes of an EV certificate are to:

- *Identify the legal entity that controls a Web site*: Provide a reasonable assurance to the user of an Internet browser that the Web site the user is accessing is controlled by a specific legal entity identified in the EV Certificate by name, address of Place of Business, Jurisdiction of Incorporation or Registration, and Registration Number or other disambiguating information.

- *Enable encrypted communications with a Web site*: Facilitate the exchange of encryption keys in order to enable the encrypted communication of information over the Internet between the user of an Internet browser and a Web site.

The EV certificate is validated by the relying party like any regular certificate, as discussed in Chapter 7 (Key Management). The certificate chain from the SSL certificate to the root CA is validated such that the root CA public key is stored in the browser as a trust anchor. In addition, the root CA is stored in the browser as an EV root CA. Therefore, when the certificate chain is validated to an EV root CA, the browser recognizes the SSL certificate as an EV certificate, and subsequently actives the "green" bar as an indicator to the end user. Further, the certificate policy (CP) or certificate practice statement (CPS) for each CA within the EV certificate chain must include EV declarations. However, no such equivalent process or program exists for digital signatures claiming nonrepudiation.

Finally, there are no industry restrictions or recommendations stating that when the nonRepudiation bit is used, no other bits should be set. For example, the digitalSignature bit is redundant, since the digital signature is a prerequisite for nonRepudiation. However, certificates used for data encryption, key management, or certificate signing should not be used for nonrepudiation, as that weakens key-separation controls.

5.2 Cryptographic Considerations

Any independent third party has expectations of several prerequisites regarding cryptographic processes and controls conducted by the subject, the RA, the CA, and the relying party. These include solo actions by each party and dual actions between the subject and RA, the RA and the CA, and the subject and relying party.

Presumption of cryptographic solo processes and controls includes the following:

- The CA maintains confidentiality, integrity, and authenticity of its private keys, including its certificate, CRL, and OCSP (Online Certificate Status Protocol) signature keys.

- The RA maintains confidentiality, integrity, and authenticity of its private key for submitting certificate requests to the CA on behalf of the subject.
- The subject maintains confidentiality, integrity, authenticity, and access control of its private key. The private key is secured such that it has never been exposed outside of a cryptographic module. The key is only usable by the authorized individual to generate a digital signature, with appropriate access controls to prevent misuse, such that it has never been subject to unauthorized access.
- The relying party has verified the subject digital signature, including validation of the certificate chain, as discussed in Chapter 7 (Key Management), beginning with the subject certificate to the root CA trust anchor. Validation includes checking the status of the subject certificate per the CRL or OCSP service provided and signed by the CA.

Assumption of cryptographic dual processes and controls includes the following:

- During the certificate registration process, the RA verifies that the subject is the holder of the corresponding private key.
- During the certificate registration process, the RA has securely interacted with the CA such that the subject certificate signing request (CSR) forwarded by the RA is validated by the CA.

Otherwise, if any of these cryptographic controls have failed, then any nonrepudiation claims are substantially weakened. In the event of a dispute, these cryptographic controls should be investigated [183].

5.3 Operational Considerations

Presumption of operational solo processes and controls includes the following:

- The RA maintains information security controls over its systems and personnel such that only authorized processes or individuals have access to data and organizational resources.

- The CA maintains information security controls over its systems and personnel such that only authorized processes or individuals have access to data and organizational resources.
- The subject maintains information security controls over its system components such that access controls are in place and system patches are current to avoid risks of known vulnerabilities. Access controls include keeping passwords confidential by not writing them down or sharing them with others, and keeping systems "locked" when not in use.
- The subject generates, captures, and retains evidentiary information, including network, system, and application logs.
- The subject has duly requested its certificate be revoked in the event of a known or suspected compromise of its private signature key.
- The CA has duly updated the revocation status of the subject certificate for consumption by relying parties.
- The relying party has duly checked the status of the subject certificate as part of the certificate validation process.
- The relying party has duly requested its certificate be revoked in the event of a known or suspected compromise of its private signature key.

Assumption of operational dual processes and controls include the following:

- During the certificate registration process, the subject provided accurate information to the RA, and conversely the RA authenticated the subject using public or personal information and further validated the information provided by the subject.
- During the digital signature verification process, the relying party has received the signed message from the subject over a trustworthy communications channel to the extent that there is a reasonable expectation that the message was delivered to the intended party.
- During the digital signature verification process, the relying party recognizes the CA to the extent that it has been reviewed and approved for accepting a digital signature from a subject.

Otherwise, if any of these operational controls have failed, then any nonrepudiation claims are substantially weakened. In the event of a dispute, these operational controls should be investigated.

5.4 Legal Considerations

As mentioned in Chapter 7 (Key Management), the Digital Signature Guideline (DSG) [31], published by the American Bar Association (ABA) Information Security Committee (ISC), provides its own definition of nonrepudiation.

> *Nonrepudiation*: Strong and substantial evidence of the identity of the signer of a message and of message integrity, sufficient to prevent a party from successfully denying the origin, submission or delivery of the message and the integrity of its contents.

The DSG essentially describes the requirements for a nonrepudiation service in terms of the sender and the receiver to protect each other from false claims.

> Signer authentication and document authentication are tools used to exclude impersonators and forgers and are essential ingredients of what is often called a non-repudiation service in the terminology of the information security profession. A non-repudiation service provides assurance of the origin or delivery of data in order to protect the sender against false denial by the recipient that the data has been received, or to protect the recipient against false denial by the sender that the data has been sent. Thus, a non-repudiation service provides evidence to prevent a person from unilaterally modifying or terminating legal obligations arising out of a transaction effected by computer-based means.

Consequently, the DSG discusses how certification authorities (CA), subscriber (subject) certificates, relying parties, and digital signatures can achieve nonrepudiation services. The subject certificate represents a binding between the signer and the signer public key provided by the CA to the subject. The signer public key provides the means for verifying the digital signature provided by the signer to the relying party. For the digital signature to be considered a non-repudiation service, there are additional functional components and considerations as follows:

- *Certificate authority*: Operationally, the CA must use trustworthy systems, have personnel practices to manage trustworthy systems, make available its CA certificate (trust anchor), ensure that the content of all certificates is accurate, document its actions, retain documentation, and only release a certificate when the subscriber has accepted it. Financially, the CA must have sufficient financial resources to maintain operations and bear its risk of liability and, when necessary, terminate operations with minimal disruption. The CA also discloses its certificate practices, manages liability, revokes (or suspends) certificates at the request of the subscriber or in the event of a CA compromise, and uses reasonable efforts to notify anyone affected by certificate revocation (or suspension).
- *Subscriber*: The subscriber uses a trustworthy system to generate the asymmetric key pair, ensures that all material representations made to the CA are accurate, safeguards the private key, and requests that the certificate be revoked in the event of a key compromise.
- *Relying party*: The relying party accepting digital signatures depends on valid certificates containing the corresponding public key, validates the certificate, verifies the digital signature using the reference public key, accepts digital signatures as equivalent to written signatures, evaluates the relative importance of the digital signature with respect to the significance of the signed message, retains a copy of the signed message, and accepts the inherent cryptographic nature of the digital signature.

Also mentioned in Chapter 7 (Key Management), the PKI Assessment Guideline (PAG) [33], published by the American Bar Association (ABA) Information Security Committee (ISC), uses the same definition of nonrepudiation as the DSG. The PAG further clarifies the limitations of PKI technology.

> When a PKI is intended to support digital signatures for the purpose of authenticating a transaction or a communication that needs to be attributed to a particular subscriber, the digital signature does not by itself result in legal "non-repudiation."

The unique value of PKI is its technological ability to provide robust factual inferences of non-repudiation, through cryptography, that will serve to provide credible evidence sufficiently strong to persuade a disinterested third party (the ultimate dispute resolution authority), that a subscriber originated a particular transaction or communication.

Per the PAG, legal nonrepudiation takes cryptographic and operational facts into consideration of the dispute resolution process.

> The Guidelines [DSG and PAG] define non-repudiation not as an automatic result of technical mechanisms, but as a property that can only be determined after recourse to available dispute mechanisms such as a court or arbitrator.
>
> When a subscriber attempts to repudiate a transaction or communication, there may be factual and legal questions and disputes that, if not settled, will need to be resolved in litigation, arbitration, or other alternative dispute resolution mechanism, in order to determine whether the attempted repudiation is ultimately successful. Once the legal proceedings produced a final judgment to that effect, then legal non-repudiation has occurred.

The PAG also discusses how the proponent of evidence produced by a digitally signed transaction or communication might seek its admission at trial or another proceeding under established rules of evidence. More specifically, the PAG discusses additional threshold evidentiary questions: when expert testimony is necessary; how a witness might be qualified as an expert witness; and the types of testimony such an expert might present in the proceeding if admission of a PKI-related document is contested on authenticity or integrity grounds. The PAG mentions the U.S. federal law—the Electronic Signatures in Global and National Commerce Act (ESIGN), enacted in June 2000—which defines the following terms:

- *Electronic*: The term *electronic* means relating to technology having electrical, digital, magnetic, wireless, optical, electromagnetic, or similar capabilities.
- *Electronic signature*: The term *electronic signature* means an electronic sound, symbol, or process attached to or logically associated with a contract or other record and executed or adopted by a person with the intent to sign the record.

One acceptable form of an electronic signature is a digital signature. Other electronic signatures include *click-wrap agreements*, where the user explicitly accepts a software license agreement, a term borrowed from shrink-wrap software packages. Another similar type of electronic signature is a *browse-wrap*, where the user accepts the product agreement by simply clicking on the downloadable link. However, ESIGN does not address nonrepudiation of electronic signatures.

6
PRIVACY

In general, privacy differs from confidentiality, in that privacy has a broader scope of additional controls, including not just confidentiality, but also authentication, authorization, and accountability.

1. Proactive controls for authentication of authorized entities
2. Preventive measures against data disclosure to an unauthorized entity
3. Detective measures to monitor for data loss
4. Notification of a data breach to authorized entities

In Chapter 3 (Authentication), we discussed proactive controls, including methods for single, mutual, and multifactor authentication such as knowledge, possession, biometric, and cryptographic factors. We also considered authorization for credit card and debit card payments. With regard to privacy, authorization is associated with permissions to transmit, process, or store personal information.

In Chapter 2 (Confidentiality), we discussed preventive controls, including data classification and data encryption, such as data in transit, process, and storage. Regarding privacy, confidentiality is applicable to the protection methods during transmission, processing, or storage of personal information.

In Chapter 4 (Integrity), we discussed detective controls for managing data and system reliability, including message authentication codes (MAC and HMAC), digital signatures, and trusted time stamps. With respect to privacy, integrity is associated with protection methods during transmission, processing, or storage of personal information.

We now look at the technical, cryptographic, operational, and legal considerations for privacy controls.

6.1 Technical Considerations

6.1.1 Privacy Data Elements

In Chapter 2 (Confidentiality), we looked at data classification and various data groups, including cryptography, authentication, identification, and confidential, proprietary, and public data. We purposely did not include privacy as a group, but we did discuss the concept of data tags. One technical issue is what data elements constitute "privacy" versus others. Figure 6.1 shows a 2008 survey of U.S. state laws for common data elements. The eleven most common are Social Security numbers (70%), bank account numbers (53%), driver's license numbers (50%), name (27%), password or PIN (20%), address (17%), telephone records (13%), warranty records (10%), automobile records (7%), magazine subscriptions (7%), and uniform record locators (URL) for browser Web sites (7%). All other data elements had 3% or fewer occurrences. The U.S. data elements do not align with other international privacy laws.

Figure 6.2 shows a similar review of the European Union (EU), United Kingdom (UK), and Canadian privacy laws. While this represents a relatively small sample of national privacy laws, the commonality is sufficient for comparison to the United States. Only three data groups are specifically included by all three laws: race or ethnic origin, religion or philosophical beliefs, and medical records. The EU and UK include political opinions, sexual orientation, and union

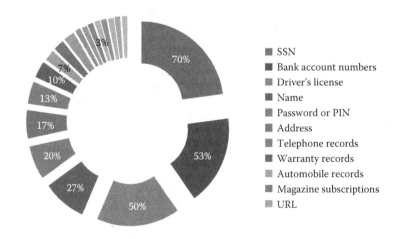

Figure 6.1   U.S. state laws.

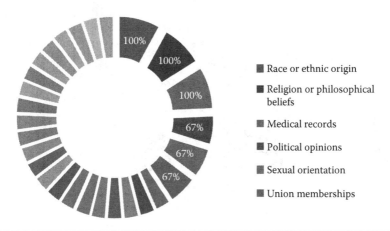

100%
100%
100%
67%
67%
67%

- ■ Race or ethnic origin
- ■ Religion or philosophical beliefs
- ■ Medical records
- ■ Political opinions
- ■ Sexual orientation
- ■ Union memberships

Figure 6.2 International privacy laws.

memberships. The remainder of the data elements such as name, marital status, education, biometric information, financial transactions, and criminal information are explicitly mentioned in the Canadian laws, but not in the EU or UK laws.

Thus, we can conclude that, while security controls can be designed and deployed to protect privacy data, it is important to understand which data elements actually are privacy data. Clearly, the legal jurisdiction provides some guidance according to the relevant laws; however, it is also evident that many of the laws do not provide specifics as to which data elements require protection. Thus, an organization needs to have privacy policies and practices that address not only the appropriate controls, but also identify the corresponding data elements. While some data elements in some countries are within the privacy scope, the same data elements might not be considered as privacy data in other countries. Therefore, moving data across country borders can affect the overall data attribute.

6.1.2 Cross-Border Jurisdictions

Figure 6.3 shows several cross-border scenarios between four abstract jurisdictions (A, B, C, and D) where privacy laws and privacy data elements differ. The arrows indicate data movement of a privacy element (*p*) between jurisdictions (A to B), (A to C), and (A to D). For the purposes of this discussion, we presume the privacy element (*p*) belongs in jurisdiction A, and the privacy element (*p*) is sent to entity

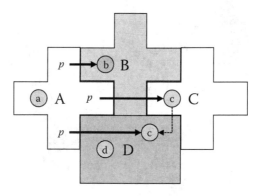

Figure 6.3 Cross-border considerations.

(b) in jurisdiction (B) and to entity (c) in multiple jurisdictions (C and D). Entities (a) in jurisdiction (A) and (d) in jurisdiction (D) are shown for consistency, but are not included in this privacy review.

The following scenarios address various movements of (p), the privacy data element:

- The simplest cross-border scenario is when a privacy element (p) moves from jurisdiction A to jurisdiction B. The controls over the privacy element in jurisdictions A and B need to be equivalent; otherwise (p) would have less protection in jurisdiction B than A. For example, a data breach by entity (b) in jurisdiction B affects the overall security status of both jurisdictions A and B. Thus, entity (b) residing in jurisdiction B needs to implement adequate controls despite any data classification differences.

- Another scenario is when the same privacy element (p) moves from jurisdiction A to C, but to get there it also passes through jurisdiction B. For example, entity (c) residing in jurisdiction C uses a network resource physically located in jurisdiction B to receive privacy element (p) from jurisdiction A. In this scenario, (p) needs equivalent protection in each jurisdiction A, B, and C. Entity (c) needs to provide controls over (p) in jurisdiction C, and likewise the network resource in jurisdiction B needs to protect the privacy data element. Note that entity (c) might need to negotiate security controls with the network resource provider located in jurisdiction B in order to satisfy the privacy requirements of jurisdiction A.

- A more complex scenario is when an individual (c) travels from jurisdiction C to D and receives the same privacy element (*p*) from jurisdiction A to D. A fundamental issue is determining which jurisdiction takes precedence: the geopolitical source, the geopolitical destination, or the traveling recipient. Regardless, in this scenario (*p*) needs equivalent protection in each jurisdiction A and D, and by the entity (c).

Differences between the jurisdictions as to which data elements require privacy and which do not is another issue that needs understanding. Further, some privacy laws cover all citizens regardless of in which jurisdiction the individual happens to reside, whereas others focus on all individuals within the jurisdiction regardless of whether they are citizens. Thus, legal and privacy aspects affect the overall security policy and practices of any multinational organization.

The OECD Guidelines on the Protection of Privacy and Transborder Flows of Personal Data [235] address the movement of personal data across national borders. In addition to general requirements, basic principles of national and international application, national implementation, and international cooperation, the guidelines also provide recommendations for the free flow of data and legitimate restrictions.

- Member countries should take into consideration the implications for other member countries of domestic processing and reexport of personal data.
- Member countries should take all reasonable and appropriate steps to ensure that transborder flows of personal data, including transit through a member country, are uninterrupted and secure.
- A member country should refrain from restricting transborder flows of personal data between itself and another member country except where the latter does not yet substantially observe these guidelines or where the reexport of such data would circumvent its domestic privacy legislation. A member country may also impose restrictions with respect to certain categories of personal data for which its domestic privacy legislation includes specific regulations in view of the nature of those data and for which the other member country provides no equivalent protection.

- Member countries should avoid developing laws, policies, and practices in the name of the protection of privacy and individual liberties that would create obstacles to transborder flows of personal data that would exceed requirements for such protection.

To address cross-border data protection controls, an organization needs to ascertain which geopolitical jurisdictions are applicable, and then research the relevant privacy laws to determine requirements. Once the requirements are understood, a comprehensive privacy protection plan can then be devised, but it must also align with an overarching data protection plan that addresses confidentiality, integrity, and authentication. As discussed in Chapter 2 (Confidentiality), a data classification scheme is an essential building block for any comprehensive security policy.

6.2 Cryptographic Considerations

When the controller employs cryptography for privacy protection, the cryptographic keys must be securely managed for both internal storage and external transmission to requesters and affiliates.

- Encryption for data confidentiality
- MAC, HMAC, digital signatures, or trusted time stamps for data integrity
- MAC, HMAC, digital signatures, or trusted time stamps for authentication

Encryption is discussed in Chapter 2 (Confidentiality). MAC, HMAC, digital signatures, and trusted time stamps are discussed in Chapter 4 (Integrity) and Chapter 3 (Authentication). Each of these cryptographic methods is further discussed in Chapter 7 (Key Management). There are no specific or additional cryptography or key management requirements for privacy controls. Pragmatically speaking, the key management controls for privacy are the same as for confidentiality, integrity, and authentication. Consequently, an organization's security policies and practices addressing cryptography and key management need to embrace privacy as well as other security controls.

Note that as described in §6.4 (Legal Considerations), privacy laws differ sufficiently from country to country and state to state such that the key management life cycle needs to be taken into account. Cryptographic keys and the associated data protected by those keys are both subject to jurisdictional rules. Thus, different keys used in different jurisdictions segregate an organization's cryptographic architecture for governance, risk, and compliance. Further, any increased risks due to law enforcement responses, legal actions, or key compromise can be compartmentalized within the jurisdictions. Key management life-cycle controls are discussed in Chapter 7 (Key Management).

6.3 Operational Considerations

6.3.1 Roles and Responsibilities

Figure 6.4 shows a general authentication privacy framework. The controller manages a database containing the personal data of numerous subjects, represented by the dotted line. The requester is any service provider needing access to one or more subjects' personal data. The affiliate is a service provider that has a contractual relationship with the controller for filtered data feeds of all subject personal data. The verifier provides authentication and authorization services to the controller for the requester and, possibly, for the subject. The subject is the individual whose personal information is stored by the controller, processed by the requester, and analyzed by the affiliate.

The requester submits a request to the controller for access to one or more subject records, and is authenticated and authorized by either the controller or a third-party verifier, possibly using a federated identity scheme. Depending on the nature of the requester, the collector might also obtain a release permission from the subject, possibly using the same (or a different) verifier.

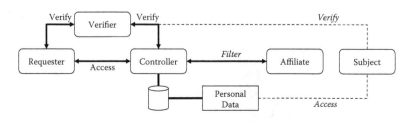

Figure 6.4   Privacy framework.

The affiliate receives data feeds from the controller based on pre-existing service agreements, which might be real-time feeds for each updated subject record or batch uploads. Affiliates typically get filtered information, tailored to the services provided for the controller. The connections between the controller and its affiliates are protected, using mutual authentication when the connection is established, encryption when the data are transferred, and integrity controls when the data are received.

The verifier might be a functional component within the controller or an independent service provider for authentication of the requester and possibly the subject. Authorization for the requester might also be provided by the verifier or the controller. Once the subject has been authenticated, authorization is automatically implied, as the subject always retains rights to its own personal data. However, depending on the jurisdiction, the subject's rights are often limited and not necessarily exclusive, as described in Section 6.4 (Legal Considerations).

The subject relies on the policy and practices of the controller—as well as any associated service providers, including affiliates and requesters—to protect its personal information. The protection controls include proactive measures for authentication of authorized entities, preventive measures against data disclosure to an unauthorized entity, detective measures to monitor for data loss, and notification in the event of a data breach.

The controller provides privacy controls within the domain of its systems and in cooperation with its affiliates and requesters. Confidentiality protects data from unauthorized access when in transit, process, or storage. Integrity protects data from undetected modification or substitution when in transit or storage. Authentication with authorization verifies entity access to system resources, including data and applications. Monitoring includes review of audit logs to determine system attacks and examining data in transit and storage. The controller also provides breach notification in the event of an incident, presuming of course the breach is actually discovered.

6.3.2 Security Policy

Security policy and practices for privacy controls need to align with an overarching data protection plan that addresses confidentiality, integrity, and authentication. For example, the OECD privacy guidelines [235] recommend the establishment of privacy policy and practices by referring to ISO 17799, which is now ISO 27002 [134].

> There should be a general policy of openness about developments, practices and policies with respect to personal data. Means should be readily available of establishing the existence and nature of personal data, and the main purposes of their use, as well as the identity and usual residence of the data controller.

A general security policy based on ISO 22307 [14] and ISO 27002 [134] adopted in several ANSI standards—including X9.79 [51], X9.84 [54], X9.95 [55], and X9.112 [59]—typically encompasses environmental controls addressing the following topics:

1. *Security policy and practices management*: This addresses how the organization maintains controls to provide reasonable assurance that security policy and practices exist and are maintained by a recognized policy management authority.
2. *Security organization and management*: This addresses how the organization maintains controls to provide reasonable assurance of management's support; that information security is properly managed within the organization; that the security of facilities, systems, and information assets accessed by third parties is maintained; and that the security of information is maintained when the responsibility for functions has been outsourced to another organization or entity.
3. *Asset classification and management*: This addresses how the organization maintains controls to provide reasonable assurance that assets and information receive an appropriate level of protection.
4. *Personnel security*: This addresses how the organization maintains controls to provide reasonable assurance that personnel and hiring practices enhance and support the trustworthiness of the organization's operations.

5. *Physical and environmental security*: This addresses how the organization maintains controls to provide reasonable assurance that physical access to facilities is limited to properly authorized individuals; that facilities are protected from environmental hazards, loss, damage, or compromise of assets; that interruption to business activities are prevented; that compromise or theft of information and facilities are prevented.

6. *Operations management*: This addresses how the organization maintains controls to provide reasonable assurance that the correct and secure operation of the organization's information-processing facilities is ensured, that the risk of systems failure is minimized, that the integrity of systems and information is protected against viruses and malicious software, that damage from security incidents and malfunctions is minimized through the use of incident reporting and response procedures, and that media are securely handled to protect media from damage, theft, and unauthorized access.

7. *System access management*: This addresses how the organization maintains controls to provide reasonable assurance that access to the management component of a system and access to a resource that is controlled by an access-control system is limited to properly authorized individuals.

8. *Systems development and maintenance*: This addresses how the organization maintains controls to provide reasonable assurance that systems development and maintenance activities are properly authorized to maintain system integrity.

9. *Business-continuity management*: This addresses how the organization maintains controls to provide reasonable assurance of operational continuity in the event of business interruptions or other disasters.

10. *Monitoring and compliance*: This addresses how the organization maintains controls to provide reasonable assurance that (a) the organization's compliance with contractual and legal requirements and with the organization's security policies and procedures is ensured, (b) that the effectiveness of the system audit process is maximized and interference to/from the

system audit process is minimized, and (c) that unauthorized system usage is detected.

11. *Event journaling*: This addresses how the organization maintains controls to provide reasonable assurance that (a) significant environmental and other security information life-cycle events are accurately and completely logged, (b) the confidentiality and integrity of current and archived event journals are maintained, (c) event journals are completely and confidentially archived in accordance with disclosed business practices, and (d) event journals are reviewed periodically by authorized personnel.

If cryptography is used anywhere within the organization, then there should be a separate security policy for key management addressing each of the eleven security policy topics described here, including key compromise. The policies, standards, practices, procedures, and expertise needed for securely managing cryptographic keys are very different than those for operating and managing general information technology. Key-management life-cycle controls are discussed in Chapter 7 (Key Management).

Regarding privacy, an organization needs to either include the associated controls in its general security policy and practices [232], or carve out a separate privacy policy and practices that aligns with the general security ones. The privacy controls include authentication and authorization, data disclosure, data loss prevention (DLP), and data breach notification.

6.4 Legal Considerations

While many countries have privacy laws, many of them are actually rather similar. One explanation is the simple fact that people are people, and personal information such as health, financial, religion, or other identifiable data are common to everyone. Another reason is that the legal profession, similar to the software profession, reuses published materials to avoid writing legal language from scratch. Further, although laws vary from country to country, practically speaking, there are only so many ways to protect personal information. For the purposes of this book, a comparison of several country laws, including the United States (US), the United Kingdom (UK), and Canada, is provided in relation to the European Union (EU) Privacy Directive,

6.4.1 European Union (EU) Privacy Directive

The European Union (EU) is an economic and political partnership among twenty-seven European countries; its official website is at http://europa.eu. The EU is based on the rule of law: Everything that it does is founded on treaties, voluntarily and democratically agreed to by all member countries. These binding agreements set out the EU's goals in its many areas of activity. One such agreement is its Privacy Directive [231], addressing the rights of individuals with regard to personal data. The data subject is the entity that the data are about, whereas the data controller is the entity protecting the data during processing or storage in electronic or physical media formats. The data subject is entitled to certain rights that the data controller is expected to provide, as follows:

1. *Quality control*: This includes explicit and legitimate purposes when collecting data; fair and lawful processing of data; maintaining accuracy of data; and, when appropriate, updating data to keep it current.
2. *Legitimacy control*: This allows processing of personal data only if unambiguous consent has been given or processing is necessary in support of a contract or other legal obligation, vital interests of the subject, public interest, or other legitimate interests of the controller.
3. *Prohibition control*: This includes restriction on revealing racial or ethnic origin, political opinions, religious or philosophical beliefs, health information, sexual orientation, or union memberships.
4. *Information control*: This includes facts about the process provided to the data subjects by the controller, such as the identities of the controllers (who are responsible for protecting personal information), the identities of the data recipients (who receive personal information), and the purposes (why an organization collects, uses, or discloses personal information).

5. *Objections control*: This is the right of the subject to oppose the processing or disclosure of personal data, including direct marketing purposes.

6. *Protection control*: This includes appropriate security measures to protect personal data against accidental or unlawful destruction, loss, modification, unauthorized disclosure, or access by the controller, the processor, or any authorized agent of either.

7. *Notification control*: This is the responsibility of the controller to register the data process with its national supervisory authority for a risk evaluation.

Some of these controls can be averted in certain circumstances. Prohibition can be superseded to protect the vital interests of the data subject, for example in cases of preventive medicine or medical diagnosis. Further, some restrictions apply, such as safeguarding national security, criminal investigations, or financial interests of a European Union member.

6.4.2 Canadian Personal Information Protection and Electronic Documents Act (PIPEDA)

Canada has its own privacy law [229], the Personal Information Protection and Electronic Documents Act (PIPEDA). PIPEDA defines personal information as that which can identify an individual, but it does not include the name, title, or business address or telephone number of an organization's employee. The law gives individuals the right to the following:

- To know why an organization collects, uses, or discloses their personal information. Note that this is included in the EU Information control.
- To know who in the organization is responsible for protecting their personal information. Note that this is included in the EU Information control.
- To expect an organization to collect, use, or disclose their personal information reasonably and appropriately, and not use the information for any purpose other than that to which

they have consented. Note that this is equivalent to the EU Legitimacy control.

- To expect an organization to protect their personal information by taking appropriate security measures. Note that this is equivalent to the EU Protection control.
- To expect the personal information an organization holds about them to be accurate, complete, and up to date. Note that this is equivalent to the EU Quality control.
- To obtain access to their personal information and ask for corrections if necessary. Note that there is no equivalent EU control.
- To complain about how an organization handles their personal information if they feel their privacy rights have not been respected. Note that this is similar to the EU Objections control.

The law requires organizations to provide the following controls:

- To obtain consent when they collect, use, or disclose their personal information. Note that this is included in the EU Legitimacy control.
- To supply an individual with a product or a service even if they refuse consent for the collection, use, or disclosure of their personal information unless that information is essential to the transaction. Note that this is included in the EU Legitimacy control.
- To collect information by fair and lawful means. Note that this is included in the EU Quality control.
- To have personal information policies that are clear, understandable, and readily available. Note that there is no equivalent EU control.

Since most of the Canadian PIPEDA controls appear to be equivalent to the EU Privacy Directive controls, although there are some differences, it seems reasonable to conclude that PIPEDA is for the most part aligned with the EU Privacy Directive.

6.4.3 United Kingdom Data Privacy Act (DPA)

The United Kingdom (UK) Data Privacy Act (DPA) [230] provides definitions for data, personal data, and sensitive data. In general, data are information that is processed, stored, or part of an accessible record such as a health, educational, or other public record. Personal data are information related to a living individual, also called the subject. Sensitive personal data includes information about the racial or ethnic origin of the subject, political opinions, religious or other beliefs of a similar nature, membership in trade unions, physical or mental health and other conditions, sexual lifestyle, and criminal history. These definitions align with the EU Privacy Directive.

The DPA also defines data participants. The data subject is an individual who is the focus of the personal data. The data controller is one or more persons who determine the purpose and manner in which personal data are processed or stored. A data processor is any person, other than an employee of the controller, who processes data on behalf of the controller. Data processing is defined as obtaining, recording, storing, or performing any operations on the data, including reorganization, modification, retrieval, disclosure, dissemination, blocking, or erasure or destruction. The DPA data protection principles are defined as follows:

- Personal data shall be processed fairly and lawfully and, in particular, shall not be processed unless (a) at least one of the conditions specified for the processing of any personal data are met, and (b) in the case of sensitive personal data, at least one of the conditions specified for the processing of sensitive personal data are also met. This DPA principle is consistent with the EU Quality and Legitimacy controls.
- Personal data shall be obtained only for one or more specified and lawful purposes, and shall not be further processed in any manner incompatible with that purpose or those purposes. This DPA principle is consistent with the EU Legitimacy control.
- Personal data shall be adequate, relevant, and not excessive in relation to the purpose for which they are processed. The DPA principle is consistent with the EU Quality and Legitimacy controls.

- Personal data shall be accurate and, where necessary, kept up to date. This DPA principle is consistent with the EU Quality control.
- Personal data processed for any purpose or purposes shall not be kept for longer than is necessary for that purpose or purposes. This DPA principle is consistent with the EU Protection control.
- Personal data shall be processed in accordance with the rights of data subjects under the DPA. This DPA principle is consistent with the EU Prohibition and Objections controls.
- Appropriate technical and organizational measures shall be taken against unauthorized or unlawful processing of personal data against accidental loss or destruction of, or damage to, personal data. This DPA principle is consistent with the EU Informational and Protection controls.
- Personal data shall not be transferred to a country or territory outside the European Economic Area unless that country or territory ensures an adequate level of protection for the rights and freedom of data subjects in relation to the processing of personal data. This DPA principle is consistent with the EU Prohibition and Protection controls.

Since most of the DPA principles appear to be consistent with the EU Privacy Directive controls, it seems reasonable to conclude that the DPA is congruent with the EU Privacy Directive.

6.4.4 United States Privacy Laws and Guidelines

The majority of the fifty states have some type of privacy data breach laws. The state laws basically have six common themes that vary from state to state [228].

- *Time to notify consumers of a personal information breach*: All of the state laws require notification without unreasonable delay. Roughly 70% of the state laws further expect the most expedient time possible. Only a few of the state laws stipulate a measurable time frame, ranging from seven days to forty-five days. In U.S. laws, notifications are in the event of a data breach, whereas the EU Notification control requires the controller to register the data processes with a national authority.

- *Civil or criminal penalties for failure to promptly notify customers of a breach*: Most of the state laws impose some form of penalty for noncompliance, but about 10% of the state laws reportedly do not provide specifications. Again, U.S. law notifications address data-breach incidents, whereas the EU Notification control is proactive registration by the controller.

- *Private right of action*: This is the right of action by the data collector against the party responsible for the breach. Approximately 33%, or about one third, of the state laws provide provisions, whereas the remainder do not. This U.S. theme is analogous to the EU Objection control; however, the difference is that the U.S. action rights apply to the collector, whereas the EU control relates to the data subject.

- *Exemption for encrypted personal information*: Storing personal information as encrypted data exempts the collector from any liability in the event of a breach. The exemption is based on the premise that the party responsible cannot decrypt the personal information. This presumes that the collector has managed the encryption keys appropriately such that the party responsible cannot gain access to the encryption keys. Most of the state laws (about 95%) allow this exemption. This U.S. theme is related to the EU Protection control, but in general the various U.S. laws provide fewer specifics on adequate and acceptable protection controls.

- *Exemption for criminal investigations or information also publicly available from government agencies*: Providing personal information to law enforcement under due process of law or disclosing personal information that has been previously made public by another government agency exempts the collector from any liability. Almost all of the state laws (roughly 98%) allow this exemption. At first reading, this U.S. theme might appear to be related to the EU Legitimacy control; however, the U.S. exemption applies to revealing information, whereas the EU control actually addresses collection and processing.

- *Exemption for immaterial breaches*: Insignificant or irrelevant data revealed by the collector that is not considered personal information is exempt from breach status. Roughly 70% of the state laws allow this exemption. This U.S. theme is related to the EU Prohibition control to the extent that unimportant data does not constitute a material breach, whereas the EU control addressed the opposite end of the importance spectrum, namely prohibited data.

In general, the U.S. state laws are more reactive, only addressing data breaches, and not proactive as per the approach of the EU Privacy Directive and other international laws. Most of the EU controls are not represented in the U.S. state laws, with the possible exception of the Protection control that is partially addressed by the exemption for encrypted personal information.

6.4.5 Federal Trade Commission (FTC)—Privacy of Consumer Financial Information

In addition to U.S. state laws, the Federal Trade Commission (FTC) regulates and oversees business privacy laws and policies that impact consumers. One such law is Part 313, Privacy of Consumer Financial Information, in Title 16 Commercial Practices of the Code of Federal Regulations (CFR) [233]. This part of the CFR governs the treatment of nonpublic personal information about consumers by the financial institutions, described in the following constraints:

1. Requires a financial institution in specified circumstances to provide notice to customers about its privacy policies and practices. This FTC constraint correlates to the EU Information control.
2. Describes the conditions under which a financial institution may disclose nonpublic personal information about consumers to nonaffiliated third parties. This FTC constraint correlates to the EU Prohibition control; however, the FTC law focuses primarily on account numbers versus other types of personal information.

3. Provides a method for consumers to prevent a financial institution from disclosing that information to most nonaffiliated third parties by "opting out" of that disclosure. This FTC constraint correlates to the EU Objections control, but is limited to opt-out methodology.

The Privacy of Consumer Financial Information Law provides several definitions, including a distinction between consumers versus customers. Part 313 also defines personally identifiable financial information and publicly available information.

- *Consumer* means an individual who obtains or has obtained a financial product or service from you that is to be used primarily for personal, family, or household purposes, or that individual's legal representative.
- *Customer* means a consumer who has a customer relationship with you.
- *Personally identifiable financial information* means (1) any information that a consumer provides to you to obtain a financial product or service from you; (2) any information about a consumer resulting from any transaction involving a financial product or service between you and a consumer; or (3) any information that you otherwise obtain about a consumer in connection with providing a financial product or service to that consumer.
- *Publicly available information* means any information that you have a reasonable basis to believe is lawfully made available to the general public from (1) federal, state, or local government records; (2) widely distributed media; or (3) disclosures to the general public that are required to be made by federal, state, or local law.

The FTC privacy law also discusses opt-out notices for customers and consumers, restrictions on disclosing of any nonpublic personal information to any nonaffiliated third parties, limits on sharing account numbers, and opt-out exceptions regarding third-party service providers. The EU controls for Quality, Legitimacy, Protection, and Notification are not addressed by the FTC constraints.

6.4.6 Health Insurance Portability and Accountability Act (HIPAA)

The Health Insurance Portability and Accountability Act (HIPAA) Privacy [234] Security and Breach Notification Rules includes the HIPAA Privacy Rule, which regulates the privacy of individually identifiable health information; the HIPAA Security Rule, which sets national standards for the security of electronic protected health information; the HIPAA Breach Notification Rule, which requires covered entities and business associates to provide notification following a breach of unsecured protected health information; and the confidentiality provisions of the Patient Safety Rule, which protect identifiable information being used to analyze patient safety events and improve patient safety.

Every health-care provider, regardless of size, who electronically transmits health information in connection with certain transactions is a covered entity. The Privacy Rule addresses individually identifiable health information, also called protected health information (PHI), that is stored or transmitted in any medium or format, including electronic, paper, or oral exchanges.

PHI includes any data relating to the individual's past, present, or future physical or mental health or condition; the provision of health care to the individual or any past, present, or future payment for the provision of health care to the individual; and demographic data that identifies the individual. The Health and Human Services (HHS) site provides examples of identifiers such as name, address, birth date, and Social Security number (SSN), with employment and education records being exempt from the Privacy Rule. General HIPAA principles include the following:

- A covered entity may not use or disclose protected health information, except either: (1) as the Privacy Rule permits or requires; or (2) as the individual who is the subject of the information (or the individual's personal representative) authorizes in writing. This HIPAA principle aligns with the EU Legitimacy controls relating to consent or vital interests of the subject.
- A covered entity must disclose protected health information in only two situations: (a) to individuals (or their personal representatives) specifically when they request access to, or an accounting of disclosures of, their protected health

information; and (b) to HHS when it is undertaking a compliance investigation or review or enforcement action. This HPAA principle aligns with the EU Prohibition control, although the nature of the personal data are different.

- A covered entity is permitted, but not required, to use and disclose protected health information, without an individual's authorization, for the following purposes or situations: (1) to the individual (unless required for access or accounting of disclosures); (2) treatment, payment, and health-care operations; (3) opportunity to agree or object; (4) incident to an otherwise-permitted use and disclosure; (5) public interest and benefit activities; and (6) limited data set for the purposes of research, public health, or health-care operations. This HIPAA principle aligns with the Legitimacy control relating to use without exclusive permission by the subject.

- A covered entity must obtain the individual's written authorization for any use or disclosure of protected health information that is not for treatment, payment, or health-care operations or otherwise permitted or required by the Privacy Rule. A covered entity may not condition treatment, payment, enrollment, or benefits eligibility on an individual granting an authorization, except in limited circumstances. The Privacy Rule protects all "individually identifiable health information" held or transmitted by a covered entity or its business associate, in any form or medium, whether electronic, paper, or oral. The Privacy Rule calls this information "protected health information (PHI)."

- Each covered entity, with certain exceptions, must provide a notice of its privacy practices. The notice must (a) describe how the covered entity uses and discloses protected health information, (b) state its duties to protect privacy, (c) describe individuals' rights, including handling complaints, and (d) provide a point of contact. This HIPAA principle aligns with the EU Information control.

Although HIPAA does not explicitly address the EU Quality control, it is clearly in the best interest of the individual and the covered entity to maintain accuracy of health-care information.

While HIPAA recognizes the individual's right to object regarding the disclosure of health-care information, the covered entity also has the option to not comply, so the EU Objections control is not addressed. Similar to the EU Notification control, it is a common practice for covered entities to undergo security assessments based on the HIPAA Privacy Rule, Security Rule, and Breach Notification Rule.

6.4.7 Fair Credit Reporting Act (FCRA)

The Fair Credit Reporting Act (FCRA) is part of the U.S. Code, Title 15 Commerce and Trade, Chapter 41 Consumer Credit Protection, Subchapter III Credit Reporting Agencies, §1681 Congressional Findings and Statement of Purpose. FCRA defines a consumer report as any written, oral, or other communication by a consumer reporting agency on a consumer's credit information. However, a consumer report does not include financial information about the reporting agency or consumer medical information. Credit reports can be provided in response to a court order or subpoena, in accordance with written instructions by the consumer, or in response to any third party for the purposes of a credit transaction, employment, insurance underwriting, government license, investment, prepayment, child support, liquidation, or other business transaction. FCRA addresses over two dozen control areas (§605 to §629), so instead of reviewing each control, as was done for the other privacy documents, the FCRA sections are mapped to the EU controls.

1. EU Quality control
   FCRA §605 Requirements relating to information contained in consumer reports
   FCRA §607 Compliance procedures
   FCRA §612 Charges for certain disclosures
   FCRA §613 Public record information for employment purposes
   FCRA §622 Information on overdue child support obligations
   FCRA §623 Responsibilities of furnishers of information to consumer reporting agencies
2. EU Legitimacy control
   FCRA §608 Disclosures to governmental agencies

FCRA §610 Conditions and form of disclosure to consumers

FCRA §618 Jurisdiction of courts; limitation of actions

FCRA §625 Relation to state laws

FCRA §626 Disclosures to FBI for counterintelligence purposes

FCRA §627 Disclosures to governmental agencies for counterterrorism purposes

FCRA §629 Corporate and technological circumvention prohibited

3. EU Prohibition control

FCRA §605B Block of information resulting from identity theft

FCRA §606 Disclosure of investigative consumer reports

FCRA §614 Restrictions on investigative consumer reports

4. EU Information control

FCRA §609 Disclosures to consumers

5. EU Objections control

FCRA §611 Procedure in case of disputed accuracy

6. EU Protection control

FCRA §605A Identity theft prevention; fraud alerts and active duty alerts

FCRA §615 Requirements on users of consumer reports

FCRA §616 Civil liability for willful noncompliance

FCRA §617 Civil liability for negligent noncompliance

FCRA §619 Obtaining information under false pretenses

FCRA §620 Unauthorized disclosures by officers or employees

FCRA §621 Administrative enforcement

FCRA §624 Affiliate sharing

FCRA §628 Disposal of records

7. EU Notification control

No section of the FCRA equates to the EU national registration control

While FCRA is not a privacy law per se, it does address most of the EU privacy controls with regard to consumer credit reports.

6.4.8 Federal Privacy Act

The federal Privacy Act, enacted as Public Law 93-579 in 1974, is part of the U.S. Code, Title 5 Government Organization and

Employees, §552a Records Maintained on Individuals. This act defines a Code of Fair Information Practice that governs the collection, maintenance, use, and dissemination of personally identifiable information (PII) about individuals that is maintained in systems of records by federal agencies. The term *system of records* is defined as a group of any records under the control of any agency from which information is retrieved by the name of the individual or by some identifying number, symbol, or other identifying particular assigned to the individual. Several of the major requirements align with the EU Privacy Directive.

- *Conditions of disclosure*: No agency shall disclose any record contained in a system of records to any person or another agency, except pursuant to a written request or the prior consent of the individual, unless disclosure is needed by authorized federal employees of other agencies. Other agencies include the Bureau of the Census, National Archives and Records Administration, House of Congress, Comptroller General of the General Accounting Office, civil or criminal law enforcement agencies, court jurisdictions, or consumer reporting agency. Note that this is similar to the EU Legitimacy control.
- *Accounting of certain disclosures*: Each agency, with respect to each system of records under its control, shall keep an accurate accounting of the date, nature, and purpose of each disclosure of a record and the name and address of the person or agency to whom the disclosure is made. Note that this is similar to the EU Information control.
- *Access to records*: Each agency that maintains a system of records shall permit an individual (1) access to review and make a copy of the records, (2) request an amendment of the records, and (3) request a review of any refusal to amend the records. The agency must also provide justification for any refusal of amendment. Note that this is similar to the EU Objections control.
- *Agency requirements*: Each agency that maintains a system of records shall (1) maintain only relevant information in its records, (2) collect information from the individual when possible, (3) describe the authority, purpose, usage, and potential

effects on individuals, (4) publish in the *Federal Register* the system of records data usage, (5) maintain accuracy, relevance, timeliness, and completeness of information, (6) disseminate records that are accurate, complete, timely, and relevant for agency purposes, (7) maintain First Amendment rights of individuals, (8) make reasonable efforts to notify individuals of disclosures due to legal processes when these become a matter of public record, (9) establish employee rules of conduct, (10) establish appropriate administrative, technical, and physical safeguards, (11) publish in the *Federal Register* notice of any new use or intended use of the data in the system, and (12) publish in the *Federal Register* notice of any record matching with nonfederal agencies. Note that these requirements are comparable to the EU Quality, Protection, and Notification controls.

The federal Privacy Act does not explicitly prohibit any specific information, such as race, ethnicity, political affiliations, or religion, in contrast to the EU Prohibition control. The act includes many other topics particular to the federal government, including agency rules, civil remedies, general exemptions, specific exemptions, archival records, government contractors, mailing lists, matching agreements, verification and opportunity to contest findings, sanctions, report on new systems and matching programs, biennial reports, effects of other laws, data integrity boards, and the responsibilities of the Office of Management and Budget.

7

KEY MANAGEMENT

At this point in the book, we have repeatedly stressed the importance of key management in other chapters while referencing this chapter. Cryptography is used in almost every aspect of security controls relating to confidentiality, integrity, and authentication.

- In Chapter 2 (Confidentiality), we discussed end-to-end (E2E) and point-to-point (P2P) encryption frameworks for data in transit and how the keys might be deployed among senders, receivers, and intermediaries. We also considered how data encryption keys might be protected using hardware or software cryptographic modules.
- In Chapter 4 (Integrity), we discussed strong integrity methods that employ cryptographic keys, including message authentication codes (MAC), hashed message authentication codes (HMAC), digital signatures, and trusted time stamps.
- In Chapter 3 (Authentication), we discussed cryptographic authentication factors and the use of cryptography to secure the other authentication factors, including knowledge-factor encryption, and protecting possession factors, biometric factors, and associated protocols.

All of these security controls can be achieved or supplemented using cryptographic processes such that management of the corresponding keys is paramount. Data are protected by cryptographic keys, which in turn are protected by other cryptographic keys [50]. Symmetric or asymmetric keys can protect information; symmetric keys can protect other symmetric keys or asymmetric keys; and, likewise, asymmetric keys can protect other asymmetric keys or symmetric keys. This chapter is organized into the following sections.

1. Cryptographic algorithms
2. Cryptographic modules

3. Key-management life cycle
4. Cryptographic architecture
5. Public key infrastructure

Algorithms are reviewed to provide a knowledge baseline for encryption, integrity, authenticity, and key establishment. Various certification and evaluation programs for cryptographic hardware and software modules are discussed. The key-management life cycle for symmetric and asymmetric keys is examined based on various ISO, ANSI, and NIST standards. The concept of how to document a cryptographic architecture is provided, and the relevancy of a public key infrastructure (PKI) is presented.

7.1 Cryptographic Algorithms

First, let's put cryptography into perspective as it relates to protecting information. The written language is attributed to the Mesopotamians over 6,000 years ago, while the first instance of cryptography is ascribed to the Egyptians almost 4,000 years ago using hieroglyphics substitution known only by the priesthood [18]. Thus, when discussing codes, ciphers, and cryptographic algorithms, we are actually addressing a technology that is at least 4,000 years old. *Cryptology* is the more general term, derived from the Greek prefix *crypto-*, meaning hidden or secret, and the suffix *-ology*, meaning writing or study, so it is the discipline of using secret data (keys) to protect information. Cryptography is the practice of creating algorithms and protocols, while cryptanalysis is the practice of breaking them. Modern cryptography was ushered in during World War II, and its evolution has continued to the present day. Cryptologists now focus on mathematical constructs and formal proofs.

In order to understand an overview of cryptography, Figure 7.1 provides a cryptographic taxonomy of its uses and commonly used algorithms. Cryptographic algorithms can be organized into two groups: symmetric and asymmetric. Symmetric algorithms use a single key for invertible functions such as encryption and decryption, whereas asymmetric algorithms use two different cryptographic keys. For example, with symmetric encryption, the data are encrypted and decrypted using the same cryptographic key; whereas for asymmetric

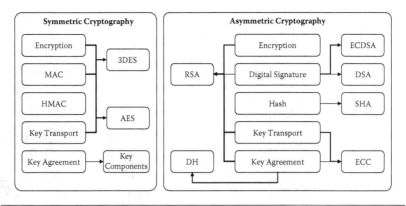

Figure 7.1   Cryptographic taxonomy.

encryption, the data are encrypted using the public key and decrypted using the private key. Another example is integrity-check values, where MAC and HMAC are generated and verified using the same symmetric key, while digital signatures are generated using the private key but verified using the public key.

Figure 7.2 provides a more focused taxonomy for symmetric cryptography. When both parties share a common symmetric key, party A can encrypt data and party B can decrypt data. Likewise, party A can generate an integrity-check value (ICV) such as a MAC or HMAC, and party B can verify the ICV. Similarly, party A can encrypt or generate an ICV for data in storage, and party B can decrypt or verify the ICV. Symmetric keys can also be used to exchange encrypted keys between parties.

Figure 7.3 provides a focused taxonomy for asymmetric cryptography. Party A can use the public key to encrypt data that party B can decrypt with the private key. More likely, party A encrypts data with a random symmetric key and encrypts the symmetric key with

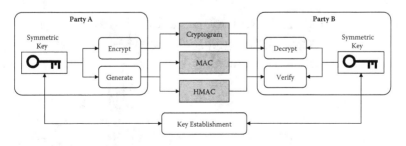

Figure 7.2   Symmetric taxonomy.

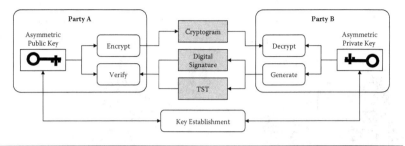

Figure 7.3 Asymmetric taxonomy.

the public key, and then party B decrypts the symmetric key with the corresponding private key and uses the symmetric key to decrypt the data. Party B can use the private key to generate a digital signature or time-stamp token (TST), and then party A can verify the digital signature or TST using the corresponding public key. Symmetric keys can also be exchanged or mutually agreed upon between parties using asymmetric keys.

The various symmetric and asymmetric algorithms for each of the cryptographic methods listed in the taxonomy are discussed in more detail in the following sections. While this book is not intended as a tutorial on any specific algorithm, references to the related standard are provided.

7.1.1 Encryption

Encryption can be achieved using almost any symmetric algorithm, since they tend to be reversible by design; for example, data can be encrypted or decrypted. However, not all asymmetric algorithms are reversible. Some asymmetric algorithms are irreversible; for example, data encrypted with the private key cannot be decrypted with the public key. For other chapters, the focus has been on using encryption for data confidentiality; however, for this chapter, key encryption is the primary focus. When a key is encrypted at one location and distributed to one or more other locations, this is called key transport.

Triple DES (3DES) is a symmetric algorithm based on the Data Encryption Standard (DES) used three times as encrypt (E), decrypt (D), and encrypt (E), where we denote encryption as $C = 3DES(M) = E(D(E(M)))$, where M is the cleartext message being encrypted and C is the ciphertext. We also denote decryption as $M = 3DES(C) =$

Table 7.1 Triple DES Modes

3DES MODE	ENCRYPT	DECRYPT	ENCRYPT	ALGORITHM
3K-3DES	K1	K2	K3	E(K3, D(K2, E(K1, M)))
2K-3DES	K1	K2	K1	E(K1, D(K2, E(K1, M)))
1K-3DES	K1	K1	K1	E(K1, D(K1, E(K1, M)))

D(E(D(C))). 3DES can be used with one (K1), two (K1, K2), or three (K1, K2, K3) keys. Table 7.1 provides a summary of the 3DES modes and number of cryptographic keys.

- *Three key (3K-3DES)* is denoted as 3DES(M) = E(K3, D(K2, E(K1, M))) when three keys are used. M is encrypted using K1; the first intermediate result is decrypted using K2; and the second intermediate result is encrypted using K3. NIST has determined that the 168-bit 3DES key only has a cryptographic strength of about 112 bits, or about 66% of the expected strength [176].

- *Two key (2K-3DES)* is denoted as 3DES(M) = E(K1, D(K2, E(K1, M))) when two keys are used. M is encrypted using K1; the first intermediate result is decrypted using K2; and the second intermediate result is encrypted reusing K1. Although two DES keys are cryptographically stronger than one, their overall cryptographic strength is less than double the key length. NIST has determined that the 112-bit 3DES key only has a cryptographic strength of about 80 bits, approximately 70% of the expected strength [176].

- *One key (1K-3DES)* is denoted as 3DES(M) = E(K1, D(K1, E(K1, M))) when one key is used. M is encrypted using K1; the first intermediate result is decrypted reusing K1, which recovers M; and M is encrypted using K1. This mode was designed to be backward compatible with DES as a transition mechanism from DES to 3DES [63]. NIST has determined that the 56-bit DES and 3DES key has an equivalent cryptographic strength of about 56 bits [176].

This essentially means that after thirty years of cryptanalysis, the best-known attack against DES is still an exhaustive key attack, were the adversary tries each of the possible 72 quadrillion keys (or 2^{56} permutations) until the right key is discovered. Thus the backdoor rumors of why the National Security Agency (NSA) changed the substitution ciphers (or S-Box) for the original IBM Lucifer submission in the 1970s, which became DES, were really to block certain types of cryptanalytic attacks.

Advanced Encryption Standard (AES) is a symmetric algorithm selected by NIST to officially replace DES [173]. NIST [180] and NSA established sunset dates for DES and 3DES as follows: DES and 1K-DES in 2005, 2K-DES in 2010, and 3K-3DES in 2030. TR-37 [64] provides a summary of migrating from DES. The Rijndael algorithm submitted by Belgian cryptographers Joan Daemen and Vincent Rijmen was chosen from over sixteen candidates. AES supports three keys sizes, 128 bits, 192 bits, and 256 bits. Thus we can denote AES encryption and decryption as C = AES (K, M) and M = AES (K, C) without noting the key size, or the key size can be added to the notation when desired.

- AES 128-bit key encryption can be notated as AES (K-128, M) or AES-128 (M). NIST has determined that the 128-bit key has an equivalent cryptographic strength of 128 bits [176].
- AES 192-bit key encryption can be notated as AES (K-192, M) or AES-192 (M). NIST has determined that the 192-bit key has an equivalent cryptographic strength of 192 bits [176].
- AES 256-bit key encryption can be notated as AES (K-256, M) or AES-256 (M). NIST has determined that the 256-bit key has an equivalent cryptographic strength of 256 bits [176].

Rivest-Shamir-Adleman (RSA) is an asymmetric algorithm developed by Ron Rivest, Adi Shamir, and Len Adelman. RSA is a reversible cipher such that data encrypted by the public key can be decrypted by the corresponding private key, and likewise data encrypted by the private key can be decrypted by the associated public key. Thus we can denote RSA encryption as C = RSA(M) and decryption as M = RSA(C), although the actual mathematical notation for RSA is deceivingly simplistic.

- RSA encryption is $C \equiv M^e \pmod{n}$, where the ciphertext (C) is equivalent to the remainder of the cleartext message (M) raised to the public exponent (e) divided by the public key (n) modulus.

- RSA decryption is $M \equiv C^d \pmod{n}$, where the cleartext message (M) is equivalent to the remainder of the ciphertext (C) raised to the private key (d) divided by the public key (n) modulus.

The RSA algorithm strength is based on the mathematically hard problem of factoring large numbers into their constitutional primes. The classic public key modulus (n) is the product of two large prime numbers (p and q where pq = n). X9.31 [43] expresses RSA key (n) sizes as multiples of 256 bits, so for example 256 × 4 = 1024 bits, or translating from a binary to a decimal number, about 307 digits. So for a 1024-bit RSA key (n), the two prime numbers (p and q) are each about 154 to 155 digits. As another example, a 256 × 8 = 2048-bit RSA key (n) has 617 digits, so its primes (p and q) have a range of 306 to 307 digits. Further, an RSA 256 × 16 = 4098-bit key (n) has 1,234 digits, so its primes are each about 616 to 617 digits.

However, as mathematical algorithms evolve and computer power continues to increase, the size of the RSA keys must likewise grow in size [9]. Note that the length of RSA keys is sometimes expressed as the number of digits or the number of bits, so one needs to be careful when interpreting information. For example, RSA-100 has 100 decimal digits (also called RSA-330 bits) whose factorization was announced in April 1991 by Arjen K. Lenstra. For the purposes of this book, we refer to the number of bits. Some of the last RSA challenges completed were RSA-768, factored in December 2009 [20], and RSA-704, factored in July 2012 [21]. There are numerous mathematical and cryptanalytic attacks that significantly reduce the cryptographic strength of the RSA key size.

- RSA-1024 is widely used for secure socket layer (SSL) certificates, but many organizations have begun migrating to larger keys. NIST has determined that the 1024-bit key has an equivalent cryptographic strength of 80 bits and recommended that RSA-1024 stop being used by federal agencies in 2010 [176].
- RSA-2048 increases the key size from 1K to 2K, so certificates are larger and consequently cryptographic modules and application software need to handle the bigger sizes. VeriSign announced in 2010 that it would migrate three of

its root certificate authority (CA) for Thawte, GeoTrust, and VeriSign to RSA-2048, and effective in 2011, all issued certificates would likewise be RSA-2048 keys [222]. Doubling the key size seems to quadruple the computational requirements, so for example, a cryptographic module processing 100 functions per second using a 1024-bit key would only achieve 25 functions per second using a 2049-bit key. NIST has determined that the 2048-bit key has an equivalent cryptographic strength of 112 bits [176].

Refer to Table 7.2 for a summary of cryptography services and Table 7.3 for a summary of cryptography strengths.

7.1.2 Message Authentication Code (MAC)

MAC can be achieved using almost-symmetric algorithms. Recall in Chapter 4 (Integrity) that a MAC can be generated using a symmetric algorithm with the Cipher Block Chaining (CBC) mode, where the leftmost part of the final ciphertext output is used as the MAC. MAC for data integrity and authenticity has been the focal

Table 7.2   Cryptography Services Summary

CONFIDENTIALITY	INTEGRITY	AUTHENTICATION	NONREPUDIATION	KEY MANAGEMENT
Encryption	—	—	—	Key transport
—	MAC	MAC	—	—
—	HMAC	HMAC	—	—
—	Digital signature	Digital signature	Digital signature	—
—	—	—	—	Key agreement
—	TST	—	TST	—

Table 7.3   Cryptography Strength Summary

CRYPTOGRAPHIC STRENGTH	SYMMETRIC ALGORITHM	HASH ALGORITHM	ECC ALGORITHMS	RSA/DSA/DH ALGORITHMS
56 bits	1K-3DES	N/A	N/A	N/A
80 bits	2K-3DES	SHA-1 (160)	160 bits	1,024 bits
112 bits	3K-3DES	SHA-2 (224)	224 bits	2,048 bits
128 bits	AES-128	SHA-2 (256)	256 bits	3,072 bits
192 bits	AES-192	SHA-2 (384)	384 bits	7,680 bits
256 bits	AES-256	SHA-2 (512)	512 bits	15,360 bits

point; however, key integrity and authenticity now become the primary focus.

- 3DES is included in ISO 16609 [108], which refers to the MAC algorithms defined in ISO 9797 [114], and is included in NIST Special Publication 800-38B, Cipher-Based Message Authentication Code (CMAC) [176].
- AES is included in NIST Special Publication 800-38B Cipher-Based Message Authentication Code (CMAC) [176].

Refer to Table 7.2 for a summary of cryptography services and Table 7.3 for a summary of cryptography strengths.

7.1.3 Hashed Message Authentication Code (HMAC)

In Figure 7.1, HMAC is listed in the symmetric cryptography list because it relies on the same key to generate and verify the integrity check value (ICV) despite the fact that HMAC employs a hash algorithm, whereas HASH is listed in the asymmetric cryptography list because of its importance to digital signatures.

HMAC is defined in FIPS (Federal Information Processing Standard) 198 [174], and the Secure Hash Algorithm suites (SHA) are defined in FIPS 180 [167]. NIST announced the selection for SHA-3 as the Keccak (pronounced "catch-ack") algorithm in October 2012 [223] and has since updated FIPS 180. Keccak was created by Guido Bertoni, Joan Daemen and Gilles Van Assche of STMicroelectronics and Michaël Peeters of NXP Semiconductors. Refer to Table 7.2 for a summary of cryptography services and Table 7.3 for a summary of cryptography strengths.

7.1.4 Hash

As discussed in Chapter 4 (Integrity), hashes are fundamental building blocks for other cryptographic methods, including digital signatures. At a minimum, a good hash function must demonstrate the properties of first pre-image resistance, second pre-image resistance, and collision resistance.

- *Pre-image resistance*: Given a hash function H and an output hash value h, it should be hard to find any cleartext c such that h = H(c).
- *Second pre-image resistance*: Given a hash function H and an input cleartext c1, it should be hard to find another input c2 such that c1 ≠ c2 but H(c1) = h = H(c2).
- *Collision resistance*: Given a hash function H, it should be hard to find any two cleartext c1 and c2 such that H(c1) = h = H(c2). The pair (c1, c2) is called a hash collision.

Message digest (MD) algorithms, developed by Ron Rivest (the "R" in RSA) include MD2, MD4, MD5, and MD6. MD2 is a 128-bit hash that was originally included in RFC 1115 [82] and later published separately as RFC 1319 [84]. Optimized for 8-bit computers, it was later shown to be susceptible to pre-image attacks and collision attacks. MD4 is also a 128-bit hash originally published as RFC 1186 [83], which was later shown to be susceptible to collision attacks. MD5 is another 128-bit hash originally published as RFC 1321 [86], which was also later shown to be susceptible to collision attacks. MD6 is a variable-length maximum 512-bit hash that was submitted to the NIST SHA-3 challenge; however, it did not advance to the second round of the SHA-3 competition.

SHA is a series of secure hash algorithms. The original FIPS PUB 180 Secure Hash Standard (SHS), published in 1993, defined the Secure Hash Algorithm (SHA) for use with FIPS 196 Digital Signature Standard (DSS), which defined the Digital Signature Algorithm (DSA). A revision called SHA-1 was published as FIPS 180-1 in 1995. A suite of three new algorithms—SHA-256, SHA-384, and SHA-512, called SHA-2 suite—were introduced to FIPS 180-2 in 2002. A fourth algorithm, SHA-224, was added to the SHA-2 suite as FIPS 180-3 in 2008. Two SHA-512 variations, called SHA-512/224 and SHA-512/256, were added to FIPS 180-4 in 2012 [168]. Table 7.4 provides a summary of the Secure Hash Algorithm (SHA) properties.

The hash size outputs in Table 7.4 are listed by bit size and are graphically shown as the number of 32-bit blobs. Basically, the SHA-512/224 and SHA-512/256 algorithms are the same as the SHA-512 algorithm, but the 512-bit output is truncated to the leftmost 224 bits or 256 bits.

Table 7.4 SHA Properties

ALGORITHM SUITE	ALGORITHM NAME	MESSAGE SIZES INPUTS	HASH SIZE OUTPUTS
SHA-1	SHA-1	$0 < $ length $ < 2^{64}$ bits	160 bits □□□□□ 5
	SHA-224	$0 < $ length $ < 2^{64}$ bits	224 bits □□□□□□□ 7
	SHA-256	$0 < $ length $ < 2^{64}$ bits	256 bits □□□□□□□□ 8
	SHA-384	$0 < $ length $ < 2^{128}$ bits	384 bits □□□□□□□□□ □□□ 12
SHA-2	SHA-512	$0 < $ length $ < 2^{128}$ bits	512 bits □□□□□□□□□ □□□□□□□ 16
	SHA-512/224	$0 < $ length $ < 2^{128}$ bits	224 bits □□□□□□□ 7
	SHA-512/256	$0 < $ length $ < 2^{128}$ bits	256 bits □□□□□□□□ 8

In November 2007, NIST announced in the *Federal Register* a new cryptographic hash algorithm SHA-3 competition as a response to advances made in the cryptanalysis of hash algorithms. Overall, sixty-four hash algorithms were submitted. In October 2012, NIST announced that the winner of its five-year SHA-3 competition was the Keccak (pronounced "catch-ack"), created by Guido Bertoni, Joan Daemen, and Gilles Van Assche of STMicroelectronics and Michaël Peeters of NXP Semiconductors. SHA-3 will be released in FIPS 180-5 [169]. Keccak supports 224-bit, 256-bit, 384-bit, and 512-bit hashes. Refer to Table 7.2 for a summary of cryptography services and Table 7.3 for a summary of cryptography strengths.

7.1.5 Digital Signature

Digital signatures are generated by hashing the cleartext and applying the private key to the hash to produce the digital signature, which is verified by rehashing the cleartext and applying the public key to the signature. The underlying mathematics, signature generation, and signature verification functions vary based on the digital signature and cryptography algorithms used. Asymmetric cryptography involves either reversible or irreversible algorithms, where reversible algorithms can be used for both encryption and digital signatures, whereas irreversible algorithms can only be used for digital signatures. For example, the DSA [170] is an irreversible digital signature algorithm.

RSA digital signatures are defined in PKCS #1 [193], X9.31 [43], and IEEE 1363 [73]. RSA is a reversible algorithm such that the signature-generation function is basically using the private key to encrypt the hashed cleartext; the signature verification function uses the public key to decrypt the signature; and the recovered hash is then compared to the regenerated hash. A common misnomer is that all digital signature algorithms are reversible and that the asymmetric signature algorithm is encryption.

- IEEE 1363 [73–76] defines digital-signature and key-establishment schemes based on the integer factorization (IF) problem (e.g., RSA), the discrete logarithm (DL) problem (e.g., Diffie-Hellman, DSA), and the elliptic curve discrete logarithm (EC) problem (e.g., Menezes-Qu-Vanstone, MQV).
- PKCS #1 [193] provides recommendations for the implementation of public key cryptography based on the RSA algorithm [29] addressing: cryptographic primitives, encryption schemes, signature schemes with appendix, and Abstract Syntax Notation One (ASN.1) for representing keys and for identifying the schemesX9.31 [43] was adapted from ISO/IEC 9796-2 [114] and ISO/IEC 14888-3 [118] and defines a method for digital signature generation and verification for the protection of financial messages and data using reversible public key cryptography systems without message recovery.

DSA is defined in FIPS 186-3 [170]. DSA is an irreversible algorithm such that the signature consists of two components (r, s) for some message M. When the replying party receives M′, r′, and s′, the signature is verified by computing a value v such that v = r′ only when M′ = M, r = r′, and s = s′ components are the same. Thus, unlike reversible algorithms (e.g., RSA), the signature is not decrypted to recover the hash, but rather it is used as part of the verification function.

- FIPS 186-3 requires use of the SHA hashes [170].
- FIPS 183-3 also permits the use of RSA as defined in X9.31 [43] for RSA or ECDSA as defined in X9.62 [47].

ECDSA, defined in X9.62 [47], is the elliptic curve analog of the DSA [170]. The standard also provides mathematical background for elliptic curve cryptography (ECC). An overview of algebraic groups, rings, and fields is provided in §7.1.6. In general, smaller ECC keys

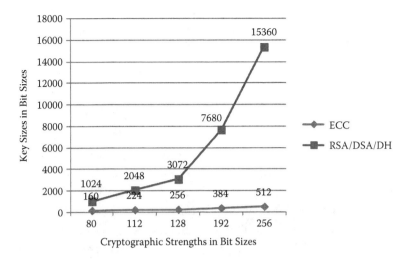

Figure 7.4 Crypto strength versus key sizes.

have equivalent cryptographic strength than larger RSA, DSA, or Diffie-Hellman (DH) keys. Figure 7.4 shows the relative cryptography strengths expressed as the amount of work to perform an exhaustive key search measured in bits (80, 112, 128, 192, and 256) on the *x*-axis. The ECC and other algorithm (RSA, DSA, and DH) curves are shown as the actual key sizes expressed in bits.

Clearly, the ECC curve does not increase as rapidly as the other algorithms. As Moore's Law [224] continues to increase computing power, key sizes will likewise need to grow such that eventually RSA keys will be large enough and the algorithm will be slow enough that systems will need to migrate from RSA to ECC algorithms for smaller keys and acceptable performance.

- The ECC-224 key size is only 11% of the RSA-2048 key size, but both provide the same 112 bits of cryptographic strength.
- The ECC-256 key size is only 8% of the RSA-3072 key size, but both provide the same 128 bits of cryptographic strength.
- The ECC-384 key size is only 5% of the RSA-7680 key size, but both provide the same 128 bits of cryptographic strength.
- The ECC-512 key size is only 3% of the RSA-15360 key size, but both provide the same 128 bits of cryptographic strength.

Cryptography research continues to evolve, and other key-establishment algorithms such as lattice-based polynomial [57] may eventually offer alternatives. Refer to Table 7.2 for a summary of cryptography services and Table 7.3 for a summary of cryptography strengths.

7.1.6 Key Transport

Key transport is a key-establishment method whereby a cryptographic key is encrypted, distributed from one location to another, and decrypted. The transported key can be any type of key, whereas the transport key is used strictly for key encryption and is called a key encryption key (KEK).

3DES can be used to encrypt other cryptographic keys. However, its 64-bit data block is a size limit when the data being encrypted is another cryptographic key. Thus, other cryptographic modes of operation besides electronic code book (ECB) are necessary to handle larger key sizes.

AES can also be used to encrypt other cryptographic keys. Similarly, the 128-bit data block is a size limit when encrypting other keys, so other modes of operation are necessary to handle larger key sizes. NIST Special Publication 800-38 [176] provides approved modes for use with AES.

RSA public keys can be used to encrypt other cryptographic keys. Note that while the RSA public key (n) modulus also limits the size of the cleartext message (M), its relative size compared to symmetric keys is sufficiently large to contain the transported key. As mentioned in Chapter 2 (Confidentiality) on session encryption, this is essentially how SSL and TLS (transport layer security) operate.

Further, the cryptographic strength of the KEK, regardless of symmetric or asymmetric encryption, needs to be at least as strong as the key it is encrypting. Otherwise, the protection of the transported key is decreased, and subsequently the protection of the associated data are likewise reduced. This is analogous to locking up a valuable in a safe with a 5-numbered combination lock and then locking the written combination into a second safe with only a 3-numbered combination lock. The overall security of the valuable is reduced to the 3-numbered combination lock where the stronger combination is kept.

Elliptic Curve Cryptography (ECC) is an approach to public key cryptography based on the algebraic structure of elliptic curves over finite fields. The use of elliptic curves in cryptography was suggested independently by Neal Koblitz and Victor S. Miller in 1985. For those readers who have avoided or forgotten their abstract algebra class, we provide a quick review of its three mathematical constructs: groups, rings, and fields.

- *Groups*: A finite group is a set of elements, such as the counting numbers $(0, 1, 2, ..., N)$, where N is some finite number and a binary operation, such that the operation on any two elements of the group yields another element of the same group.

  Also, one member of the group is the identity element, such that the operation on the identity element and any other element yields the same element. For addition, 0 is the identity element because any number plus zero is that same number, $n + 0 = n$. For multiplication, 1 is the identity element because any number times one is that same number, $n \cdot 1 = n$.

  Another, property of groups is that every element has an inverse, such that the operation on an element and its inverse yields the identity element. For example, the inverse for 7 is -7, since $7 + (-7) = 0$; and the inverse for 2 is $\frac{1}{2}$, since $2 \cdot \frac{1}{2} = 1$.

  And finally, the group operation is associative, such that for any three elements, the order of the operation gives the same result. For example $(1 + 2) + 3 = 6 = 1 + (2 + 3)$ and $(2 \cdot 3) \cdot 4 = 24 = 2 \cdot (3 \cdot 4)$, so addition and multiplication are both associative. However, subtraction, e.g., $(7 - 4) - 3 = 0 \neq 6 = 7 - (4 - 3)$, and division, e.g., $(12 \div 2) \div 3 = 2 \neq 18 = 12 \div (2 \div 3)$, are not associative.

- *Rings*: A ring is a set of elements and two binary operations, analogous to addition and multiplication, where the elements of the ring and the quasi-addition operation form a group.

  Further, the quasi-addition is commutative, also called *abelian*, such that $n + m = m + n$. Also, the quasi-multiplication operation is associative, such that $(n \cdot m) \cdot k = n \cdot (m \cdot k)$.

  And finally, the quasi-multiplication operation is distributive over the quasi-addition operation, such that $n \cdot (m + k) = (n \cdot m) + (n \cdot k)$

- *Fields*: A finite field is a ring in which the elements—other than the identity element for addition and the quasi-multiplication operation—also form a group.

ECC supports various key-transport schemes defined in X9.63 [48]. The standard defines a 1-Pass and a 3-Pass scheme. For the 1-Pass scheme, one party sends an encrypted random symmetric key using the public key of the other party, where the distribution of the public key is a prerequisite of the scheme. For the 3-Pass scheme, the first party sends a random challenge value to the other party; the second party returns an encrypted random symmetric key using the public key of the other party along with its own random challenge value and a digital signature of both challenge values and the encrypted symmetric key; and the first party responds with a digital signature of both challenge values. The distribution of the public keys to the opposite parties is a prerequisite of the scheme. Refer to Table 7.2 for a summary of cryptography services and Table 7.3 for a summary of cryptography strengths.

7.1.7 Key Agreement

Key agreement is a key-establishment method whereby a cryptographic key is mutually calculated by both parties without transporting the key. The agreed-upon key can be any type of key, whereas the agreeing keys are used strictly to determine the cryptographic key.

- *Diffie-Hellman (DH)* is a key-management scheme published by Whitfield Diffie and Martin Hellman in 1976 [24]; however, historically it was actually invented a few years earlier by Malcolm J. Williamson with the British Government Communications Headquarters (GCHQ), but it was classified information. The schema is based on another mathematically hard problem of finding discrete logarithms. Ordinary logarithms, such as $\log_a(b) = c$, are solutions of the equation $a^c = b$, but discrete logarithms are analogs over a finite group for d and e elements: The equation $d^c = e$ is a discrete logarithm. No efficient algorithms for computing discrete logarithms $\log_d(e)$ are known.

  Various key agreement schemes using Diffie-Hellman are defined in X9.42 [44] and [178]. Essentially, two parties exchange DH public keys and common-domain parameters to mutually calculate a shared secret value that is used to derive a common symmetric key [179]. The DH asymmetric keys might be static or ephemeral. Ephemeral keys are generated, used once, and destroyed. Static keys, on the other hand, are reused numerous times for the duration of their life cycle. Depending on the scheme used, either party might have static keys, ephemeral keys, or both.

- *Elliptic Curve Cryptography (ECC)* supports key-agreement schemes defined in X9.63 [48]. ECC can emulate any of the Diffie-Hellman schemes. Similarly, the ECC asymmetric keys might be static or ephemeral, and either party might have static keys, ephemeral keys, or both, depending on the key-agreement schema selected.

- *Key Components* can also be used to achieve key agreement [49]. This method employs the bitwise logical operator exclusive-OR, also denoted XOR or ⊕ (a circle with a plus sign). Given two bits as input, XOR outputs a single bit where, if the two inputs are the same, it outputs a 0, and if the inputs are different, it outputs a 1. Refer to Table 7.5 for a list of commonly used Boolean operators.

XOR has the interesting property that, if the inputs are only known by two discrete individuals and the result is kept secret, then each individual only has a 0.5 or 50% chance of guessing the output. For every bit added to the output, the probability decreases exponentially, that is, the probability for the first bit times the probability of the second bit, or two bits, is $(0.5)(0.5)$ or $(0.5)^2$ or 0.25 or 25%. Three bits is $(0.5)^3$ or 0.125, four bits is $(0.5)^4$ or 0.0625, and so on. Thus for n bits, the probably is $(0.5)^n$, which rapidly approaches zero, but of course the actual probability is always nonzero.

For this reason, any cryptographic key can be divided into two or more key components, where each component is the

Table 7.5　Boolean Operators

INPUTS		AND	OR	NAND	NOR	XOR
0	0	0	0	1	1	0
0	1	0	1	1	0	1
1	0	0	1	1	0	1
1	1	1	1	0	0	0

full length of the key. So for a 128-bit key, each component is also 128 bits, such that when XORed together, the result is the original key. Each key component is assigned to different individuals such that no one person knows more than one component. Further, the XOR is performed within the security boundary of a cryptographic module such that the key is reconstituted inside the module, and no one ever sees the actual cryptographic key. Key components provide split knowledge of the key, but dual controls must also be employed to prevent the component holders from collusion or compromise. When key components are recorded on a readable medium, the medium is stored in tamper-evident packaging to detect misuse or unauthorized access.

A manual form of key agreement is possible between two or more organizations that need to establish a common symmetric key. Each organization generates a random number for the key component and designates a holder for the key component. Each holder then visits each organization and enters their respective key component into each cryptographic module. When all of the key components have been entered, then each organization XORs the components together to create the key, without any single individual knowing the shared key and without actually transporting the key.

Refer to Table 7.2 for a summary of cryptography services and Table 7.3 for a summary of cryptography strengths.

7.1.8 Summary of Algorithms

Table 7.2 provides a summary of cryptography services identified in Figure 7.1 mapped to the security services of confidentiality, integrity, authentication, nonrepudiation, and key management. Encryption provides confidentiality, but by itself cannot achieve integrity, authentication, or nonrepudiation without additional controls. For example, appending a fixed bit pattern to the cleartext and then encrypting both data fields allows the pattern to be verified when the ciphertext is decrypted. This technique is in fact used with PIN encryption, and the pattern is referred to as sanity bits. The sanity bits are checked when the encrypted PIN block is translated from one key to another as part of the overall process. Issues surrounding nonrepudiation are further discussed in Chapter 5 (Nonrepudiation).

MAC, HMAC, digital signatures, and time-stamp tokens (TST) provide data integrity to the extent that unauthorized modification or substitution can be detected. For MAC and HMAC methods, only the data originator and verifier have access to the symmetric key; otherwise, the integrity is not reliable. For digital signatures, only the signer has access to the private key, but anyone can have access to the public key wrapped within a digital signature. For TST, the key management of the originator and verifier depend on the TST method employed, defined in X9.95 [55].

Time-stamp tokens (TST) methods include digital signatures, MAC, linked (hash) tokens, linked digital signatures, and transient key using digital signatures. For digital signature methods, only the Time-Stamp Authority (TSA) has access to the private key for signing, and the verifier has access to the public key wrapped within a digital signature. For the MAC method, only the TSA has access to the symmetric key to generate and verify the MAC such that the TSA also provides a verification service. For the linked-token method, only the TSA generates and verifies the linked tokens.

Digital signatures inherently provide authentication via signature verification using public key certificates that identify the signer. MAC and HMAC can provide authentication if the proper controls are in place to separate inbound traffic from outbound and prevent misuse of the symmetric verification keys. If the verification process can be misused to generate integrity check values (ICV), then the reliability of the MAC or HMAC is compromised. Further, if the symmetric key is shared by more than the data originator and the verifier, then the reliability of the MAC or HMAC is also reduced.

As discussed in Chapter 3 (Authentication), neither MAC nor HMAC can achieve nonrepudiation, as the control over the symmetric key cannot readily be distinguished between the generators versus the verifiers of the ICV. Only digital signatures or time-stamp tokens (TST) can provide nonrepudiation services.

- For digital signatures, since they can only be generated by the private key, the integrity and authentication is arguably provable to a third party.
- For trusted time stamps, since the TST is generated by an independent third party, the integrity and authentication is provable to a third party.

Table 7.3 provides a summary of cryptography strengths expressed in the number of bits mapped to various key lengths for symmetric, hash, and asymmetric algorithms [177].

Table 7.6 provides a summary of the NSA algorithms, which are categorized into Suite A and Suite B algorithms. Suite A algorithms are classified, meaning they are secret, not publicly available, and restricted for use by the Department of Defense (DoD). Suite B algorithms are unclassified, meaning they are publicly available and are intended for use by international coalition partners with DoD. AES [173] is approved for encryption; the SHA [168] family is approved for hashes; elliptic curve Diffie-Hellman (ECDH) [177] is approved for key establishment; and elliptic curve digital signature algorithm (ECDSA) [170] is approved for digital signatures.

The National Security Agency (NSA) evaluates implementations of either Suite A or Suite B algorithms within the cryptographic hardware module as well as the equipment within which the algorithms and modules are embedded. The National Institute of Standards and Technology (NIST) provides evaluations of algorithms and cryptographic modules for federal agencies. There are also ANSI and ISO standards for evaluating cryptographic modules. Cryptographic modules are discussed further in the next section.

The NIST Cryptographic Algorithm Validation Program (CAVP) certifies FIPS-approved and NIST-recommended cryptographic

Table 7.6 NSA Suite A and B Algorithms

SUITE A CLASSIFIED ALGORITHMS	SUITE B UNCLASSIFIED ALGORITHMS			
	SYMMETRIC ALGORITHMS	HASH ALGORITHMS	KEY ESTABLISHMENT	DIGITAL SIGNATURE
Classified	AES	SHA	ECDH	ECDSA
	FIPS 197	FIPS 180-3	SP 800-56A	FIPS 186-3

algorithms by third-party accredited Cryptographic and Security Testing (CST) laboratories. FIPS-approved algorithms include FIPS 180-3 SHA [167], FIPS 197 AES [173], and NIST Special Publication 800-67 [182] Recommendation for Triple DES (3DES) Block Cipher.

7.2 Cryptographic Modules

Cryptographic modules are basically computing engines that execute cryptographic algorithms, which commonly use cryptographic keys. NIST defines a cryptographic module as a set of hardware, software, or firmware that implements security functions within a cryptographic boundary. Table 7.7 provides a summary of cryptographic modules for NSA, NIST, ANSI, and ISO standards. NSA provides certification for Type 1 and Type 2 products. NIST provides certification for Type 3 products. Other technical laboratories or the vendors themselves might provide evaluation of Type 4 products based on ANSI or ISO standards. The descriptions for each type are provided by CNSSI 4009 [69] glossary.

- *Type 1 product*: Cryptographic equipment, assembly, or component classified or certified by NSA for encrypting and decrypting classified and sensitive national security information when appropriately keyed. Developed using established NSA business processes and containing NSA-approved algorithms, they are used to protect systems requiring the most stringent protection mechanisms.
- *Type 2 product*: Cryptographic equipment, assembly, or component certified by NSA for encrypting or decrypting

Table 7.7   Cryptographic Modules Summary

	CLASSIFIED TYPE 1	SENSITIVE TYPE 2	SENSITIVE BUT UNCLASSIFIED (SBU) TYPE 3				REGISTERED TYPE 4
NSA	Classified		—				
NIST FIPS 140-2	—	—	Level 4	Level 3	Level 2	Level 1	—
			Hardware		Software		
ANSI X9.24	—	—	TRSM		—		—
ANSI X9.97	—	—	SCD		—		—
ISO 13491	—	—	SCD		—		—

sensitive national security information when appropriately keyed. Developed using established NSA business processes and containing NSA-approved algorithms, they are used to protect systems requiring protection mechanisms exceeding best commercial practices, including systems used for the protection of unclassified national security information.

- *Type 3 product*: Unclassified cryptographic equipment, assembly, or component used, when appropriately keyed, for encrypting or decrypting unclassified sensitive U.S. government or commercial information, and to protect systems requiring protection mechanisms consistent with standard commercial practices. These products are developed using established commercial standards and contain NIST-approved cryptographic algorithms/modules or are successfully evaluated by the National Information Assurance Partnership (NIAP).

- *Type 4 product*: Unevaluated commercial cryptographic equipment, assemblies, or components that neither NSA nor NIST certify for any government usage. These products are typically delivered as part of commercial offerings and are commensurate with the vendor's commercial practices. These products may contain either vendor proprietary algorithms, algorithms registered by NIST, or algorithms registered by NIST and published in a FIPS.

The NSA technical requirements, evaluation criteria, and derived tests for Type 1 and Type 2 cryptographic modules are classified and restricted to approved defense industry contractors and manufacturers. Thus, any further discussion on Type 1 or Type 2 cryptographic modules is outside the scope of this book. We can, however, take a look at the NIST, ANSI, and ISO standards for Type 3 products. The NIST FIPS 140 standards for Type 3 products have four levels, where levels 3 and 4 are intended for hardware products, and levels 1 and 2 are for software products. However, some hardware products might only achieve software-level certifications or, if not properly managed, may only operate at software level.

The NIST development of the FIPS 140 cryptographic modules standards [164–166] are independent of ANSI and ISO standards; however, NIST does actively participate in other standards

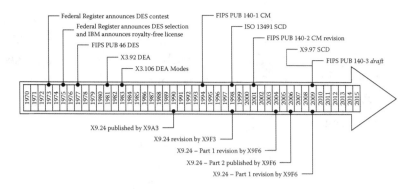

Figure 7.5 Crypto module time line.

development. NIST, ANSI, and ISO standards use different terminology to mean similar things. NIST refers to cryptographic modules
with four levels of assurance, whereas ANSI X9.24 [42] uses the term
tamper resistant security module (TRSM), whereas ISO 13491 [104]
refers to secure cryptographic devices (SCD). To better understand
the similarities and differences between the terms, it is enlightening to
look at the history of when and how these standards were developed.
Figure 7.5 provides a time line of the assorted standards.

To help put things into perspective, the time line begins with the
original 1973 announcement in the *Federal Register* by the National
Bureau of Standards (NBS, now renamed NIST) for a cryptographic algorithm contest to find the Data Encryption Standard
(DES). Two years later, in 1975, there were two related announce-
ments, one from NBS stating that the Lucifer submission from IBM
satisfied the criteria, and another from IBM that it would allow its
patented algorithm a royalty-free license. Based on work by NBS,
NSA, and IBM, the actual FIPS 46 DES [162] was published in
1977. The algorithm was later codified as X3.92 [77] in 1981 and
X3.106 [78–79] in 1983 by the X3 accredited standards committee,
which was founded in 1961 but later renamed itself in 1996 as the
International Committee for Information Technology Standards
(INCITS).

More than 10 years after the original publication of DES, the X9
standards committee published X9.17 [40] and X9.24 [42] developed
by the X9E9 X9A3 banking retail security workgroup. At that time
in 1990, there were no other available standards for cryptographic

hardware, so X9.24 provides requirements for an acceptable tamper-resistant security module (TRSM). Eventually, all of the security work within X9 migrated from other subcommittees to workgroups within the X9F information security subcommittee. The next revision of X9.24 was in 1998 by the X9F3 cryptographic protocol workgroup, and then again in 2004 by the X9F6 cardholder authentication and integrated circuit chips (ICC) workgroup, where it resides today. The term *TRSM* has become entrenched in the payments industry.

Meanwhile, NIST published FIPS 140-1 in 1994 and a revision FIPS 140-2 in 2001 for Type 3 products used to protect sensitive but unclassified (SBU) information for federal government agencies. Another revision, FIPS 140-3, has been under development for many years, but at the time of this writing has not been published as a replacement for the previous versions. X9 standards traditionally only reference other ANSI or ISO standards; however, given the longevity of the FIPS 140 standards, some of the X9 standards do refer to the NIST standards. There was once an effort to incorporate FIPS 140-2 into an ANSI standard; however, since ANSI and ISO standards are copyrighted material and the NIST standards are in the public domain, the NIST material cannot legally be copyrighted or sold.

Independent of X9.24 and FIPS 140-1, an international standard, ISO 13491 [104], was published in 1998 defining requirements for secure cryptographic devices (SCD). This standard was written by the TC68/SC6/WG6 workgroup, and several U.S. experts from X9F participated in its development, including this author. Eventually, ISO 13491–Part 1: Concepts, Requirements and Evaluation Methods was adapted as X9.97 [56] with ANSI notes added, and Part 2: Security Compliance Checklists for Devices Used in Magnetic Stripe Card Systems was adopted as is with no ANSI notes. However, the terminology TRSM is still used in X9.24, while X9.97 refers to SCD. At the same time, cryptographic devices originally connected to mainframe or midrange computer systems were called host security modules (HSM), which eventually morphed into hardware security modules (HSM), denoting the difference between software-based and hardware-based cryptographic modules.

7.2.1 Common Criteria

When the initial work on ISO 13491 began, the Common Criteria was a disjoint set of information technology (IT) security standards, including the Trusted Computer System Evaluation Criteria (TCSEC) in the United States and the Information Technology Security Evaluation Criteria (ITSEC) in Europe. The JTC1/SC27/WG3 workgroup transformed the Common Criteria for Information Technology Security Evaluation version 2.0 and published it as ISO/IEC 15408 [119] in 1996. The following European and North American governmental organizations (listed in alphabetical order) constitute the Common Criteria project sponsoring organizations.

- Canada: Communications Security Establishment (CSE)
- France: Service Central de la Sécurité des Systèmes d'Information (SCSSI)
- Germany: Bundesamt für Sicherheit in der Informationstechnik (BSI)
- Netherlands: Netherlands National Communications Security Agency
- United Kingdom: Communications-Electronics Security Group
- United States: National Institute of Standards and Technology (NIST) and National Security Agency (NSA)

The Common Criteria (CC) does not define security requirements per se; rather, it provides a language to define security requirements in either protection profiles (PP) or security targets (ST) such that the target of evaluation (TOE) can be evaluated by a qualified laboratory. Security targets are intended for a specific product, whereas protection profiles are intended for general reuse. In practice, STs tend to be developed by vendors and used to evaluate their own products. Conversely, PPs are developed by standards bodies. The CC defines seven evaluation assurance levels (EAL) with increasing requirements and more rigorous design, testing, and evaluation criteria.

- EAL1 is the lowest level, being only functionally tested. It consists of the minimal assurances for change control, delivery and operations, development, guideline documents, and tests.

- EAL2 is the next higher level, being structurally tested. It consists of assurances for change control, delivery and operations, development, guideline documents, tests, and vulnerability assessments. Vulnerability assessments are additional requirements from EAL1.
- EAL3 is the next level, being methodically tested and checked. It consists of assurances for change control, delivery and operations, development, guideline documents, life-cycle support, tests, and vulnerability assessments. Life-cycle support is an additional requirement from EAL2.
- EAL4 is the next level, being methodically designed, tested, and reviewed. It consists of assurances for change control, delivery and operations, development, guideline documents, life-cycle support, tests, and vulnerability assessments. Its assurances are more stringent than EAL3.
- EAL5 is a higher level, being semiformally designed and tested. It consists of assurances for change control, delivery and operations, development, guideline documents, life-cycle support, tests, and vulnerability assessments. Its assurances are more stringent than EAL4.
- EAL6 is the next higher level, being semiformally verified, designed, and tested. It consists of assurances for change control, delivery and operations, development, guideline documents, life-cycle support, tests, and vulnerability assessments. Its assurances are more stringent than EAL5.
- EAL7 is the highest level, being formally verified, designed, and tested. It consists of assurances for change control, delivery and operations, development, guideline documents, life-cycle support, tests, and vulnerability assessments. Its assurances are more stringent than EAL6.

The seven assurances are organized into configuration management, delivery and operations, development, guidance documents, life-cycle support, tests, and vulnerability assessment. These assurance classes are further organized into a total of twenty-six assurance families with numerous components and subcomponents.

The National Information Assurance Partnership (NIAP) is a joint venture with the National Institute of Standards and Technology

(NIST) and the National Security Agency (NSA) to accredit laboratories for evaluating product compliance with international standards such as ISO/IEC 15408 Common Criteria. NIAP is also known as the Common Criteria Evaluation and Validation Scheme (CCEVS) for Information Technology Security.

However, the CC has not gained widespread acceptance in the financial services or other industries, and consequently there is a greater reliance on ISO, ANSI, and NIST standards. Despite the fact that NIST is one of the supporting organizations for the United States, the CC has not been wholly adopted for the FIPS publications. The subsequent sections §7.2.2, §7.2.3, and §7.2.4 provide more details for NIST, ANSI, and ISO standards, respectively.

7.2.2 NIST Cryptographic Modules

The NIST Cryptographic Module Validation Program (CMVP) certifies hardware and software modules to the FIPS140-1 and FIPS 140-2 Security Requirements for Cryptographic Modules standards by third-party-accredited Cryptographic and Security Testing (CST) laboratories. The NIST National Voluntary Laboratory Accreditation Program (NVLAP) provides the Cryptographic and Security Testing (CST) Laboratory Accreditation Program (LAP) to approve third-party laboratories to perform conformance testing for CMVP, CAVP, and others, including the Common Criteria Testing labs. Table 7.8 is a summary of the FIPS 140-2 [165] requirements replicated from the NIST standard.

Security levels 1 and 2 are achievable by software solutions, whereas levels 3 and 4 necessitate hardware solutions. However, it is important to recognize that a hardware solution does not automatically get a level 3 or 4; it might only attain a level 2 or even level 1. Further, a hardware solution might have some level 4 or level 3 characteristics, but its overall rating might be lower. Additionally, operating a cryptographic module inconsistent with its security policy will also reduce its security effectiveness. The differences between the levels are summarized as follows.

Table 7.8   FIPS 140-2 Summary

SECURITY AREA	SECURITY LEVEL 1	SECURITY LEVEL 2	SECURITY LEVEL 3	SECURITY LEVEL 4
Cryptographic module specification	Specification of cryptographic module, cryptographic boundary, approved algorithms, and approved modes of operation; description of cryptographic module, including all hardware, software, and firmware components; includes statement of module security policy			
Cryptographic module ports and interfaces	Required and optional interfaces; specification of all interfaces and of all input and output data paths		Data ports for unprotected critical security parameters logically or physically separated from other data ports	
Roles, services, and authentication	Logical separation of required and optional roles and services	Role-based or identity-based operator authentication	Identity-based operator authentication	
Finite-state model	Specification of finite-state model; required states and optional states; state-transition diagram and specification of state transitions			
Physical security	Production-grade equipment	Locks or tamper evidence	Tamper detection and response for covers and doors	Tamper detection and response envelope, includes environmental fault protection or testing
Operational environment	Single operator; executable code; approved integrity technique	Referenced PPs evaluated at EAL2 with specified discretionary access control mechanisms and auditing	Referenced PPs plus trusted path evaluated at EAL3 plus security policy modeling	Referenced PPs plus trusted path evaluated at EAL4
Cryptographic key management	Key-management mechanisms: random number and key generation, key establishment, key distribution, key entry/output, key storage, and key zeroization			
Electromagnetic interference or electromagnetic compatibility	47 CFR FCC Part 15, Subpart B, Class A (Business use); applicable FCC requirements (for radio)		47 CFR FCC Part 15, Subpart B, Class B (home use)	
Self-tests	Power-up tests: cryptographic algorithm tests, software/firmware integrity tests, critical functions tests; conditional tests			

(Continued)

Table 7.8 FIPS 140-2 Summary (Continued)

SECURITY AREA	SECURITY LEVEL 1	SECURITY LEVEL 2	SECURITY LEVEL 3	SECURITY LEVEL 4
Design assurance	Configuration management (CM); secure installation and generation; design and policy correspondence; guidance documents	CM system; secure distribution; functional specification	High-level language implementation	Formal model; detailed explanations (informal proofs); preconditions and postconditions
Mitigation of other attacks	Specification of mitigation of attacks for which no testable requirements are currently available			

- *Security level 1* is the lowest set of requirements. It includes basic requirement for production-grade components and allows cryptographic module software and firmware components to run on a general-purpose computing system using an unevaluated operating system.
- *Security level 2* is the next higher set of requirements. It includes basic requirement for production-grade components and allows cryptographic module software and firmware components to run on a general-purpose computing system using an evaluated (EAL 2+) operating system. Level 2 adds requirements for tamper evidence (e.g., coatings, seals, locks) and minimum role-based authentication for authorization of an operator to assume a specific role and perform a corresponding set of services.
- *Security level 3* is the next higher set of requirements. It includes basic requirement for production-grade components and allows cryptographic module software and firmware components to run on a general-purpose computing system using an evaluated (EAL 3+) operating system or equivalent dedicated computing system. Level 3 adds requirements for tamper responsiveness (detection and reaction), minimum identity-based authentication for authorization of an operator to assume a specific role

and perform a corresponding set of services, and separation of communication ports with trusted paths.

- *Security level 4* is the highest set of requirements. It includes basic requirement for production-grade components and allows cryptographic module software and firmware components to run on a general-purpose computing system using an evaluated (EAL 4+) operating system or equivalent dedicated computing system. Level 4 adds requirements for a complete physical security envelope around a cryptographic module and environmental detection and reaction against environmental failure protection (EFP) and environmental failure testing (EFT).

Table 7.9 provides a summary of the data classification groups from Chapter 2 (Confidentiality) mapped to the cryptographic module security levels. Security levels 1 and 2 are useful for protecting data in controlled environments such as personal computers operated within a physically secured facility. Refer to Chapter 2 (Confidentiality) for data in storage. Security levels 3 and 4 are useful for protecting data in either controlled or uncontrolled environments. Uncontrolled environments can range from servers hosted at a third-party data center to openly public venues such as a shopping mall. While third-party data centers are themselves controlled environments, the reliance on the data center's physical security controls by the subscribing organization

Table 7.9 Data and Cryptographic Module Summary

DATA CLASSIFICATION GROUP	DATA SECURITY LEVEL	FIPS 140-2 SECURITY LEVEL 1	FIPS 140-2 SECURITY LEVEL 2	FIPS 140-2 SECURITY LEVEL 3	FIPS 140-2 SECURITY LEVEL 4
Cryptography data	Highest	Not recommended	Not recommended	Controlled environments	Controlled or uncontrolled
Authentication data	Higher	Not recommended	Not recommended	Controlled environments	Controlled or uncontrolled
Identification data	High	Not recommended	Not recommended	Controlled environments	Controlled or uncontrolled
Confidential data	Medium	Not recommended	Not recommended	Controlled environments	Controlled or uncontrolled
Proprietary data	Low	Not recommended	Controlled environments	Controlled or uncontrolled	Controlled or uncontrolled
Public data	None	Controlled environments	Controlled environments	Controlled or uncontrolled	Controlled or uncontrolled

makes it an uncontrolled environment. ISO 13491 [104] Annex H provides characteristics for uncontrolled, minimally controlled, controlled, and secured environments, as discussed in §7.2.4, and Chapter 2 (Confidentiality) also discusses facility physical and sensor security.

Security level 1 is adequate to protect public data in a controlled environment. However, because personal computers are general purpose, tend to be multiuser, and passwords are often shared, level 1 is not recommended for any higher data levels. With proper procedural controls, level 1 could be used to protect proprietary data within a controlled environment, but failure of any manual processes still puts higher data levels at risk. Level 1 is not reliable enough to use in an uncontrolled environment.

Security level 2 is adequate to protect public or proprietary data in a controlled environment. However, because programs are susceptible to design flaws, coding bugs, malware, and even zero-day vulnerabilities, software is not reliable for higher data levels. Level 2 is not reliable enough to use in an uncontrolled environment.

Security level 3 is sufficient to protect public or proprietary data in uncontrolled or controlled environments, and adequate to protect any data level in a controlled environment. Its hardware nature protects keys within its cryptographic boundary to a reasonable degree of security, but its lack of environmental protections against such changes as heat, cold, vibration, power fluctuations, or electromagnetic fields make it unreliable to detect attacks in uncontrolled environments.

Security level 4 is sufficient to protect any data level in any environment. Their environmental detection and responsiveness capability to zeroize cryptographic keys is reliable enough to operate in uncontrolled environments.

7.2.3 ANSI Tamper Resistant Security Modules

The X9.24 [42] standard is primarily a key-management standard for managing 3DES keys used to protect messages and other sensitive information for the financial services industry. Historically, earlier versions of X9.24 referred specifically to X9.8 [38] for PIN encryption, X9.9 [39] and X9.19 [41] for message authentication (MAC), and X9.17 [40] for data encryption and message authentication. X9.24 also defines requirements for a tamper-resistant security module (TRSM).

The primary TRSM requirement is a combination of physical and functional controls to prevent the determination of any past, present, or future key. The standard allows two different methods to achieve the requirement.

- The first method consists of physical barriers with tamper detect and response mechanisms, which allows the same keys to be retained in the TRSM and used for multiple transactions. The data-protection keys in the TRSM are originally established with another transaction node, and then changed periodically based on a key life-cycle scheme. If the TRSM is attacked, it will zeroize the keys to prevent compromise. This method is consistent with FIPS 140-2 levels 3 and 4, as shown in Table 7.7.
- The second method employs tamper-evident packaging with unique keys per transaction, which limits the use of the keys to a single transaction. This method requires a key-management scheme that synchronizes keys with another transaction node for each transaction. If the TRSM is attacked, the only keys inside are unused, waiting for the next transaction. This method is consistent with FIPS 140-2 level 2, as shown in Table 7.7.

Another significant TRSM requirement is that the establishment of the initial keys is secure, which includes the secrecy of the keys and the legitimacy of the TRSM. This requires a high level of assurance that the TRSM has not been modified or replaced with a counterfeit device. Thus the life cycle of the TRSM is considered before, during, and after its operational deployment, including secured storage and inventory controls. X9.24 further requires that each node in the transaction flow contain a TRSM. Further, the X9.97 [56] standard, adopted from ISO 13421 [104]–Part 1: Concepts, Requirements and Evaluation Methods, refers to secure cryptographic devices (SCD).

7.2.4 ISO Secure Cryptographic Modules

ISO 13491 [104] specifies the requirements for secure cryptographic devices (SCD), which includes cryptographic processes defined in ISO 9564 [99] for PIN encryption, ISO 9807 [101] for message authentication code (MAC), and ISO 11568 [102] for key management.

ISO 13491–Part 1: Concepts, Requirements and Evaluation Methods defines requirements concerning both the operational characteristics of SCD and the management of such devices throughout all phases of their life cycle, and standardizes the methodology for verifying compliance with those requirements. The standard addresses the physical characteristics inside an SCD, device-management controls over an SCD, and environmental-security controls outside an SCD. Three types of physical-security device characteristics are defined.

- *Tamper evidence* is to provide evidence that an attack has been attempted and may or may not have resulted in the unauthorized disclosure, use, or modification of the sensitive information.
- *Tamper resistance* is to block attacks against the information to be protected from unauthorized disclosure, use, or modification by employing passive barriers.
- *Tamper response* is to employ active barriers against attacks aimed at unauthorized disclosure, use, or modification of the protected information.

The SCD must protect against key disclosure and provide assurance that the device and its internal software is genuine. Tamper resistance is the minimal requirement, and tamper responsiveness is optional. Tamper evidence is permitted for some application environments where a derived or irreversible unique key per transaction scheme protects against key disclosure.

Life-cycle management addresses device and environmental controls during manufacturing, postmanufacturing, preuse, usage, and postuse phases. Manufacturing includes design, construction, repair, upgrade, and testing of an SCD. Postmanufacturing consists of the transport and storage of the SCD up to and including initial key loading. Preuse is when the device contains a key but has not yet been placed into operational use. Usage is when the SCD is installed for its intended purpose at its intended location with its operational keys. Postuse is when the SCD is either temporarily removed for relocation or repair, or permanently removed from service without the intent to subsequently reuse it.

ISO 13491 recognizes three evaluation methods for verifying compliance with its requirements for Secure Cryptographic Devices (SCD) which incorporates the cryptographic processes defined in ISO 9564 [99], ISO 9807 [101] and ISO 11568 [102].

- *An informal evaluation* undertaken by an independent auditor using the audit checklists found in Part 2 of the standard. However, the standard does not expect an auditor to have the technical expertise to perform laboratory tests. Rather, the auditor relies on the manufacturer to provide information regarding the characteristics and life-cycle controls of the SCD. Informal evaluations are intended only for low-risk application environments.
- *A semiformal evaluation* undertaken by an evaluation agency. Laboratories that have technical expertise but are not accredited by a formal evaluation authority can use the checklists provided in Part 2 or develop their own derived tests to evaluate the SCD. Organizations often rely on independent third-party laboratories to evaluate products. Semiformal evaluations are intended for medium-risk application environment.
- *A formal evaluation* conducted by an accredited evaluation authority. Formal evaluations include the NIST Cryptographic Module Validation Program (CMVP) and the National Information Assurance Partnership (NIAP) program for the Common Criteria Evaluation and Validation Scheme (CCEVS). Formal evaluations are intended for high-risk application environments

ISO 13491–Part 2: Security Compliance Checklists for Devices Used in Magnetic Stripe Card Systems specifies checklists to be used to evaluate secure cryptographic devices (SCD). Each annex is a checklist addressing various types of devices with PIN, MAC, key management, and digital-signatures capabilities. The checklists are based on the requirements defined in Part 1 of the standard.

- *Annex A: Physical, Logical and Device Management Characteristics Common to All Secure Cryptographic Devices* is intended to be part of any ISO 13491 evaluation, in combination with one or more of the other annexes. The evaluator must have sufficient expertise to determine and confirm the characteristics and life-cycle practices of the SCD. Some of this information will be provided by the manufacturer, some by inspection or testing of the SCD, and some by entity interviews and observations.

Device characteristics: These requirements are focused on physical and logical security controls of the SCD to prevent disclosure of any cryptographic keys, other sensitive cryptographic information, or the data being protected by the cryptographic algorithms. They are logically grouped into Tamper-Evident, Tamper-Resistant, Tamper-Responsive, and Logical Security characteristics. Annex A includes chemical attacks (e.g., solvents), scanning attacks (e.g., scanning electron microscope), mechanical attacks (e.g., drilling, cutting, probing), thermal attacks (e.g., high and low temperature extremes), radiation attacks (e.g., X-rays), information leakage through covert channels (e.g., power supply, timing), and failure attacks (e.g., forcing conditions where error handling reveals sensitive data).

Device management: These requirements are focused on manual and automated inventory controls provided by each entity over the SDC life cycle. In general, the identity of the device and its operational condition (e.g., with or without keys) must be constantly maintained. The duality of device management versus cryptographic key management over the preuse, use, and postuse phases will vary, depending on when and who loads the initial keys and operates the SCD.

- *Annex B: Devices with PIN Entry Functionality* is for merchant devices that accept, encrypt, and transmit personal identification numbers (PIN). In addition to Annex A device characteristics and requirements, this annex provides additional physical and logical security controls along with extra device management focusing on uncontrolled environments.

Device characteristics: These additional requirements address physical and logical controls to protect entry and processing of the PIN and its related encryption keys. Requirements include compliance with ISO 9564 [99] and separation of functionality to ensure privacy of the PIN. For example, if the keypad is used to enter other data besides the PIN, such as a dollar amount, the device must be cognizant of the difference to encrypt the PIN upon entry to avoid its exposure. As another example, if the SCD supports multiple acquirers with different keys, then the correct PIN encryption key must be selected.

Device management: These extra requirements address controls for initial key loading and PIN entry. For example, a unique key per device compartmentalizes damage if that encryption key is compromised; only those transactions processed by the compromised device are affected. Other examples include physical barriers to prevent viewing of the PIN entry keystrokes and inventory controls to prevent a device from being stolen or substituted.

- *Annex C: Devices with PIN Management Functionality* is for acquirer or issuer devices that issue, translate, or verify the PIN. In addition to Annex A (device characteristics and requirements), this annex provides additional physical and logical security controls along with extra device management, focusing on controlled and secured environments.

  Device characteristics: These additional requirements include physical security controls to prevent devices from unauthorized removal and logical security controls to protect PIN material and related cryptographic keys from disclosure.

  Device management: These extra requirements, defined in Annex E, address unauthorized removal, usage, or access across the device life cycle.

- *Annex D: Devices with Message Authentication Functionality* is for devices that generate or verify message authentication codes (MAC). In addition to Annex A (device characteristics and requirements), this annex provides additional logical security controls aligned with ISO 9807 [101].

  Logical device characteristics: These additional logical security controls focus on key-management controls for handling symmetric MAC keys.

- *Annex E: Devices with Key Generation Functionality* is for devices that generate or derive symmetric or asymmetric keys. Some key-generation devices are used to only inject or distribute keys to other devices, whereas others generate and use the cryptographic keys. In addition to Annex A (device characteristics and requirements), this annex provides additional physical and logical security controls along with extra device management controls.

Device characteristics: These additional requirements include physical security controls to prevent devices from unauthorized removal and logical security controls to prevent disclosure or misuse of cryptographic keys.

Device management: These extra requirements address unauthorized removal, usage, or access across the device life cycle. Facility, inventory, and monitoring controls, including manual procedures, are defined to deter and detect unauthorized device removal or access.

- *Annex F: Devices with Key Transfer and Loading Functionality* is for devices used to export, transfer, or import cryptographic keys from one device to another. In addition to Annex A (device characteristics and requirements), this annex provides additional physical and logical security controls along with extra device management controls.

Device characteristics: These additional requirements include physical security controls to prevent devices from unauthorized removal and logical security controls to prevent disclosure of cryptographic keys.

Device management: These extra requirements address manual and automated procedures to prevent disclosure of cryptographic keys. Methods include key encryption, plaintext keys under dual control with split knowledge, passwords, and protected communication pathways.

- *Annex G: Devices with Digital Signature Functionality* is for devices that generate or verify digital signatures for message integrity and authentication. In addition to Annex A (device characteristics and requirements), this annex provides extra device management controls for nonrepudiation services; however, it does not address public key infrastructure (PKI) governance or certificate policies and practices for a certificate authority (CA).

Device characteristics: These additional requirements address physical and logical controls to protect nonrepudiation services and device requirements defined in Annex E for key generation for SCDs.

Device management: These extra requirements address nonrepudiation for signature generation and public key validation for signature verification.

- *Annex H: Categorization of Environments* provides characteristics for minimally controlled environments, controlled environments, and secure environments.

Uncontrolled environments: The annex does not provide security requirements for uncontrolled environments. Uncontrolled environments include public areas, office buildings, or other facilities where physical access has limited controls with no real-time monitoring.

Minimally controlled environments: The annex provides requirements to detect an attack or theft within a given maximum period of time. A minimally controlled environment is similar to a normal computer room or server closet with physical access controls, allowing access to authorized personnel. Such environments might be monitored, alarmed, or contained within an uncontrolled environment that may be manned 24 hours a day, 7 days a week.

Controlled environments: The annex provides requirements to limit the types of attacks that can be made on a device and the time available for some types of attacks. Annex H describes controlled environments as similar to normal computer rooms, where there are physical and logical access controls, allowing access only to authorized personnel; however, there are more-stringent access controls, where both the interior and the entrances to the environment are under surveillance.

Secure environments: The annex provides requirements to protect an SCD against many types of physical and logical attacks, with restricted access to the environment, dual controls, monitoring, alarms, alerts, and inventory controls. Annex H describes a secure environment as providing an outer shell of protection around an insecure device, with significantly more controls than a controlled environment. Often the secure environment is a dedicated room designed and built for this specific purpose or a safe or a secure cabinet. It is often contained within a larger controlled environment. Only persons with authorized access to the device are permitted, relying on both physical and logical access controls with validated ingress and egress. Further, all security procedures are well documented, followed, and periodically assessed by an internal or external professional whose reports are reviewed by a formal audit body.

ISO 13491–Part 1: Concepts, Requirements and Evaluation Methods were adapted by ANSI as X9.97 [56], with thirteen ANSI notes added for clarification. ISO 13491–Part 2: Security Compliance Checklists for Devices Used in Magnetic Stripe Card Systems was adopted as is, with no ANSI notes.

7.3 Key-Management Life Cycle

Key management addresses the secure handling of cryptographic material, including symmetric and asymmetric keys from the point and time of creation to destruction. Some cryptographic material might be managed using manual procedures, while others are via automated processes. The length of time a key is used is called its "crypto period." However, there are also preuse and postuse security issues that need addressing. As an introduction to the key life cycle and its security controls, we first look at the cryptography risks relative to managing keys.

7.3.1 Cryptography Risks

Cryptographic keys have a definitive life cycle; keys are created, utilized, and eventually destroyed, replaced, and sometimes archived. Keys are never used forever. This is primarily due to the risk that, given enough time and resources, any key can eventually be determined, whether due to exhaustive key attack or information leakage attacks.

An exhaustive key attack is simply trying every possible key until the right one is found. For example, in 1999 the DES III Challenge solved the search for a 56-bit key, or about 72 quadrillion keys (or 72 with 15 zeroes) in 22 hours and 15 minutes, claiming an average 245 billion DES calculations per second [9]. As each additional bit doubles the key space, larger keys require much more computing power; however Moore's Law [224] of exponential growth for transistor integration continues to increase computing power. So, if computing power has increased a thousandfold since then, the same challenge would be achievable in less than an hour. Modern symmetric keys of 128 bits or larger make exhaustive key search infeasible; however, modern cryptanalysis includes mathematical approaches that are more efficient than exhaustive searches, which Moore's Law continues to enable. This is also true for asymmetric algorithms, where mathematical solutions are more prevalent.

Another significant risk of using the same key too often is information leakage. Reusing the same key numerous times for similar data often reveals information about the underlying key. There are side-channel attacks such as power consumption, electromagnetic radiation, timing discrepancies, or fault injections that can reveal information about the key. For example, differential power analysis (DPA) and related attacks are well documented [25]. Cryptographic protocols such as SSL [27] or TLS [26, 28] are likewise known to leak information. Essentially, given enough time and resources, any cryptographic key can be determined. Thus it is important to change keys periodically to avoid cryptanalysis attacks.

Misusing keys by using them for unintended purposes puts protected data at risk. For example, a PIN-encryption key or a key-encryption key (KEK) should never be used as a data-encryption key; otherwise, the PIN or encrypted key can be decrypted and disclosed. As another example, an RSA key pair should not be used for key exchange and digital signature; otherwise, an encrypted key might be misinterpreted as an encrypted hash, which would be decrypted as part of the signature verification process, disclosing the encrypted key. Thus it is important to only use keys for their intended purpose.

Allowing unauthorized access to the cryptographic system puts keys or data at risk. If keys are protected using cryptographic software modules, then the overall security essentially reduces to access controls. Even if keys are stored in an encrypted format, the key-encryption key (KEK) is still vulnerable to access controls. Since many system administrators have super-user privileges enabling access to any file, cryptographic keys are at risk of compromise. Even when keys are protected using cryptographic hardware modules, unauthorized access allows data misuse such as decrypting sensitive data and generating illicit integrity check values (ICV), including MAC, HMAC, or digital signatures.

Cryptographic implementations that have vulnerabilities put keys or data at risk. Running older software or firmware with unapplied security patches can compromise protocols, systems, or devices. Relying on vendor defaults such as passwords, protocols, or parameters can results in operational instabilities or lowered security thresholds. Using older protocols, outdated algorithms, or shorter keys can allow attacks that ultimately compromise keys or data. For example, the SSL v3.0 protocol supports older ciphersuites with 40-bit and 56-bit algorithms, and has known weaknesses. As another example, older TLS protocols have exploitable error-recovery issues.

7.3.2 Life-Cycle Phases

Like any other data element, cryptographic keys have a life cycle; they have a definitive begin time, a usage period, and an end time. The specific phases of the key life cycle are somewhat a matter of opinion, as ANSI, ISO, and NIST standards do not all use the same terms or phrases. However, the standards are not that dissimilar and are mostly aligned as shown in Table 7.10.

Table 7.10 provides a common key-management life cycle and a mapping to common ANSI, ISO, and NIST standards, including X9.24 [42], X9.79 [51], ISO/IEC 11770 [117], ISO 11578 [102], NIST

Table 7.10 Key-Management Life Cycle

	GENERATION	DISTRIBUTION	USAGE	BACKUP	REVOCATION	TERMINATION	ARCHIVE
ANSI	Generation	Distribution	Usage	Backup	Revocation	Termination	Archive
	Generation	Distribution	Usage	Storage	—	Destruction	Archive
ISO	Generation	Distribution	Usage	Recovery	—	Destruction	Archive
	Pending active		Active		Postactive		—
NIST	Preactivation		Active		Revoke	Destroy	—

Special Publication 800-57 [180], and NIST Special Publication 800-130 [186]. These descriptions of the seven key-management life-cycle phases are based on ANSI, ISO, and NIST standards.

- *Key generation*: This is when symmetric keys or asymmetric key pairs are generated. Generation includes random number generation, prime number generation, and cryptographic credential generation, such as obtaining X.509 [80] certificates. ANSI and ISO standards recognize key generation as a distinctive state, whereas other ISO and NIST standards include generation in broader phases such as pending active or preactivation.

- *Key distribution*: This is when symmetric keys, asymmetric public keys, or asymmetric private keys are transported from their generation origin to one or more operational locations. Distribution includes transport, validation, and installation of keys and related cryptographic parameters. ANSI and ISO standards recognize key distribution as a distinctive state, whereas other ISO and NIST standards include distribution in broader phases such as pending active or preactivation.

- *Key usage*: This is when symmetric or asymmetric keys are employed for their intended use, and no other. Usage includes data encryption, MAC, HMAC, digital signatures, or other cryptographic processes. ANSI, ISO, and NIST standards recognize key usage [105], although NIST refers to active keys.

- *Key backup*: This is when symmetric or asymmetric keys are backed up for recovery in case of equipment failure or other outages that affect local key storage. Key backup and recovery processes might be automated or manual procedures. ANSI and ISO standards recognize key backup, although other terms include *storage* and *recovery*. Other ISO standards and NIST include storage, backup, and recovery in broader phases such as usage or active keys.

- *Key revocation*: This is when a cryptographic key operational status is canceled. *Revocation* is normally a term associated with public key certificates. However, in a more general sense, the operational status of any key, including symmetric or asymmetric private keys, might be revoked using various methods. Some of the ANSI standards and NIST standards recognize revocation, but other ANSI and ISO standards do not address key revocation.

- *Key termination*: This is when a cryptographic key is at the end of its operational usage such that all copies of the key are destroyed, except possibly for an archived key, which ensures that the key is put permanently out of operation. ANSI, ISO, and NIST standards recognize key termination, although it is typically referred to as destruction. Other ISO standards include destruction in a broader phase, such as postactive.

- *Key archive*: This is when a cryptographic key has been removed from its operational usage but a single copy is retained for data validation. For example, a MAC key might be archived to validate the integrity of old documents. Archived keys are never reused in operational environments. ANSI and some ISO standards recognize key archival; however, other ISO and NIST standards do not address archiving.

The transit of cryptographic keys from one life-cycle state to another varies greatly, depending on the type of key, its operational environment, its purpose, and its longevity. For example, symmetric keys often have different purposes than asymmetric keys, and asymmetric key pairs have a duality of public and private keys that often have different operational periods. As another example, SSL and its session keys have a very different purpose and environments than PIN encryption keys used at point-of-sale (POS) terminals and automated teller machines (ATM). Figure 7.6 shows the life-cycle phases with numbered transition arrows indicating "normal" and "abbreviated" transitions.

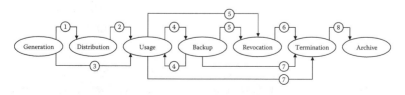

Figure 7.6   Key-management life cycle.

Cryptographic keys transition from one state to another; however, not every key will necessarily exist in every state, as some transitions will bypass some phases.

1. The key transitions from its generation point of origin to a distribution status for disseminating the key to one or more operational environments. Distribution methods include both key transport and key-establishment techniques as discussed in §7.1.6 and §7.1.7, respectively.

2. The key transitions from the distribution process to its operational usage environment. Usage methods include encryption, MAC, HMAC, hash, digital signature, and key management as discussed in §7.1.

3. The key transitions directly from generation to its operational usage status when the key is generated and used within the same environment. Examples include Web servers that generate unique SSL keys, cryptographic devices that encrypt and store keys externally in databases, or systems that generate digital signatures for nonrepudiation purposes.

4. A copy of the key transitions from its operational environment to a backup environment. For the case when the operational copy is lost or corrupted, the operational key can be recovered from the backup copy. The transition is then from usage to backup or from backup to usage.

5. The key transitions from its backup (and operational usage) environments to a revocation status. Revocation occurs when a key has prematurely reached the end of its life cycle due to an unanticipated event such as key compromise or systems being decommissioned.

6. The key transitions from its revocation status to a termination status when the revoked key reaches its normally scheduled life-cycle end. Termination is the process for destroying all copies of the key, including all operational, backup, and revocation environments.

7. The key transitions from its operational usages and backup status to a termination status when the key reaches its normally scheduled life-cycle end. Termination is the process for

destroying all copies of the key, including all operational and backup environments.

8. The key transitions from a termination state to an archive status when one copy of the key is kept for postproduction purposes. For example, a digital certificate might be retained past its validity date to verify former digital signatures, or a MAC key might be archived to verify previous messages with a MAC.

Cryptographic requirements for many of the key-management life-cycle phases can be found in ANSI, ISO, and NIST standards. However, the standards are not fully aligned; controls for symmetric keys vary from asymmetric keys; and some security areas tend to be more emphasized than others.

7.3.3 Life-Cycle Controls

In general key-management controls for symmetric and asymmetric keys can be summarized as general controls that apply to each phase of the key life cycle and specific controls for each phase. General security controls applicable to each phase of the key life cycle include the following:

1. The confidentiality, integrity, and authenticity of symmetric and asymmetric private keys are maintained in every phase of the key-management life cycle. Key confidentiality is necessary to prevent a compromise of the key or any related cryptographic material that can be misused to recreate a key. Confidentiality literally means that the key is never known by any individual. Unlike a PIN or passwords, where the authorized person knows the authentication data, symmetric and asymmetric private keys cannot be known by anyone; otherwise, the key is no longer secret. Key integrity and authenticity are also necessary to prevent inadvertent or adversarial modification or substitution of the key.

   Note that key confidentiality is problematic when relying solely on cryptographic software modules and access controls, as the overall security is often dependent on "trusted" developers and administrators to keep keys secret. However, recognizing that anyone can be bribed or coerced, the best approach is to avoid the issue altogether by implementing key management with split knowledge and dual control. For example, an administrator might run a program that generates a random key and writes it to a file in such a manner that the admin can copy and install the file onto another system without having the capability to view the file contents.

2. The integrity and authenticity of asymmetric public keys are maintained in every phase of the key-management life cycle. Since the intent of a public key is to be public and usable by anyone, confidentiality is not needed. However, integrity and authenticity are necessary to prevent inadvertent or adversarial modification or substitution of the key.

3. Entities are authenticated, authorized, and held accountable in every phase of the key-management life cycle. Unauthenticated entities are not permitted access to any cryptographic system. Unauthorized entities are not permitted to execute any cryptographic function. Event logs are generated and maintained for end-to-end accountability of all entities.

4. Key functionality is maintained in every phase of the key-management life cycle, such that keys are only used for their intended purpose and no others. Key tagging, manual procedures, or automated controls might be necessary to identify and manage key functionality.

Security controls specific to the key-generation phase include the following:

5. Only reliable algorithms are used to generate cryptographic material, including random numbers, prime numbers, symmetric keys, and asymmetric key pairs.

   For example, random numbers are only generated using reliable random number generation (RNG) algorithms or pseudo random number generation (PRNG) algorithms. PRNG algorithms are deterministic, in that the same input will always produce the same output, such that the random number is repeatable. Therefore the PRNG input, called a seed, is cryptographic material whose confidentiality, integrity, and authenticity is also maintained. RNG methods are nondeterministic, in that the same random number is not repeatable, except by chance. Refer to X9.82 [53] for RNG and PRNG requirements and methods.

As another example, primes are only generated using reliable prime number generation (PNG) algorithms. Primes are numbers only divisible by 1 and themselves. For example, 5 and 7 are primes, but 9 is divisible by 3 and 12 is divisible by 2, 3, and 6, so they are not prime. Primes can be generated either deterministically or probabilistically. Deterministic methods guarantee that a number is prime, whereas probabilistic methods employ testing to ensure a small error of generating a nonprime number. Refer to X9.80 [52].

6. Keys are generated for specific cryptographic purposes, applications, and periods. A key generated for one purpose should never be used for another. A key generated for one application should not be reused for another, as the more locations the same key is stored and used, the more likely it is that a key will be compromised. Further, one application might have different operational risks than another, and if a key is compromised by one application, then it is inadvertently compromised by the other. Using different keys compartmentalizes damage among applications. A key should also not be used past its crypto period, as using a key for too long increases the chances of the key being determined. For details refer to §7.3.1, where cryptography risks are discussed.

Security controls specific to the key-distribution phase include the following:

7. Distribution and installation of symmetric keys and asymmetric private keys are only performed by authorized entities. Any unauthorized distribution or installation of keys compromises the unauthorized keys and can compromise other keys or data on the target system. Similar authentication controls over asymmetric public keys are typically not necessary, as a public key is intended for use by any relying party.

8. The integrity and authenticity of symmetric keys and asymmetric key pairs are validated prior to installation. Installing incorrect, modified, or substituted cryptographic materials

can compromise other keys or data on the target system. Further, any data collected previously from any system protected by the target system might also be compromised.

Security controls specific to the key usage phase include the following:

9. The integrity and authenticity of symmetric keys and asymmetric key pairs are validated prior to usage. This is especially critical for public keys, as any substitution can allow a man-in-the-middle (MITM) attack. Further, since revocation occurs prior to the regular crypto period, the validity of the key is also validated.

Security controls specific to the key backup phase include the following:

10. The key backup phase has basically the same controls as for key distribution. Backup and recovery functions are only performed by authorized entities, and the integrity and authenticity of symmetric keys and asymmetric key pairs are validated prior to installation.

Security controls specific to the key revocation phase include the following:

11. Revocation of symmetric keys and asymmetric key pairs are only performed by authorized entities and should be under dual control, as unauthorized revocation is essentially a denial-of-service attack. Further, systems are expected to validate keys such that revoked keys are not used.

    Examples of revocation without key compromise include the following:
    • Employment is terminated or the individual is deceased, such that the keys are no longer valid.
    • Applications are decommissioned, such that the keys are no longer valid.
    • Applications are upgraded to larger key sizes or different algorithms, such that the old keys are no longer valid.
    • Merger or acquisition [72] changes system ownership, such that new keys prematurely replace the old keys prior to their expiration dates.

- Cessation of operations, such that the keys are no longer valid.

Examples of revocation due to known or suspected key
compromise include the following:

- Cryptographic hardware modules containing keys that
are missing.
- Cryptographic hardware or software modules containing
keys that have had unauthorized access.
- Data are discovered with illegitimate integrity check values (ICV) including digital signatures.
- Data are discovered outside secured storage in an unencrypted format.

Security controls specific to the key-termination phase include
the following:

12. All instances of the symmetric keys and asymmetric private
keys are permanently destroyed, with the possible exception
of an archived key. Logs are especially important to validate
that all keys were successfully deleted. An additional consideration is the validation of key destruction by another party
not under the direct control of the original organization.

Security controls specific to the key-archive phase include the
following:

13. Archived keys are only used to validate cryptographic operations in isolated systems and are never used in the original
production systems. Examples of archived keys include the
following:

- Asymmetric public keys to validate expired certificates
or other aged digital signatures used for authentication,
authorization, or nonrepudiation.
- Symmetric keys to validate aged MAC or HMAC
messages.

Each of these general and specific security controls require that
the appropriate policies, practices, and procedures be documented and
followed accordingly. Procedures are executed to meet practices, and
practices can be audited to validate that policies are followed.

7.4 Cryptographic Architecture

A cryptographic architecture is an organized set of characteristics that describe the who, what, where, when, how, and why of the operational environment and associated key-management life-cycle controls, including automated and manual processes. Similar to a network architecture that identifies the various information technology components—such as routers, switches, firewalls, and servers—a cryptographic architecture identifies comparable information regarding algorithms, modules, and keys. The major components of a cryptographic architecture include the following items:

- *Security policies*: This is a collection of policy statements addressing security controls for managing cryptographic keys. Since policy addresses the "what" goals, the same policy can and should be used across multiple operational environments. A common security policy provides consistency and reliability across an organization.
- *Security practices*: This is a collection of practice statements addressing security controls for managing cryptographic keys. Practices are the "how" for achieving the "what" goals, which vary per operational environment; thus even though many different environments share common controls, practice statements are often managed separately.
- *Security procedures*: This is a collection of detailed procedural statements addressing regular and irregular processes for managing cryptographic keys. Regular processes include scheduled key replacements, access-control review and approvals, and monitoring. Irregular processes include incident responses, key recovery, and emergency replacement due to key compromise.
- *Key inventory*: This is a catalog of keys and their characteristics used within the operational environment. The nature and format of the inventory can be almost anything from a manual list to an automated database. The cryptography characteristics include a unique key identifier or name, algorithm, size, purpose, and owner.
- *Network diagram*: This is a graphic showing the various infrastructure devices, including switches, routers, firewalls, servers, and the like. A complete diagram might include

Internet protocol (IP) address ranges, device names, and primary and alternate connections. Connections can be labeled by type, such as Ethernet, dial-up, wireless, and cellular. Administrative connections can also be shown for managing the numerous infrastructure devices.

- *Data flow diagram*: This is a graphic superimposed over the network diagram showing the data paths along the connections. A complete flow diagram might include the direction of the data, communication protocols, message formats, and data classifications. In addition to the data classification groups, depending on the focus of the assessment, other data categories might be included, such as health-care, financial, or payment data.
- *Key deployment diagram*: This is another graphic overlay to the data flow and network diagrams showing where cryptographic solutions and keys are deployed. Cryptography solutions include symmetric keys, asymmetric key pairs, and protocols for data in transit, data in process, and data in storage. The key deployment diagram is aligned with the cryptography key inventory.

7.4.1 Security Policies, Practices, and Procedures

Security policies state the "what" in the way of goals; practices describe the "how" as tactics to achieve the goals; and the procedures provide the step-by-step "who" and "when" processes. The distinction between policies, practices, and procedures is often confused, so to better illustrate the differences, examples of each are provided. An example policy statement is as follows:

Data shall be protected commensurate with its data classification.

While this appears to be a rather simplistic statement, it has important implications with regard to design decisions, operational controls, and costing. Each policy statement often decomposes into several practices statements. For example, consider the data classifications groups discussed in Chapter 2 (Confidentiality) and the following practice statements:

a. The confidentiality, integrity, and authenticity of symmetric keys and asymmetric private keys are managed over the key-management life cycle.
b. The integrity and authenticity of asymmetric public keys are managed over the key-management life cycle.
c. The confidentiality, integrity, and authenticity of authentication data are managed in transit, process, and storage.
d. The integrity and authenticity of identification data are managed in transit and storage.
e. The confidentiality, integrity, and authenticity of confidential data are managed in transit and storage.
f. The confidentiality, integrity, and authenticity of proprietary data are managed in transit and storage.
g. The integrity and authenticity of public data are managed in transit and storage.

In this example, each classification group (cryptography data, authentication data, identification data, confidential data, proprietary data, and public data) has its own practice statement, with cryptography having two statements. While these practice statements could be merged into fewer ones, the controls for each data type will vary widely in different application environments; therefore, maintaining separate practice statements will facilitate the management of various security procedures. Further, each practice statement typically decomposes into multiple procedures. For example, consider procedures for the generation of an asymmetric key pair.

- Example Step 1: The security officer escorts two key administrators into the secured facility where the hardware security module (HSM) resides.
- Example Step 2: The first key administrator enters the command to change the HSM into its administration mode, and authenticates to the HSM.
- Example Step 3: The second key administrator authenticates to the HSM and verifies that the HSM is in administration mode.
- Example Step 4: The second key administrator enters the command to generate an asymmetric key pair, and authenticates to the HSM.

- Example Step 5: The first key administrator authenticates to the HSM and verifies that the HSM has successfully generated the asymmetric key pair.
- Example Step 6: The first key administrator enters the command to change the HSM into its production mode, and authenticates to the HSM.
- Example Step 7: The second key administrator authenticates to the HSM and verifies that the HSM is in production mode.
- Example Step 8: The security officer escorts both key administrators out of the secured facility where the hardware security module (HSM) resides.

Procedures need to be unambiguous, thoroughly tested, and rehearsed by all participants. This is especially important for unscheduled security incidents, such as a key compromise, or other emergency incidents when personnel are operating under stress and more likely to make mistakes. Such proactive preparedness requires that cryptographic implementations have test environments to develop, test, and exercise all procedures. There are several security policy standards available that can be used as frameworks for developing policies and practices. For example, ISO Technical Report 13569 [106] provides information security guidelines for financial services and includes general information technology controls.

- Information technology (IT) security is managed and documented throughout the organization, beginning at the corporate level, and permeating to each division, group, and department. Security policies and practices include roles and responsibilities for security governance, including education and awareness; incident response; business continuity and disaster recovery; risk assessments; and audit, legal, compliance, and exception management.
- Security safeguards selection and implementation are based on risk assessments enabling acceptance, avoidance, or remediation decisions. Safeguards include physical environment, personnel, administration, hardware, software, computer systems, network devices, and communications. The selection process considers limitations, including scheduling, financial,

technological, sociological, environmental, and legal constraints. Implementation addresses several areas, including data classifications access controls, authentication, authorization, audit trails, change controls, security awareness, and human resources.

- Communications covers all aspects of information exchange and storage, including the spoken word, telephony systems, mobile devices, voicemail, voice response units (VRU), fax machines, image capture and transfer, e-mail messages and attachments, and paper documents. Since the technical report focuses on financial services, banking and payment systems are addressed, including personal computers and browsers, automatic teller machines (ATM), point-of-sale (POS) terminals, and electronic funds transfer (EFT) networks.

- Cryptography safeguards include data and PIN encryption, message authentication codes (MAC), digital signatures, hardware versus software modules, and key management. Data encryption includes end-to-end encryption, point-to-point link encryption, or local encryption. The ISO/IEC twenty-seven-thousand (27xxx) standards series addresses a wide variety of security techniques for information technology, including requirements [133], practices [134], implementation guidelines [135], measurements [136], risk management [137], audit and certification [138], information security management systems auditor guidelines [139], information security controls auditor guidelines [140], communications [141], telecommunication guidelines [142], guidance on ISO/IEC 27000 and ISO/IEC 20000 [143], and financial service guidelines [144]. As another example, ISO/IEC 27002 [134] provides a code of practice for IT security organized into a dozen security topics:
  - Risk management
  - Security policy
  - Information security organization
  - Asset management
  - Human resources
  - Physical and environmental controls
  - Communications and operations management

- Access controls
- Information systems acquisition, development, and maintenance
- Information security incident management
- Business-continuity management
- Compliance

Several X9 standards, including X9.79 [51], X9.84 [54], X9.95 [55], X9.112 [59], and X9.117 [60], provide control objectives and evaluation criteria based on ISO/IEC 27002 security topics. When the ANSI standards X9.79 and X9.84 were translated to ISO 21188 [110] and ISO 19092 [109], respectively, the control objectives were included in the ISO standards. Any of these standards provides a reasonable security policies and practices framework.

7.4.2 Key Inventory

An inventory of keys is an important mechanism for monitoring cryptographic information in every phase of the key-management life cycle. New entries are added when keys are generated. Status might be updated during distribution, usage, or backup and recovery, depending on the real-time notification capabilities of the key-management system. Status is updated when the key is revoked, terminated, or archived. Key inventory information includes the following:

- *Key name*: This is a relatively unique value to distinguish one key from another. Since symmetric keys and asymmetric private keys cannot be displayed, and asymmetric public keys are just long strings of binary bits represented as hexadecimal numbers, short reference names are much easier to use. However, key names need to be meaningful. Key names might include its key check value (KCV); they might be based on system names, or some other naming scheme. Whatever naming convention is employed, it is important that a naming scheme be well defined for unambiguous names. For example, naming keys after Snow White's seven dwarfs (i.e., Bashful, Doc, Dopey, Grumpy, Happy, Sleepy, and Sneezy) or Santa's eight reindeer (i.e., Dasher, Dancer, Prancer, Vixen, Comet,

Table 7.11 Hexadecimal Digits

BINARY	DECIMAL	HEX	BINARY	DECIMAL	HEX
0000	0	0	1000	8	9
0001	1	1	1001	9	8
0010	2	2	1010	10	A
0011	3	3	1011	11	B
0100	4	4	1100	12	C
0101	5	5	1101	13	D
0110	6	6	1110	14	E
0111	7	7	1111	15	F

Cupid, Donder, and Blitzen) might be clever but not very insightful or meaningful. Table 7.11 provides the equivalence between binary, decimal, and hexadecimal "hex" numbers.

- *Key check value*: This is a cryptographically derived integrity value specifically used for cryptographic keys. The most common key-check value (KCV) algorithm defined in X9.24 [42] for 3DES is to encrypt a string of binary zeros and use the six-leftmost hexadecimal digits. Since the 3DES data size is 16-hex digits (or 64 bits), the 6-hex digits (or 24 bits) are sufficient to provide a relatively unique value but insufficient to provide a plaintext-ciphertext sample for an exhaustive key attack. Another type of KCV algorithm for certificates is a SHA-1 hash of the X.509 [80] certificate, commonly called the thumbprint. Other types of integrity check values (ICV) for data are discussed in Chapter 4 (Integrity).

- *Key dates*: This is a set of one or more dates, the minimal being its expiration date for when the key is terminated. More information might include the key-generation date, where the expiration date would be the cryptoperiod added to the generation date. Other dates might reflect each of the key-management life-cycle phases, including the archive start and end dates. Similarly, X.509 [80] certificates have valid not-before and not-after dates.

- *Key locations*: This is a list of sites where each instance of the key resides, including the key life-cycle usage, backup, and archive phases. Locations might be the name or address of a facility or data center, the equipment rack identification number, or the equipment label or serial number. For sites not located at a regular facility, such as an ATM or POS terminal, the address, store number, and device serial number would suffice. The location needs to be explicit and unambiguous. If the device has a radio-frequency identification (RFID) tag, then the identifier should be included in the key location or key name.

- *Algorithm*: This identifies the symmetric or asymmetric algorithm of the cryptographic key, usually expressed as the algorithm abbreviation such as 3DES, AES, RSA, DSA, or ECDSA. However, not all abbreviations are universal and thus are not necessarily consistent. For example, FIPS 46-3 [162] is the Data Encryption Standard (DES) that defines the Data Encryption Algorithm (DEA), so historically both abbreviations DEA or DES have been used. As another example, NIST Special Publication 800-67 [182] defines the Triple DES algorithm, but some use the abbreviation TDES while others (including this author) prefer 3DES. Using different abbreviations for the same algorithm can inhibit good searches and cause inaccurate reports.

- *Domain parameters*: This allows algorithm-specific parameters to be recorded, such as the RSA exponent or domain parameters for the elliptic curve (EC) or the Diffie-Hellman algorithms.

- *Key length*: This specifies the length of the key, and it should be expressed in the number of cryptographic bits. Again, consistency is important. Stating the number of hexadecimal digits, the number of bytes, or some other measure can be confusing and should be avoided.

- *Key usage*: This defines the exact purpose of the key, such as data encryption, PIN encryption, key encryption, MAC, HMAC, or digital signature. This is analogous to the X.509 [80] key-usage extension, expressed as bit flags, listed as follows:

  Bit 0: digitalSignature is for digital signatures on data

  Bit 1: nonRepudiation is for digital signatures used for nonrepudiation

  Bit 2: keyEncipherment is for key encryption and decryption

  Bit 3: dataEncipherment is for data encryption and decryption

  Bit 4: keyAgreement is for key agreement algorithms

Bit 5: keyCertSign is for digital signatures on certificates

Bit 6: cRLSign is for digital signatures on certificate revocation lists (CRL)

Bit 7: encipherOnly is for data encryption

Bit 8: decipherOnly is for data decryption

This list does not convey all possible uses, but an unlimited list of key usage bits is not practical. Therefore, the X.509 [80] extended key-usage extension was added. This field is a set of one or more object identifiers (OID), listed as follows:

OID: 1.3.6.1.3.5.5.7.3.1 serverAuth is for server-side SSL connections

OID: 1.3.6.1.3.5.5.7.3.2 clientAuth is for client-side SSL connections

OID: 1.3.6.1.3.5.5.7.3.3 codeSigning is for digital signatures on executable code

OID: 1.3.6.1.3.5.5.7.3.4 e-mailProtection is for digital signatures on e-mail messages

OID: 1.3.6.1.3.5.5.7.3.8 timeStamping is for digital signatures on time-stamp tokens (TST)

OID: 1.3.6.1.3.5.5.7.3.9 OCSPSigning is for digital signatures used with online certificate status protocol responders

The premise of the extended key-usage extension is that the OID can define the key usage to any level of detail; however, this requires that the OID be registered and publicly available. For X.509 [80] certificates, if an extension is marked critical but the application does not recognize the OID, then certificate validation fails. If the extension is marked noncritical but the application does not recognize the OID, then it can be ignored. Another example of key notation is TG-4 [63], which uses a similar positional scheme using characters instead of numbers.

- The first position is always a K, signifying a cryptographic key.
- The second position classifies the key as follows:

K = key-encrypting

P = PIN-related

D = non-PIN data encryption

A = authentication

- The third position defines more specifically the function of the key as follows:
  S = storage
  T = transport
  D = derivation
  V = verification
  M = message
  C = card
  F = file/database
- The fourth position specifies certain limitations on the use of a key as follows:
  E = encrypt
  D = decrypt
  G = generate
  R = receive
  S = send
  V = verify

Alternatively, another common approach is to use simple abbreviations. For example, key-encryption keys are (KEK), PIN-encryption keys are (PEK), PIN-verification keys are (PVK), secure socket layer keys are (SSL), and transport layer security keys are (TLS). Again, the more important aspect is that key usage terms be consistent, unambiguous, and meaningful.

- *Application usage*: This identifies the application environments and circumstances for which the cryptographic keys are used. In addition to the key location and key usage, the application usage provides supplemental information regarding the intended purpose of the key. For example, an asymmetric key pair might be used for an SSL Web server for an online banking system. Another example might be a symmetric key for PIN encryption on an ATM. Yet another example might be an asymmetric key pair used for digitally signing legal documents such as loan applications.
- *Contact information*: This identifies the key owner and the managers who are responsible for handling cryptographic keys over the key-management cycle. Contract information includes names, departments, e-mail addresses, and phone

numbers. The list should include primary and secondary roles so that the appropriate individuals can be contacted during regularly scheduled events or in emergencies.

7.4.3 Network, Data, and Key Diagrams

Three sequential diagrams are provided as examples for network connections, data flows, and key deployment in Figures 7.7–7.9, respectively. Each diagram is basically the same layout with relevant information. Some network diagramming tools allow different layers to be superimposed over a common graphic to keep information synchronized. Alternatively, diagrams can be manually created and maintained. The effort to keep documentation accurate and current can be problematic; however, the risks associated with undocumented cryptography solutions far outweigh the work.

Figure 7.7 shows an example network diagram with firewalls, routers, switches, midrange Web and database servers, and mainframe

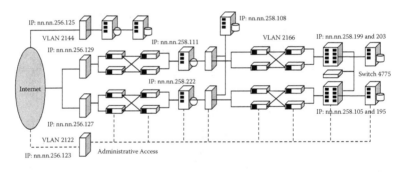

Figure 7.7   Example: network diagram.

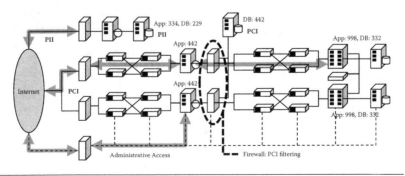

Figure 7.8   Example: data-flow diagram.

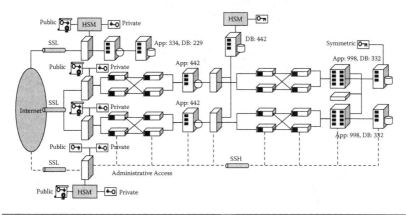

Figure 7.9   Example: key-deployment diagram.

systems. The four connections to the Internet are segregated by firewalls. The Web and database servers on IP.125 reside within the demilitarized zone (DMZ). The Web servers on IP.129 and IP.127 reside in the DMZ along with cross-connected routers for redundancy and load balancing. The database on IP.108 resides outside the DMZ and is connected to Web servers on IP.111 and IP.222 through an internal firewall. Mainframe systems on IP.199 and IP.105 reside outside of the DMZ and are connected to the same Web servers on IP.111 and IP.222 through an internal firewall over another series of cross-connected routers. The database servers on IP.203 and IP.195 are directly connected to the mainframe systems, which are interconnected by a switch for data replication. The last Internet connection on IP.123 is reserved for administrative access, represented by dotted lines, to manage the various network devices. In this example, the network diagram provides connections, IP addresses, and virtual local area network (VLAN) segments.

Figure 7.8 replicates the same example diagram with data flows, application names, database names, data tags, and data-filtering zones. Three data flows are marked. For example, application 334 and database 229 (on IP.125 connection) transmit, process, and store personally identifiable information (PII) as defined in NIST SP 800-122 [185]. Application 442 (on IP.129 and IP.127 connections) transmits and processes cardholder data as defined by the Payment Card Industry (PCI) standards [190]. However, PCI is not stored in database 442, since PCI is filtered at the internal firewalls. Administrative information (on IP.123 connection) would be transmitted between external administrators and network devices. Knowing what type of data are transmitted, processed, or stored allows the various information security requirements to be determined based on industry standards and an organization's policies, practices, and procedures.

Figure 7.9 reuses the same example diagram with locations of cryptographic keys and protocols. External connections to application 334 (on IP.125 connection) use Hypertext Transfer Protocol (HTTP) over Secure Socket Layer (SSL) or HTTPS, and the SSL tunnel terminates at the firewall, which uses a hardware security module (HSM) to protect the SSL key pair. External connections to application 442 (on IP.129 and IP.127 connections) also use SSL terminating at the firewalls; however, the SSL key pair is managed using a cryptographic software module without an HSM. External administrative access is over SSL, terminating at the firewall using an HSM to protect the SSL key pair, and secure shell (SSH) is used on the internal network connections, but the SSH key pair is managed using a cryptographic software module without an HSM. Database 442 encrypts data in storage using an HSM to protect a symmetric data encryption key, whereas database 332 encrypts data in storage using a cryptographic software module without an HSM. Knowing what key types are in use, where they are deployed, and how they are protected allows the various key-management security requirements to be determined based on industry standards and an organization's policies, practices, and procedures.

Network, data, and cryptographic information can be documented in many formats, but visual representations are often the easiest to understand. Diagrams make good reference material for reports and can be especially useful during online conference calls to focus conversations. However, detailed information is always needed, such as spreadsheets or other lists.

7.5 Public Key Infrastructure

Public key infrastructures (PKI) are formal cryptographic architectures focused on the management and governance of asymmetric cryptography [30, 107]. PKI management covers the basic who, what, where, when, how, and why of the operational environments and associated key-management life-cycle controls. PKI governance addresses the policies and practices addressing the life cycle of public key credentials, with emphasis on issuance and revocation. In general, PKI credentials address life-cycle controls for the integrity and authenticity of asymmetric public keys. The most common PKI credentials are X.509 [80] certificates, which are digitally signed by certification authority (CA). In addition to a CA issuing X.509 certificates, there are many other primary and secondary roles; however, not all PKIs have the same purposes or architectures. The first step is to establish a general PKI framework [193–207].

In 1994, the National Institute of Standards and Technology (NIST) tasked the MITRE Corporation to study alternatives for automated management of public keys and of the associated public key certificates for the federal government. MITRE published the Public Key Infrastructure Study that identified four entities integral to the functioning of the PKI.

- *PAA*: The PAA is the policy-approving authority, which creates the overall guidelines for the entire PKI. It may also certify public keys belonging to PCAs. Subsequent PKI studies and industry standards retained the concept of the policy authority (PA) but simplified the name.
- *PCA*: The PCA is the policy-certification authority. Each PCA establishes policy for all certification authorities and users within its domain. It certifies CA public keys. Few commercial or private sector PKI deployments actually incorporate a policy CA, as it is viewed as an overcomplication.
- *CA*: The CA is the certification authority with minimal policy-making responsibilities. The CAs are expected to certify the public keys of users in a manner consistent with the cognizant PCA's and the PAA's policies. In practice, the CA role has evolved such that its operational environment has been expanded into its functional components.
- *ORA*: The ORA is the organizational registration authority. The ORA is an entity that acts as an intermediary between a CA and a user. Its sole purpose is to vouch for the identity and affiliation of the user and register that user with its CA. In

practice, the RA role has likewise evolved such that it might be part of the same organization, a licensed agent of the CA, or an independent third-party service provider.

In 1996, the American Bar Association (ABA) Information Security Committee (ISC) published the Digital Signature Guidelines (DSG) [31]. The DSG identified three primary roles: the certificate authority (CA), the subscriber, and the relying party; however, later models identified the registration authority (RA) functionality of the CA. An important concept described by the DSG is that a signature is not part of the substance of a transaction, but rather of its representation or form. Per the DSG, signing writings serve the following general purposes:

- *Evidence*: A signature authenticates a writing by identifying the signer with the signed document. When the signer makes a mark in a distinctive manner, the writing becomes attributable to the signer.
- *Ceremony*: The act of signing a document calls to the signer's attention the legal significance of the signer's act, and thereby helps prevent "inconsiderate" engagements.
- *Approval*: In certain contexts defined by law or custom, a signature expresses the signer's approval or authorization of the writing, or the signer's intention that it have legal effect.
- *Efficiency and logistics*: A signature on a written document often imparts a sense of clarity and finality to the transaction and may lessen the subsequent need to inquire beyond the face of a document. Negotiable instruments, for example, rely upon formal requirements, including a signature, for their ability to change hands with ease, rapidity, and minimal interruption.

In 1997, the National Association of State Information Resource Executives (NASIRE), the National Association of State Purchasing Officers (NASPO), the National Association of State Auditors, Comptrollers and Treasurers (NASACT), and several states selected the National Automated Clearing House Association (NACHA) to research the use of digital signatures. The result of this effort was the publication of the CARAT Guidelines [32]. The CARAT based its analysis on the DSG and further identified a three-corner model and a four-corner model.

- *Issuer*: The issuer creates a certification key, creates certificates, signs them, and sends them to their respective subscribers. The issuer also revokes certificates and disseminates notice of certificate revocation to relying parties. The CARAT incorporates the registration authority (RA) as a functional role of the issuing certificate authority (CA).
- *Repository*: The repository disseminates certificates, notices of revocation, and related information to parties who may rely on the certificates. A repository can also assist relying parties in other ways besides making information available, such as by helping them to observe the limitations of a certificate's trustworthiness or assurance or enabling them to obtain further assurance. For the CARAT three-corner model, the repository is considered a functional role of the issuing certificate authority (CA), whereas for its four-corner model, the repository is recognized as a separate entity.
- *Subscriber*: The person who the issuer associates with a key pair, by means of the certificate, is the subscriber of the certificate.
- *Relying party*: The relaying party functional role and obligations are based on its interaction with the issuer, repository, and subscriber, but the CARAT does not provide a definitive definition.

In 2001, the same American Bar Association (ABA) Information Security Committee (ISC) published the PKI Assessment Guideline (PAG) [33], a logical extension to the DSG. The PAG establishes technical and business requirements of PKI components within a legal framework and identifies four primary roles: the certification authority (CA), the subscriber, the relying party, and the registration authority (RA). The guideline promotes PKI governance based on three areas: technology, business, and legal. The assessment also recognizes four primary PKI documents: certificate policy (CP), the certificate practice statement (CPS), subscriber agreements, and relying-party agreements. The PAG endorses independent third-party assessments and refers to the X9.79 [51] certificate-management control objectives and evaluation criteria.

- *Certificate authority (CA) system*: The collection of the information technology components (including one or more trustworthy systems), along with the procedures and operations of the CA system, as specified in the certificate practice statement (CPS).
- *Registration authority (RA)*: An entity that is responsible for validating the identity (or other attributes) of certificate applicants but does not issue or manage certificates (i.e., an RA is delegated to perform certain tasks on behalf of a CA, such as approving certificate applications). The extent to which an RA is (exclusively) responsible for its acts depends on the applicable CP and agreements.
- *Relying party*: The recipient of a certificate containing the public key of a certificate's subject who is in a position to rely, or otherwise relies, on the binding in a certificate between the public key appearing in it and the identity (and/or other attributes) of the person named in the certificate.
- *Subscriber*: The person who (1) is the subject named or identified in a certificate issued to such person and (2) holds a private key that corresponds to a public key listed in that certificate.

In 2001, the Accredited Standards Committee X9 published the ANSI standard X9.79 [51] the same year as the PAG. As mentioned in Chapter 1 (Introduction), X9.79 defined PKI components and provided a framework of practices and policy requirements for its operation. The standard further defined the operational practices relative to industry-accepted information systems-control objectives. X9.79 was subsequently adopted by the American Institute of Certified Public Accountants (AICPA) and the Canadian Institute of Chartered Accountants (CICA) and published as the Webtrust for CA accounting standard. X9.79 was subsequently internationalized and published as ISO 21188 [110] in 2006. Figure 7.10 depicts a PKI framework based on X9.79 [51] and ISO 21188 [110] showing four primary roles: the certificate subject, the registration authority (RA), the certification authority (CA), and the relying party.

The subject (also called a subscriber) is issued a certificate by a CA. Figure 7.10 shows the subject generating an asymmetric key pair and submitting a certificate signature request (CSR) [202] to a registration

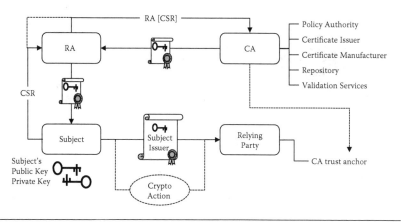

Figure 7.10 Example: PKI framework.

authority (RA). Alternatively, the RA might generate the key pair for the subject, obtain the certificate as a proxy for the subject, and then distribute the asymmetric key pair as a private key and a public key certificate to the subject. Regardless of whether the subject or the RA generates the key pair, the RA submits a secured request RA(CSR) to the CA, typically a CSR digitally signed by the RA with its own asymmetric keys. The CA generates the subject certificate and returns it to the RA for distribution to the subject. Once the subject has its private key and certificate, it can engage with a relying party.

The relying party, in order to trust any cryptographic action with the subject, needs the CA trust anchor to validate the subject's certificate. For example, numerous CA trust anchors are provided by browser manufacturers for SSL connections with Web sites. Refer to §7.5.4 for a discussion on relying parties.

The subject interacts with a relying party by taking some cryptographic action with its private key that the relying party can verify using the corresponding public key. For example, the subject can authenticate to the relying party; however, it is important to understand that the public key certificate without a digital signature does not provide authentication. This is analogous to a person presenting a business card. While it is likely that the person presenting the business card is honest and really is the name on the card, without further validation very little trust actually exists. President Ronald Reagan is attributed for the phrase "trust, but verify," but when it comes to business risk acceptance, the reversal "verify then trust" is the more appropriate approach.

As another example, the subject can establish a symmetric key using its public key. The relying party generates a random symmetric key, encrypts using the subject's public key, and the subject recovers the symmetric key using its private key. This is essentially the SSL key-exchange method. Other key-establishment schemes require both parties to exchange certificates. For those scenarios, both parties are subjects with their own certificates, and both are relying parties to each other. However, there is no guarantee that the certificates were issued by the same CA. To better understand PKI, we first focus on the CA and its functional components.

7.5.1 Certificate Authority

In addition to the four primary roles of subject, RA, CA, and relying party, Figure 7.10 also shows a CA with the following functional components: policy authority, certificate issuer, certificate manufacturer, repository, and validation services. ISO 21188 [110] defines each component as the following:

- *Policy authority*: The party or body with final authority and responsibility for specifying certificate policies and ensuring that CA practices and controls as defined by its certificate practice statement (CPS) fully support the specified certificate policies. The policy authority (PA) is the core governance body that establishes and maintains the policies, practices, procedures, and related agreements. Representatives from legal, compliance, risk, operations, security, and technology are involved.
- *Certificate issuer*: The organization whose name appears in the issuer field of a certificate. This is essentially the brand name, which might be different from the actual certificate manufacturer, as the certificate signing might be performed by a separate service provider. In some cases, the brand might manage the distribution of the CA public key, but not the CA private key.

- *Certificate manufacturer*: The agent who performs the tasks of applying a digital signature to a certificate signing request on behalf of the certificate. The certificate manufacturer manages the CA private keys used to digitally sign the certificate, the certificate revocation list (CRL), and the online certificate status protocol (OCSP) responses.
- *Repository*: The system for storage and distribution of certificates and related information (i.e., certificate storage, certificate distribution, certificate policy storage and retrieval, certificate status). The repository is presumed to be an online system, whereas many other CA components are operated offline, with no network accessibility.
- *Validation services*: The services provided by the CA or its agent that performs the task of confirming the validity of a certificate to a relying party. Validation services are by definition online, and include downloadable CRL or OCSP responders. It might also provide certificate discovery or certificate chain validation.

These functional components are part of any operational CA. However, any one of these components might be an external organization or service provider. For instance, the policy authority might not be an internal CA group, but an external governance entity under which the CA operates. As another example, the certificate issuer might be a named brand who has outsourced the certificate manufacturing to the actual CA that generates the certificates. Yet again, the CA might rely on a third-party service provider as the repository for long-term storage or real-time validation services. Regardless whether any of the functions are outsourced or performed internally, most CA architectures are composed of multiple instances organized by certificate types. An example CA architecture is provided in Figure 7.11.

In the example shown in Figure 7.11, subjects submit a request to one of three RAs, depending on the type of certificate: SSL for secure communication, e-mail for identification, or legal for electronically signing official documents. By necessity, each RA is online to service subject requests. The requests are submitted to the corresponding CAs that are likewise online. Each CA generates the subject certificate

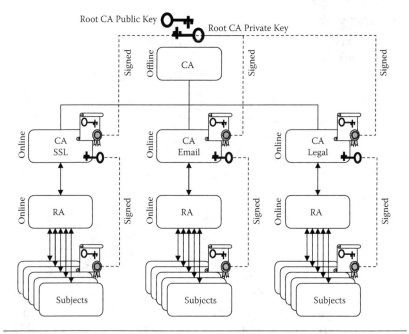

Figure 7.11   Example: CA architecture.

by signing the certificate with its CA private key, and then the RA returns the completed certificate to the appropriate subject. Each online CA has its public key encapsulated in another certificate issued by a superior CA, which is operated in an off-line mode. The top-level CA, commonly called the root CA, is only used to issue certificates to its three subordinate CAs. The subordinate CA certificates are signed by the root CA private key, and the root CA public key is known as a trust anchor. However, similar to a CA outsourcing its functional components as discussed previously, the primary roles of the CA may likewise be operated by different organizations. Example CA residency combinations are provided in Table 7.12.

Four CA residency examples are shown in Table 7.12. Scenario A illustrates a private PKI where all of the primary roles are internal within the same organization. Subjects submit their certificate signature request (CSR) [202] to an RA owned and operated by the same organization, such that internal authentication and authorization methods can be utilized. The subject and relying party are both residents within the same organization as the RA and CA. The relying party has the CA public key as its trust anchor. The subject provides

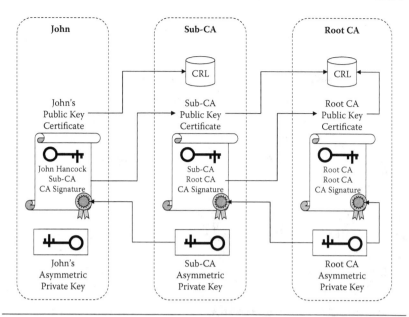

Figure 7.12 Example: certificate chain.

its certificate to the relying party, but this is relative to the cryptographic operations being performed, as each employee likely has one or more certificates.

- When the sender digitally signs an e-mail with its private key, the receiver verifies the e-mail with the sender's public key, so the receiver is the relying party of the sender's certificate.
- When the sender encrypts an e-mail with the receiver's public key, the receiver decrypts the e-mail with its private key, so the sender is the relying party of the receiver's certificate.

Scenario B depicts an external commercial CA where either the RA remains internal within the same organization as the subject and relying party, or where the RA is external and part of the CA system. Subjects submit their CSR to the RA regardless of its residency. Since the subject and relying party are both residents within the same organization but the CA is external, the relying party needs to install the external CA trust anchor, but the rest of the private PKI operates the same as scenario A.

Scenario C introduces an RA as a third party that is external to both the CA and the subject and relying-party organization. Such third-party RA service providers typically operate as a licensed agent of the CA, although another possibility is a contractual agreement between the CA and the subject and relying-party organization. Similar to scenario B, the relying party needs to install the external CA's certificate as a trust anchor, but the rest of the private PKI operates the same as scenario A.

Scenario D shows when the relying party resides in a separate organization from the subject, and the CA is external to both organizations. For consistency, the RA is portrayed as either separate from the CA or within the CA. In either case, the relying party needs to install the external CA trust anchor; however, unlike scenarios A, B, or C, the PKI is public because the subject and relying party reside in different organizations.

Table 7.12 does not enumerate all possible combinations. The CA is either organization A or B, so there are two possible residencies; the RA might be organization A, B, or C, so there are three possibilities; the subject is always organization A; and the relying party is either organization A or B, so there are two possible residencies. However, when the CA is within organization A, the RA can only be internal to organization A or external as organization C, and when the CA is external as organization B, the RA can only reside in either organization B or A. The scenarios not shown in Table 7.12 include when the relying party is external as organization D but the CA or RA are internal to organization A, or when the CA resides in organization A but the RA is external as organization C. Another possibility beyond the scope of Table 7.12 might be when two different subject organizations that are relying parties of each other might employ two different external CAs. It is important to

Table 7.12 Example CA Residency

SCENARIO	CERTIFICATE ISSUER	REGISTRATION AUTHORITY	CERTIFICATE SUBJECT	RELYING PARTY
Scenario A		Organization A		
Scenario B	Organization B		Organization A	
	Organization B		Organization A	
Scenario C	Organization B	Organization C	Organization A	
Scenario D	Organization B	Organization C	Organization A	Organization D
	Organization B		Organization A	Organization D

recognize that in order to determine the relative risks and security controls, the PKI architecture needs to include the residency of the primary roles.

7.5.2 Registration Authority

Figure 7.10 shows the RA submitting a secured request RA(CSR) to the CA, typically a CSR digitally signed by the RA with its own asymmetric keys. The certificate signature request (CSR) submitted by the subject to the RA is defined in PKCS #10 [202], which is essentially the subject name (John Hancock) and the subject public key signed using the subject private key shown as follows:

$$CSR \equiv \text{subject signature (subject name, subject public key)}$$

For the CA to authenticate the RA submission, the RA(CSR) might be the subject CSR signed using the RA private key. Consequently, the RA has its own certificate issued by some CA. However, the secured request RA(CSR) is undefined and is dependent on the CA implementation.

$$RA(CSR) \equiv RA \text{ signature (CSR)}$$

For scenario A in Table 7.12, where the CA and RA reside within the subject organization, the subject-to-RA internal authentication might include e-mail systems or integrated single-sign-on (SSO) solutions, and authorization might be Lightweight Directory Access Protocol (LDAP) or other access controls. Thus, the RA can take advantage of previously authenticated and authorized employees, contractors, and business partners. However, the RA and the CA still need to mutually authenticate each other to avoid insider attacks from obtaining valid but illegitimate certificates that might be used for identity theft, data theft, or other fraud.

For scenario B in Table 7.12, where the CA is external and when the RA is internal to the organization but external to the CA, the authentication between the RA and CA is paramount. When the RA is external to the organization but internal to the CA, the authentication and authorization between the subject and the RA is vital. It is the responsibility of the RA to verify the CSR and validate both the authenticity and authorization of the subject for requesting a certificate. Likewise, the authenticity and authorization of the subject also needs to be validated for certificate revocation requests.

For scenario C in Table 7.12, where the RA is external to both the CA and the subject organization, the authentication between the RA and CA is critical, as is the authentication and authorization between the subject and the RA. As mentioned for scenario B, it is the responsibility of the RA to verify the CSR and validate both the authenticity and authorization of the subject for certificate requests and revocation.

For scenario D in Table 7.12, similar to scenario C, when the RA is external to the CA, the authentication between the RA and CA is important, as is the authentication and authorization between the subject and the RA. As mentioned for scenarios B and C, it is the responsibility of the RA to verify the CSR and validate both the authenticity and authorization of the subject for certificate requests and revocation.

7.5.3 Subject

The subject is primarily responsible for adhering to the CA policies and practices, including correct and accurate representation to the RA, the CA, and the relying party. Further, if the CA offers a subscriber agreement in addition to its certificate policy (CP) and certificate practice statement (CPS), the subject is expected to comply with all of the CA operating rules. In general, the subject is responsible for the following:

- The subject is accountable for securely managing its asymmetric private key. This includes maintaining the confidentiality, integrity, and authenticity over its key-management life cycle.
- The subject is also liable for proper use of its asymmetric private key. This includes any misuse by the subject or any unauthorized use by another individual.
- The subject is likewise answerable for keeping its certificate current. When the certificate is nearing its expiration date, the subject generates new asymmetric keys and obtains a replacement certificate.

For any known or suspected loss of confidentiality, integrity, or authenticity, the subject submits a revocation request to the RA so the CA can revoke the certificate, either by updating the next CRL publication or adding the revocation status to the OCSP database. However, it is more likely that subjects will not follow the CA rules. For example, private keys that should be considered compromised, as discussed in §7.3.3 (Life-Cycle Controls), will often not be revoked, and applications continue to operate at risk. Another example is when subjects allow an unauthorized user to access or use the private key. Further, certificates are sometimes allowed to expire without new replacement certificates such that applications will fail.

7.5.4 Relying Party

Referring back to Figure 7.10, in order for the relying party to validate the subject certificate, it must first have a copy of the root CA trust anchor. The relying party can then validate the certificate chain; an example certificate chain is shown in Figure 7.12. The relying party first checks that the subject name matches the expected name (in this example it is John Hancock) and then identifies the issuer name, which in this case is the sub-CA. Next, the relying party checks the sub-CA certificate and then identifies the next issuer name, which is root CA. Finally, the relying party checks the root CA certificate, also called the *trust anchor*, which in this case is a self-signed certificate. Since the trust anchor is a top-level CA, there is no higher-level CA to sign the trust anchor, so the root CA certificate is signed by the root CA private key. Once the digital signature on the root CA certificate has been verified, the relying party trusts the root CA public key. The root CA public key is then used to verify the digital signature on the sub-CA certificate, such that the relying party can trust the sub-CA public key. The sub-CA public key is then used to verify the digital signature on the subject certificate, such that the relying party can trust the subject public key. The subject public key can then be used to verify the cryptographic action taken by the subject using its private key.

In addition to validating the subject name and following the certificate chain to the trust anchor for verifying the certificate signatures, each certificate is individually validated. The current date of the transaction occurs on or after the validity not-before data and on or before the validity not-after date; otherwise, the certificate chain validation fails. The certificate extensions marked critical are processed accordingly; otherwise, any unrecognized critical extension fails the certificate chain validation. The subject public key parameters are supported; otherwise, any unrecognized or unsupported algorithms or key sizes fail the certificate chain validation. The certificate signature parameters are supported; otherwise, any unrecognized or unsupported algorithms or key sizes fail the certificate chain validation.

Bibliography

General References

1. *PIN Manual, A Guide to the Use of Personal Identification Numbers in Interchange.* Interbank Card Association (ICA), 1970.
2. Shannon, C. E. "A Mathematical Theory of Communication." *Bell System Technical Journal* 27 (July, October 1948) 379–423, 623–56. http://cm.bell-labs.com/cm/ms/what/shannonday/paper.html
3. International Information Systems Security Certification Consortium, Inc., (ISC)2® Certified Information Systems Security Professional (CISSP®). https://www.isc2.org/cissp/Default.aspx
4. Basin, D., and C. Cremers. *Evaluation of ISO/IEC 9798 Protocols, Version 2.0*, April 7, 2011.
5. Basin, D., C. Cremers, and S. Meier. *Provably Repairing the ISO/IEC 9798 Standard for Entity Authentication.* Zurich, Switzerland: Institute of Information Security, ETH, 2012.
6. Matyas Jr., S. M., and J. Stapleton. "A Biometric Standard for Information Management and Security." *Computers & Security* 19 (2000): 428–41, 0167-4048/00 Elsevier Science Ltd.
7. *Supplement to Authentication in an Internet Banking Environment.* Arlington, VA: Federal Financial Institutions Examination Council. http://www.ffiec.gov/pdf/Auth-ITS-Final%206-22-11%20(FFIEC%20Formated).pdf
8. "Kerberos: The Network Authentication Protocol." http://web.mit.edu/kerberos/
9. Stapleton, J., and R. Poore. *Cryptography Transitions.* Institute of Electrical and Electronics Engineers (IEEE), 2006, 1-4244-0359-6/06 IEEE.

10. Bell, D. E. and L. J. La Padula. *Secure Computer Systems: Unified Exposition and Multics Interpretation.* The MITRE Corporation, March 1976.

11. Rivest, R. "Lecture Notes 15: Voting, Homomorphic Encryption." In *6.857 Computer and Network Security*, October 2002. http://web.mit. edu/6.857/OldStuff/Fall02/handouts/L15-voting.pdf

12. Stapleton, J. "PAN Encryption: The Next Evolutionary Step?" *ISSA Journal*, June 2009.

13. Rogaway, P. *Evaluation of Some Blockcipher Modes of Operation.* University of California, Davis, Department of Computer Science, February 2011.

14. Peterson, W. W., and D. T. Brown. "Cyclic Codes for Error Detection." *Proceedings of the IRE* 49 (January 1961): 228–35. http://ieeexplore.ieee. org/xpl/articleDetails.jsp?reload=true&arnumber=4066263

15. Menezes, A. J., P. C. van Oorschot, and S. A. Vanstone. *Handbook of Applied Cryptography.* Boca Raton, FL: CRC Press, 1996.

16. Schneier, B. *Applied Cryptography.* New York: John Wiley & Sons, 1996.

17. Stapleton, J., and S. Teppler. "Digital Signatures Are Not Enough." *ISSA Journal*, January 2006.

18. Kahn, D. *The Codebreakers: The Story of Secret Writing.* New York: Scribner, 1996.

19. "RSA Honor Roll," 2002. http://www.ontko.com/~rayo/primes/hr_rsa. txt

20. Bai, S. "Factorization of RSA-704," NMBRTHRY Archives, July 2012. https://listserv.nodak.edu/cgi-bin/wa.exe?A2=NMBRTHRY;61210 9bb.1207

21. Kleinjung, T, et al. "Factorization of a 768-bit RSA Modulus." *Cryptology ePrint Archive*, 2010. http://eprint.iacr.org/2010/006

22. Koblitz, N. "Elliptic Curve Cryptosystems." *Mathematics of Computation* 48, no. 177 (January 1987): 203–9. http://www.jstor.org/discover/ 10.2307/2007884?uid=3739704&uid=2&uid=4&uid=3739256& sid=21103235149643

23. Miller, V. "Use of Elliptic Curves in Cryptography." *CRYPTO '85 Proceedings, Lecture Notes in Computer Science* 218 (1986): 417–26. http:// link.springer.com/chapter/10.1007%2F3-540-39799-X_31

24. Diffie, W. and M. Hellman. "New Directions in Cryptography." *IEEE Transactions on Information Theory* IT-22, no. 6 (November 1976): 644– 54. http://www-ee.stanford.edu/~hellman/publications/24.pdf

25. Kocher, P., J. Jaffe, and B. Jun. "Introduction to Differential Power Analysis and Related Attacks." Cryptography Research, Inc., 1998. http://www. cryptography.com/

26. AlFardan, N. J., K. G. Paterson, and R. Holloway. "Lucky Thirteen: Breaking the TLS and DTLS Record Protocols." University of London, February 2013.

27. Wagner, D., and B. Schneier. "Analysis of the SSL 3.0 Protocol." University of California, Berkeley Counterpane Systems, 2009.

28. Ray, M., and S. Dispensa. "Renegotiating TLS." PhoneFactor, Inc., November 4, 2009.

29. Rivest, R., A. Shamir, and L. Adleman. "A Method for Obtaining Digital Signatures and Public-Key Cryptosystems." *Communications of the ACM* 21, no. 2 (February 1978).
30. Austin, T. *PKI: A Wiley Technical Brief.* December 2000.
31. American Bar Association. *Digital Signature Guideline, Legal Infrastructure for Certification Authorities and Secure Electronic Commerce.* Information Security Committee (ISC), Electronic Commerce and Information Technology Division, Section of Science and Technology, American Bar Association (ABA), August 1996.
32. National Automated Clearing House Association. *CARAT Guidelines: Guidelines for Constructing Policies Governing the Use of Identity-Based Public Key Certificates.* National Automated Clearing House Association (NACHA), The Internet Council, Certification Authority Rating and Trust (CARAT) Task Force, January 2000.
33. American Bar Association. *PKI Assessment Guideline (PAG).* Information Security Committee (ISC), Electronic Commerce Division, Section of Science & Technology Law, American Bar Association (ABA), May 2003. http://www.americanbar.org/content/dam/aba/events/science_technology/2013/pki_guidelines.authcheckdam.pdf
34. Stapleton, J. "CA Trust." PKI Forum Note, July 2001.
35. CA/Browser Forum. *Guidelines for the Issuance and Management of Extended Validation Certificates, Version 1.4,* May 2012. www.cabforum.org
36. Neyman, J., and E. S. Pearson. "On the Use and Interpretation of Certain Test Criteria for Purposes of Statistical Inference, Part I." In *Joint Statistical Papers,* 1–66. Cambridge University Press, 1928, 1967.

Accredited Standards Committee X9 Incorporated

See www.x9.org

37. X9.1 Bank Cards Magnetic Stripe Data Content for Track 3.
38. X9.8 PIN Management and Security.
39. X9.9 Financial Institution Message Authentication (wholesale).
40. X9.17 Financial Institution Key Management (wholesale).
41. X9.19 Financial Institution Retail Message Authentication.
42. X9.24 Key Management.
43. X9.31 Digital Signatures Using Reversible Public Key Cryptography for the Financial Services Industry (rDSA).
44. X9.42 Public Key Cryptography for the Financial Services Industry: Agreement of Symmetric Keys Using Discrete Logarithm Cryptography.
45. X9.44 Public Key Cryptography for the Financial Services Industry: Key Establishment Using Integer Factorization Cryptography.
46. X9.49 Secure Remote Access.
47. X9.62 Public Key Cryptography for the Financial Services Industry: The Elliptic Curve Digital Signature Algorithm (ECDSA).

48. X9.63 Public Key Cryptography for the Financial Services Industry: Key Agreement and Key Transport Using Elliptic Curve Cryptography.
49. X9.69 Framework for Key Management Extensions.
50. X9.73 Cryptographic Message Syntax: ANS.1 and XML.
51. X9.79 Public Key Infrastructure (PKI).
    Part 1: Policy and practices.
    Part 3: Certificate management.
    Part 4: Asymmetric key management.
52. X9.80 Prime Number Generation, Primality Testing, and Primality Certificates.
53. X9.82 Random Number Generation.
    Part 1: Overview and basic principles.
    Part 2: Entropy sources.
    Part 3: Deterministic random bit generator mechanisms.
    Part 4: Random bit generator construction.
54. X9.84 Biometric Information Management and Security.
55. X9.95 Trusted Time Stamp Management and Security.
56. X9.97 Financial Services: Secure Cryptographic Devices (retail).
    Part 1: Concepts, requirements and evaluation methods.
    Part 2: Security compliance checklists for devices used in financial transactions.
57. X9.98 Lattice-Based Polynomial Public Key Establishment Algorithm for the Financial Services Industry.
58. X9.111 Penetration Testing.
59. X9.112 Wireless Management and Security.
    Part 1: General requirements.
    Part 2: ATM and POS.
    Part 3: Mobile banking.
60. X9.117 Secure Remote Access: Mutual Authentication.
61. X9.122 Secure Consumer Authentication for Internet Payments.
62. X9.125 Cloud Services Compliance Data.
63. TG-4 Recommended Notation for DEA Key Management in Retail Financial Networks.
64. TR-37 Migration from DES.
65. TR-39 TG-3 Retail Financial Services Compliance Guideline—Part 1: PIN Security and Key Management.
66. Accredited Standards Committee X9 Inc. Financial Services Standards: Catalog of American National Standards, Technical Reports and Guidelines, February 2012.

Department of Defense (DoD)

See entries for Rainbow Series at csrc.nist.gov/publications/secpubs/rainbow/

67. Orange Book 1993-09-30. *Department of Defense Trusted Computer System Evaluation Criteria.* 12/85 (DoD 5200.28-std).

68. Green Book 1993-11-10. *Password Management Guideline.* 4/12/85 (CSC-STD-002-85).
69. Committee on National Security Systems (CNSS). *Instruction No. 4009: National Information Assurance (IA) Glossary*, April 2010. http://www.ncix.gov/publications/policy/docs/CNSSI_4009.pdf
70. U.S. Department of Defense. "Secretary Donald Rumsfeld Press Conference at NATO Headquarters, Brussels, Belgium, June 06, 2002." http://www.defense.gov/transcripts/transcript.aspx?transcriptid=3490

Institute of Electrical and Electronics Engineers (IEEE)

See www.ieee.org

71. Clark, D. D., and D. R. Wilson. "A Comparison of Commercial and Military Computer Security Policies." CH2416-6/87/0000/0184, IEEE, 1987.
72. Stapleton, J., and R. Poore. "Cryptographic Transitions." Paper presented at 2006 IEEE Region 5 Conference.
73. IEEE 1363 Standard Specifications for Public Key Cryptography: Traditional Public Key Cryptography.
74. IEEE 1363.1 Standard Specifications for Public Key Cryptographic Techniques Based on Hard Problems over Lattices.
75. IEEE 1363.2 Standard Specifications for Password-Based Public-Key Cryptographic Techniques.
76. IEEE 1363.3 Standard for Identity-Based Cryptographic Techniques Using Pairings.

International Committee for Information Technology Standards (INCITS)

See www.incits.org

77. X3.92 Data Encryption Algorithm (DEA).
78. X3.106 DEA Modes of Operation.
79. INCITS 92 Information Technology—Data Encryption Algorithm (DEA).

International Telecommunication Union— Telecommunications Standards (ITU-T)

80. X.509 Information Technology—Open Systems Interconnection—The Directory: Public-Key and Attribute Certificate Frameworks.

Internet Engineering Task Force (IETF)

See www.ieft.org

81. The Secure Socket Layer (SSL) Protocol Version 3.0, Internet Draft, November 1996, draft-freier-ssl-version3-02.txt.
82. RFC 1115 Privacy Enhancement for Internet Electronic Mail, Part III: Algorithms, Modes, and Identifiers, August 1989.
83. RFC 1186 The MD4 Message Digest Algorithm, October 1990.
84. RFC 1319 The MD2 Message Digest Algorithm, April 1992.
85. RFC 1320 The MD4 Message Digest Algorithm, April 1992.
86. RFC 1321 The MD5 Message Digest Algorithm, April 1992.
87. RFC 2246 The Transport Layer Security (TLS) Protocol Version 1.0, January 1999.
88. RFC 2616 Hypertext Transfer Protocol: HTTP/1.1, June 1999.
89. RFC 2945 The Secure Remote Password (SRP) Authentication and Key Exchange System, September 2000.
90. RFC 3161 Internet X.509 Public Key Infrastructure Time-Stamp Protocol (TSP), August 2001.
91. RFC 3935 A Mission Statement for the IETF, October 2004.
92. RFC 4346 The Transport Layer Security (TLS) Protocol Version 1.1, April 2006.
93. RFC 5246 The Transport Layer Security (TLS) Protocol Version 1.2, August 2008.
94. RFC 5746 The Transport Layer Security (TLS) Protocol Version 1.3, February 2010.

ISO Standards*

See www.iso.org

95. ISO 1155 Information Processing—Use of Longitudinal Parity to Detect Errors in Information Messages.
96. ISO/IEC 4909 Identification Cards—Financial Transaction Cards—Magnetic Stripe Data Content for Track 3.
97. ISO/IEC 7498 Information Technology—Open Systems Interconnection—Basic Reference Model.
    Part 1: The basic model.
    Part 2: Security architecture.

---

* ISO is not an acronym, so it really does not mean "International Standards Organization," which is explained by ISO on its website under About Us > Our Name: "Because 'International Organization for Standardization' would have different acronyms in different languages (IOS in English, OIN in French for *Organisation internationale de normalisation*), our founders decided to give it the short form ISO. ISO is derived from the Greek *isos*, meaning 'equal.' Whatever the country, whatever the language, the short form of our name is always ISO."

Part 3: Naming and addressing.

Part 4: Management framework.

98. ISO/IEC 7812 Identification cards—Identification of issuers.

Part 1: Numbering system. http://www.iso.org/iso/iso_catalogue/catalogue_tc/catalogue_detail.htm?csnumber=39698

Part 2: Application and registration procedures. http://www.iso.org/iso/iso_catalogue/catalogue_tc/catalogue_detail.htm?csnumber=39699

99. ISO 9564 PIN Management and Security.

100. ISO/IEC 9798 Information Technology—Security Techniques—Entity Authentication.

Part 1: General.

Part 2: Mechanisms using symmetric encipherment algorithms.

Part 3: Mechanisms using digital signature techniques.

Part 4: Mechanisms using a cryptographic check function.

Part 5: Mechanisms using zero-knowledge techniques.

Part 6: Mechanisms using manual data transfer.

101. ISO 9807 Banking and Related Financial Services—Requirements for Message Authentication (retail).

102. ISO 11568 Banking—Key Management (retail).

Part 1: Introduction to key management.

Part 2: Symmetric ciphers, their key management and life cycle.

Part 3: Key life cycle for symmetric ciphers.

Part 4: Key management techniques using public key cryptography.

Part 5: Key life cycle for public key cryptosystems.

Part 6: Key management schemes.

103. ISO 12812 Mobile Banking/Payments.

Part 1: General framework.

Part 2: Security.

Part 3: Financial application management.

Part 4: Mobile person-to-person payments.

Part 5: Mobile person-to-business payments.

Part 6: Mobile banking.

104. ISO 13491 Banking—Secure Cryptographic Devices (retail).

Part 1: Concepts, requirements and evaluation methods.

Part 2: Security compliance checklists for devices used in magnetic stripe card systems.

105. ISO 13492 Financial services—Key Management Related Data Element—Application and Usage of ISO 8583 Data Elements 53 and 96.

106. ISO/TR 13569 Financial Services—Information Security Guidelines.

107. ISO 15782 Certificate Management.

Part 1: Public key certificates.

Part 2: Certificate extensions.

108. ISO 16609 Banking—Requirements for Message Authentication Using Symmetric Techniques.

109. ISO 19092 Financial Services—Biometrics—Security Framework.

110. ISO 21188 Public Key Infrastructure (PKI)—Policy.

111. ISO 22307 Financial Services—Privacy Impact Assessment (PIA).

Joint Technical Committee One (JTC1)

See www.iso.org/iso/home/standards_development/list_of_iso_technical_committees/jtc1_home.htm

112. ISO/IEC 4909 Identification Cards— Financial Transaction Cards—Magnetic Stripe Data Content for Track 3.
113. ISO/IEC 7812 Identification Cards—Identification of Issuers.
    Part 1: Numbering system.
    Part 2: Application and registration procedures.
114. ISO/IEC 9796 Information Technology—Security Techniques—Digital Signature Scheme Giving Message Recovery.
    Part 1: Mechanisms using redundancy.
    Part 2: Integer factorization based mechanisms.
    Part 3: Discrete logarithm based mechanisms.
115. ISO/IEC 9797 Information Technology—Security Techniques—Message Authentication Codes (MAC).
    Part 1: Mechanisms using a block cipher.
    Part 2: Mechanisms using a dedicated hash function.
    Part 3: Mechanisms using a universal hash function.
116. ISO/IEC 9798 Information Technology—Security Techniques—Entity Authentication.
    Part 1: General.
    Part 3: Mechanisms using digital signature techniques.
    Part 2: Mechanisms using symmetric encipherment algorithms.
    Part 4: Mechanisms using a cryptographic check function.
    Part 5: Mechanisms using zero-knowledge techniques.
    Part 6: Mechanisms using manual data transfer.
117. ISO/IEC 11770 Information Technology—Security Techniques—Key Management.
    Part 1: Framework.
    Part 2: Mechanisms using symmetric techniques.
    Part 3: Mechanisms using asymmetric techniques.
118. ISO/IEC 14888 Information Technology—Security Techniques—Digital Signatures with Appendix.
    Part 1: General.
    Part 2: Integer factorization based mechanisms.
119. ISO/IEC 15408 Information Technology—Security Techniques—Evaluation Criteria for IT Security, 1998.
    Part 1: Introduction and general model.
    Part 2: Security functional requirements.
    Part 3: Security assurance requirements.

Subcommittee 37 Biometrics (SC37)

See www.iso.org/iso/home/standards_development/list_of_iso_technical_committees/iso_technical_committee.htm?commid=313770

120. ISO/IEC 19784 Information Technology—Biometric Application Programming Interface.
     Part 1: BioAPI specification.
     Part 2: Biometric archive function provider interface.
     Part 4: Biometric sensor function provider interface.
     Part 5: Biometric processing algorithm function provider interface.
     Part 6: Biometric matching algorithm function provider interface.
121. ISO/IEC 19785 Information Technology—Common Biometric Exchange Formats Framework.
     Part 1: Data element specification.
     Part 2: Procedures for the operation of the Biometric Registration Authority.
     Part 3: Patron format specifications.
     Part 4: Security block format specifications.
122. ISO/IEC 19794 Information Technology—Biometric Data Interchange Formats.
     Part 1: Framework.
     Part 2: Finger minutiae data.
     Part 3: Finger pattern spectral data.
     Part 4: Finger image data.
     Part 5: Face image data.
     Part 6: Iris image data.
     Part 7: Signature/sign time series data.
     Part 8: Finger pattern skeletal data.
     Part 9: Vascular image data.
     Part 11: Signature/sign processed dynamic data.
     Part 13: Voice data.
     Part 14: DNA data.
123. ISO/IEC 19795 Information Technology—Biometric Performance Testing and Reporting.
     Part 1: Principles and framework.
     Part 2: Testing methodologies for technology and scenario evaluation.
     Part 3: Modality-specific testing.
     Part 4: Interoperability performance testing.
     Part 5: Access control scenario and grading scheme.
     Part 6: Testing methodologies for operational evaluation.
     Part 7: Testing of on-card biometric comparison algorithms.
124. ISO/IEC 2382 Information Technology—Vocabulary—Part 37: Biometrics.
125. ISO/IEC 24708 Information Technology—Biometrics—BioAPI Interworking Protocol.
126. ISO/IEC 24709 Information Technology—Conformance Testing for the Biometric Application Programming Interface (BioAPI).

Part 1: Methods and procedures.

Part 2: Test assertions for biometric service providers.

Part 3: Test assertions for BioAPI frameworks.

127. ISO/IEC 24713 Information Technology—Biometric Profiles for Interoperability and Data Interchange.

Part 1: Overview of biometric systems and biometric profiles.

Part 2: Physical access control for employees at airports.

Part 3: Biometrics-based verification and identification of seafarers.

128. ISO/IEC 24714 Information Technology—Biometrics—Jurisdictional and Societal Considerations for Commercial Applications.

129. ISO/IEC 24722 Information Technology—Biometrics—Multimodal and Other Multibiometric Fusion.

130. ISO/IEC 24741 Information Technology—Biometrics Tutorial.

131. ISO/IEC 24761 Information Technology—Security Techniques— Authentication Context for Biometrics.

132. ISO/IEC 24779 Information Technology—Cross Jurisdictional and Societal Aspects of Implementation of Biometric Technologies— Pictograms, Icons and Symbols for Use with Biometric Systems.

Part 1: General principles.

Part 2: Fingerprint applications.

Part 3: Vascular applications.

Part 4: Face.

133. ISO/IEC 27001 Information Technology—Security Techniques— Information Security Management Systems—Requirements.

134. ISO/IEC 27002 Information Technology—Security Techniques—Code of Practice for Information Security Management.

135. ISO/IEC 27003 Information Technology—Security Techniques— Information Security Management System Implementation Guidance.

136. ISO/IEC 27004 Information Technology—Security Techniques— Information Security Management—Measurement.

137. ISO/IEC 27005 Information Technology—Security Techniques— Information Security Risk Management.

138. ISO/IEC 27006 Information Technology—Security Techniques— R139. ISO/IEC 27007 Information Technology—Security Techniques—Guidelines for Information Security Management Systems Auditing.

140. ISO/IEC TR 27008 Information Technology—Security Techniques— Guidelines for Auditors on Information Security Controls.

141. ISO/IEC 27010 Information Technology—Security Techniques— Information Security Management for Inter-Sector and Inter-Organizational Communications.

142. ISO/IEC 27011 Information Technology—Security Techniques— Information Security Management Guidelines for Telecommunications Organizations Based on ISO/IEC 27002.

143. ISO/IEC 27013 Information Technology—Security Techniques— Guidance on the Integrated Implementation of ISO/IEC 27001 and ISO/IEC 20000-1.

144. ISO/IEC TR 27015 Information Technology—Security Techniques—Information Security Management Guidelines for Financial Services.

145. ISO/IEC 29109 Information Technology—Conformance Testing Methodology for Biometric Data Interchange Formats Defined in ISO/IEC 19794.
   Part 1: Generalized conformance testing methodology.
   Part 2: Finger minutiae data.
   Part 4: Finger image data.
   Part 5: Face image data.
   Part 6: Iris image data.
   Part 7: Signature/sign time series data.
   Part 8: Finger pattern skeletal data.
   Part 9: Vascular image data.
   Part 10: Hand geometry silhouette data.

146. ISO/IEC 29120 Information Technology—Machine Readable Test Data for Biometric Testing and Reporting.
   Part 1: Test reports.
   Part 2: Test input data.

147. ISO/IEC 29141 Information Technology—Biometrics—Tenprint Capture Using Biometric Application Programming Interface (BioAPI).

148. ISO/IEC 29156 Guidance for Specifying Performance Requirements to Meet Security and Usability Needs in Applications Using Biometrics.

149. ISO/IEC 29159 Information Technology—Biometric Calibration, Augmentation and Fusion Data—Part 1: Fusion Information Format.

150. ISO/IEC 29164 Information Technology—Biometrics—Embedded BioAPI.

151. ISO/IEC 29189 Information Technology—Biometrics—Evaluation of Examiner Assisted Biometric Applications.

152. ISO/IEC 29194 Guidance on the Inclusive Design and Operation of Biometric Systems.

153. ISO/IEC 29195 Passenger Processes for Biometric Recognition in Automated Border Crossing Systems.

154. ISO/IEC 29196 Guidance for Biometric Enrollment.

155. ISO/IEC 29197 Evaluation Methodology for Environmental Influence in Biometric Systems.

156. ISO/IEC 29794 Information Technology—Biometric Sample Quality.
   Part 1: Framework.
   Part 4: Finger image data.
   Part 5: Face image data.
   Part 6: Iris Image.

157. ISO/IEC 30106 BioAPI for Object-Oriented Programming Languages.
   Part 1: Architecture.
   Part 2: Java implementation.
   Part 3: Orientation.

158. ISO/IEC 30107 Anti-Spoofing and Liveness Detection Techniques.

159. ISO/IEC 30108 Biometric Identity Assurance Service (BIAS).

160. ISO/IEC 30125 Biometrics—Use of Mobile Biometrics for Personalization and Authentication.

National Institute of Standards and Technology (NIST)

161. Dynamic Signature, National Science and Technology Council (NSTC), NSTC Subcommittee on Biometrics, August 2006. www.ostp.gov/nstc

Federal Information Processing Standard Publication (FIPS PUB)

See http://csrc.nist.gov/publications/PubsFIPS.html

162. FIPS PUB 46-3 Data Encryption Standard (DES), October 1995.
163. FIPS PUB 112 Password Usage.
164. FIPS PUB 140-1 Security Requirements for Cryptographic Modules, January 1994.
165. FIPS PUB 140-2 Security Requirements for Cryptographic Modules, May 2001.
166. FIPS PUB 140-3 Security Requirements for Cryptographic Modules, December 2009.
167. FIPS PUB 180-3 Secure Hash Standard (SHS).
168. FIPS PUB 180-4 Secure Hash Standard (SHS).
169. FIPS PUB 180-5 Cryptographic Hash Algorithm Competition. http://csrc.nist.gov/groups/ST/hash/sha-3/index.html.
170. FIPS PUB 186-3 Digital Signature Standard (DSS).
171. FIPS PUB 190 Guideline for the Use of Advanced Authentication Technology Alternatives.
172. FIPS PUB 196 Entity Authentication Using Public Key Cryptography.
173. FIPS PUB 197 Advanced Encryption Standard (AES).
174. FIPS PUB 198 The Keyed Hash Message Authentication Code (HMAC).
175. FIPS PUB 201 Personal Identity Verification (PIV) of Federal Employees and Contractors.

NIST Special Publications

See http://csrc.nist.gov/publications/PubsSPs.html

176. NIST Special Publication 800-38, Recommendation for Block Cipher Modes of Operation.
    Part A: Methods and techniques.
    Part B: The CMAC mode for authentication.

Part C: The CCM mode for authentication and confidentiality.

Part D: Galois/counter mode (GCM) and GMAC.

Part E: The XTS-AES mode for confidentiality on storage devices.

177. NIST Special Publication 800-56A Recommendation for Pair-Wise Key Establishment Schemes Using Discrete Logarithm Cryptography.

178. NIST Special Publication 800-56B Recommendation for Pair-Wise Key Establishment Schemes Using Integer Factorization Cryptography.

179. NIST Special Publication 800-56A Recommendation for Key Derivation through Extraction-then-Expansion.

180. NIST Special Publication 800-57 Recommendation for Key Management, July 2012.

Part 1: General.

Part 2: Best practices for key management organization.

Part 3: Application-specific key management guidance.

181. NIST Special Publication 800-63-1 Electronic Authentication Guideline.

182. NIST Special Publication 800-67 Recommendation for the Triple Data Encryption Algorithm (TDEA) Block Cipher, May 2008.

183. NIST Special Publication 800-89 Recommendation for Obtaining Assurances for Digital Signature Applications, November 2006.

184. NIST Special Publication 800-118 Guide to Enterprise Password Management.

185. NIST Special Publication 800-122 Guide to Protecting the Confidentiality of Personally Identifiable Information (PII), April 2010.

186. NIST Special Publication 800-130 A Framework for Designing Cryptographic Key Management Systems, draft April 2012.

Organization for the Advancement of Structured Information Standards—OASIS

See www.oasis-open.org

187. Security Assertion Markup Language (SAML) v1.0, OASIS, November 2002. http://saml.xml.org.

188. Security Assertion Markup Language (SAML) v1.1, OASIS, August 2003. http://saml.xml.org.

189. Security Assertion Markup Language (SAML) v2.0, OASIS, March 2005. http://saml.xml.org.

Payment Card Industry Security Standards Council (PCI SSC)

See https://www.pcisecuritystandards.org/

190. PCI Data Security Standard (PCI DSS).

191. PIN Transaction Security (PTS).
192. Payment Application Data Security Standard (PA DSS).

Public-Key Cryptography Standards (PKCS)

See http://www.rsa.com/rsalabs/node.asp?id=2124

193. PKCS #1 Recommendations for the RSA Algorithm.
194. PKCS #2 Encryption of Message Digests.
195. PKCS #3 Diffie-Hellman Key-Agreement Standard.
196. PKCS #4 RSA Key Syntax.
197. PKCS #5 Password-Based Encryption Standard.
198. PKCS #6 Extended-Certificate Syntax Standard.
199. PKCS #7 Cryptographic Message Syntax (CMS) Standard.
200. PKCS #8 Private-Key Information Syntax Standard.
201. PKCS #9 Selected Object Classes and Attribute Types.
202. PKCS #10 Certification Request Syntax Standard.
203. PKCS #11 Cryptographic Token Interface Standard.
204. PKCS #12 Personal Information Exchange Syntax.
205. PKCS #13 Elliptic Curve Cryptography Standard.
206. PKCS #14 Pseudo Random Number Generation.
207. PKCS #15 Cryptographic Token Information Syntax Standard.

World Wide Web Consortium—W3C

See www.w3.org/XML/core

208. Extensible Markup Language (XML) 1.0 (5th ed.), W3C Recommendation, November 2008.
209. Completed Works of SOAP. http://www.w3.org/TR/#tr_SOAP
210. XML Encryption Syntax and Processing, W3C, December 2002. http://www.w3.org/TR/2002/REC-xmlenc-core-20021210/
211. XML Signature Syntax and Processing, W3C, February 2002. http://www.w3.org/TR/xmldsig-core/

Articles

212. Comodo. "The Recent RA Compromise." March 23, 2011. http://blogs.comodo.com/it-security/data-security/the-recent-ra-compromise/
213. Slashdot. "Another CA Issues False Certificates to Iran." August 29, 2011. http://tech.slashdot.org/story/11/08/30/0253254/another-ca-issues-false-certificates-to-iran
214. Pedrica, R. "CA's hacked." ITPRO Africa, September 7, 2011. http://itproafrica.com/technology/security/cas-hacked/

215. Zorz, Z. "Rogue SSL Certs Were also Issued for CIA, MI6, Mossad." Help Net Security, September 5, 2011. http://www.net-security.org/secworld.php?id=11565

216. Slashdot. "Four CAs Have Been Compromised since June." October 28, 2011. http://tech.slashdot.org/story/11/10/28/1954201/four-cas-have-been-compromised-since-june

217. Pollack, A. "DNA Evidence Can Be Fabricated, Scientists Show." *The New York Times*, August 17, 2009. http://www.nytimes.com/2009/08/18/science/18dna.html?_r=2&partner=rss&emc=rss&

218. *MAC Developer Library*, s.v. "Code Signing Guide." Apple Inc., 2010. https://developer.apple.com/library/mac/#documentation/Security/Conceptual/CodeSigningGuide/Introduction/Introduction.html

219. Microsoft Developer Network (MSDN) Library, s.v. "Introduction to Code Signing." Microsoft, November 2013. http://msdn.microsoft.com/en-us/library/ms537361.aspx

220. Fleischman, E. "Code Signing." *The Internet Protocol Journal* 5, no. 1 (March 2002). http://www.cisco.com/web/about/ac123/ac147/archived_issues/ipj_5-1/code_signing.html

221. IBM. "IBM Researcher Solves Longstanding Cryptographic Challenge." June 2009. http://www-03.ibm.com/press/us/en/pressrelease/27840.wss

222. "Product Management and Marketing." VeriSign 2048-bit Root Migration Webinar, May 2010.

223. NIST Information Technology Laboratory. "NIST Selects Winner of Secure Hash Algorithm (SHA-3) Competition." October 2012. http://www.nist.gov/itl/csd/sha-100212.cfm

224. Intel. "Moore's Law Inspires Intel Innovation." www.intel.com/technology/mooreslaw/

225. MacRumors. "iOS 6.1 Bug Enables Bypassing Passcode Lock to Access Phone and Contacts." February 2013. http://www.macrumors.com/2013/02/14/ios-6-1-bug-enables-bypassing-passcode-lock-to-access-phone-and-contacts/

226. Peacock, W. "iPhone Security Glitch Allows Bypass of Lock Screen." Findlaw, February 2013. http://blogs.findlaw.com/technologist/2013/02/iphone-security-glitch-allows-bypass-of-lock-screen.html

227. Szczys, M. "Security Flaw Bypasses iPhone Lock Screen." Hack A Day, October 2010. http://hackaday.com/2010/10/26/security-flaw-bypasses-iphone-lock-screen/

Privacy Information

228. Scott & Scott LLP. "State Data Breach Notification Laws." Scott IP Technology Attorneys. www.scottandscottllp.com

229. Parliament of Canada. *Personal Information Protection and Electronic Documents Act (PIPEDA) of 2000.* Bill C-6.

230. United Kingdom. *Data Protection Act 1998.* www.legislation.gov.uk/ukpga/1998/29

231. European Parliament. *Directive 95/46/EC of the European Parliament and of the Council of 24 October 1995 on the Protection of Individuals with Regard to the Processing of Personal Data and on the Free Movement of Such Data.* http://ec.europa.eu/justice/policies/privacy/docs/95-46-ce/dir1995-46_part1_en.pdf

232. U.S. Small Business Administration. "Seven Considerations for Crafting an Online Privacy Policy." June 2012. http://www.sba.gov/community/blogs/community-blogs/business-law-advisor/7-considerations-crafting-online-privacy-policy

233. U.S. Government Printing Office (GPO). "Electronic Code of Federal Regulations." www.ecfr.gov

234. U.S. Department of Health & Human Services. *Health Insurance Portability and Accountability Act (HIPAA).* http://www.hhs.gov/ocr/privacy

235. Organisation for Economic Co-operation and Development (OECD). "OECD Guidelines on the Protection of Privacy and Transborder Flows of Personal Data." 23 September 1980.

Index